FACES OF COMMU

Immigrant Massachusetts, 1860-2000

MASSACHUSETTS HISTORICAL SOCIETY
STUDIES IN AMERICAN HISTORY AND CULTURE

FACES *of* COMMUNITY

Immigrant Massachusetts
1860-2000

EDITED BY
Reed Ueda *and*
Conrad Edick Wright

PUBLISHED BY THE
Massachusetts Historical Society
Boston, 2003

DISTRIBUTED BY
Northeastern University Press, *Boston*

Massachusetts Historical Society
Studies in American History and Culture, No. 7
© 2003 Massachusetts Historical Society
All Rights Reserved

Published with the assistance of a grant from Citizens Bank
Editing of this book was made possible in part by the proceeds of
an endowment fund created with the assistance of a Challenge Grant
from the National Endowment for the Humanities, a federal agency that
supports research, education, and public programming in the humanities.

Designed by Steve Dyer

Library of Congress Cataloging-in-Publication Data
Faces of community: immigrant Massachusetts, 1860–2000 / edited by
Conrad Edick Wright and Reed Ueda.
p. cm. — (Massachusetts Historical Society studies in American
history and culture; 7)
Includes bibliographica references and index.
ISBN 0-934909-80-6 (hardcover)
ISBN 0-934909-82-2 (paperback)
1. Immigrants—Massachusetts—History. 2. Massachusetts—Emigration
and immigration—History. I. Wright, Conrad Edick. II. Ueda, Reed.
III. Series.
F75.A1 F33 2003
304.8′744′009034—dc21
2002151537

CONTENTS

INTRODUCTION

"I WAS BORN, I have lived, and I have been made over," Mary Antin declared in her 1912 autobiography, *The Promised Land*. Mary had immigrated from Polotzk, Russia, to Boston in 1894, and a little less than two decades later she was impressed by how profoundly her exodus had reshaped her. "I am the spiritual offspring of the marriage within my conscious experience of the Past and the Present," she wrote. No longer the same person she was when she first set foot in Boston, a thirteen-year-old Yiddish-speaking Jewish girl, at thirty she considered herself very much an American.[1]

For Mary Antin and for countless others, coming to Massachusetts meant exchanging one community for another. No matter where they were from—whether from an ocean away or from a distant part of the United States or Canada—most immigrants to Massachusetts discovered that their birthplaces were culturally distinct from what they found in Boston or Worcester or Springfield. Whether home was originally an Irish tenant farm or the slave quarters of a Piedmont Virginia plantation or an Eastern European ghetto, whether its mention evoked warm memories or nightmares, migration required adopting a new identity consonant with new circumstances. Men who considered themselves Avellinesi moved to Boston's North End and became Italian Americans; women who identified themselves with rural Quebec turned into Franco Americans when they began to attend *Notre-Dame-Des-Canadiens* in Worcester.

The immigrants' composite identities defined the changing outlines of their evolving communities. In a process that was common to all major immigrant groups, newcomers drew from particular inherited traditions and practices while at the same time adapting themselves to their new surroundings. Thus this volume, while recognizing how immigrant communities reflected each group's unique cultural heritage, also pays attention to the shared pattern of community creation and development that linked their various ethnic experiences—Irish, French Canadian, Jewish, Italian, Swedish, and even African American.

Because the Bay State was a primary destination for immigrants experiencing the social changes of industrial and urban development, this volume's contributions offer important case studies, with national significance, of how newcomers and natives adjusted to each other and reshaped the boundaries of public interaction. For the purposes of this collection, we have considered immigrants to be men, women, and children whose birthplaces were culturally distinct from what they found in Massachusetts, whether or not their odysseys carried them across national borders.

Reed Ueda, in his study of Massachusetts as a laboratory for civic experimentation, describes how immigrants entered the public sphere through local involvement. By a process of Americanization through naturalization, and by connecting civic patriotism to ethnic pluralism, immigrants engaged their communities in the dialogues and debates of the public arena. Sharing the platform of civic Americanism, immigrants discovered broader identities, which they defined, for example, as Polish American, Jewish American, Irish American, or Greek American. Group leaders increasingly advocated an ethnic loyalty that was compatible with pluralistic democracy. Lawrence H. Fuchs, an expert on immigration studies, has described this process as "ethnic Americanization." Through it, Fuchs explains, "ancestral loyalties (religious, linguistic, and cultural) are changed (and in some ways strengthened) to American circumstances even as immigrants and their children embrace American political ideals and participate in American political institutions."[2]

In Janette Thomas Greenwood's study of the formation of the African American community in Worcester, she reconstitutes a "pioneering" experience comparable in ways to that of first-generation Jewish, Irish, or Italian immigrants. Worcester's local and historical circumstances determined how migrants refashioned themselves under conditions very different from those of their birthplaces. During and after the Civil War, Southern black migrants faced the challenge of rebuilding their lives as a minority within a minority community. Furthermore, the existing black community had to participate in accommodating the new arrivals from the South to create a broader African American community, much as German Jews in Boston, New York, and elsewhere had to learn to make room for Jewish immigrants from Russia. The organized efforts of outreach and sanctuary extended by Worcester citizens to blacks fleeing from the South also suggest an historical parallel with the assistance offered by modern nongovernmental organizations to forced migrants from foreign countries.

Worcester's African Americans were taking in newcomers from the South at the same time that from the North another stream of immigrants to the city was producing a new community of French Canadian Americans. John F. McClymer explores the ambivalence of this group's assimilating experience in a micro-historical study of the community issues facing religious leaders of an immigrant population. Detective-like, McClymer describes the search for the functional balance between being French Canadian and being American that lay at the heart of the church-building efforts of religious leaders. In the public realm of institutional religion, complex feelings about assimilation emerged, especially as immigrants became progressively more involved in patterns of cultural change and interaction with the surrounding community. Even for the immigrant who determines "not to change," as historian Oscar Handlin reminds us, "change comes" inescapably as "new words and ways insidiously filter in."[3]

Massachusetts policymakers and newcomers together helped to redraw the boundaries of community through their search for an inclusive form of citizenship. The relationship between periodic waves of mass immigration and the boundaries of the national community is a key theme in immigration history. The rise of the modern liberal state transformed the concepts of national membership which policymakers codified into the law of citizenship. In his study of U.S. Senator George Frisbie Hoar's role in the debate over the admission of Chinese immigrants, Jonathan Chu traces the intellectual history of citizenship policies and their role in immigration control. Chu begins by describing the complexity and diversity of nineteenth-century political ideas about race, then explores the legislative career of Hoar, who played a central role in working out a liberal nationalist view of these doctrines. Finally, Chu demonstrates how historical conceptions of race affected the making of public policy. As he shows, Hoar attacked philosophies of racial determinism and cultural essentialism in his opposition to legislation that would exclude Chinese immigrants. Hoar's efforts carried the Massachusetts vision of Reconstruction-era social egalitarianism into the national arena of immigration policymaking.

Religious institutions were frequently at the center of ethnic American communities, acting as gathering places for immigrants as well as a means to foster connections with the old country and its values, but the relationship between newcomers and their ancestral spiritual homes took a variety of forms. Paula M. Kane examines key moments of a community's emergence into the public sphere in her study of the expressive social function of Boston church architecture. The evolution of architectural aesthetics was a proxy for ethnic (particularly Irish) and Catholic identity in Boston. Kane demonstrates that religious architecture assumed a vital role in asserting the growing public importance of a Catholic minority. Focusing on the changing architectural form of the local parish church, she explores how it functioned in an interpretative and communicative way, as Boston Catholics experienced the pressure of assimilation at a unique moment in its history. Kane argues that, at this turning point, church architecture provided a means for expressing symbolically a community's claims to wider visibility, representativeness, and influence.

At the same time that ethnic religious institutions were beginning to assert themselves, however, some individuals began to question the faith of their fathers, at least in its organized form. Inherited beliefs and customs did not suit every circumstance. In her study of changing religious identities, Kristen Petersen Farmelant examines the dynamic quality of personal spiritual experience. She demonstrates how a voluntary religious pluralism lay at the heart of the ethnic community pattern created by immigration. Farmelant discovers a setting in which churches competed for immigrants and immigrants made strategic choices about becoming church members. She breaks new ground by providing evidence that to treat immigrant religious affiliation as a linear and continuous process is to oversimplify. The guided transplantation of religious heritages occurred in a challenging and disruptive atmosphere shaped by unprecedented opportunities for creative voluntarism. Also, to the extent that immigrants were exercising individual judgment and choice in public institutional participation, their behavior expressed the strategic self-interest associated with assimilation.

Both Kane and Farmelant remind us that the enclaves that immigrants constructed in Massachusetts were never isolated or sheltered hiding places from the wider world. Whether asserting themselves to others in granite forms or losing potential members who had decided that other spiritual communities better served their needs, newcomers' churches and synagogues always actively engaged with other groups, both native-born and foreign.

By the late nineteenth century, the ethnic communities of Massachusetts—particularly those with a long history in the Commonwealth—

stood firmly on the public stage. As groups, they alternately challenged each other and cooperated with each other in many different public settings. James J. Connolly's study of "grass roots" politics in Boston's West End shows how an immigrant enclave, filled with aliens and fledgling voters, organized itself for self-empowerment against the entrenched interests of ward bosses. Revising the image of "Czar" Martin Lomasney, Connolly provides a new account of the forces underlying the shift in urban politics from the late nineteenth century to the Progressive era, the transition from party-based politics to extra-partisan and community-mobilization politics. He uncovers the historical roots of a pattern of ethnic interest-group politics similar to the phenomenon Nathan Glazer and Daniel Patrick Moynihan described for New York City in the mid twentieth century in *Beyond the Melting Pot*.[4]

Throughout Massachusetts, different groups of immigrants created communal subcultures that assumed a place in, and that percolated into, a pluralist public life affecting all people. Acculturation was patterned by the historically shaped neighborhood subcultures as much as by the force of group solidarity or formal institutions such as schools. The ecology of local subcultures mediated between immigrants and a changing public mainstream.

Public recreation and leisure activity provided common venues for cultural mediation. As Mark Herlihy shows in his study of Revere Beach, the urban beach park became a public institution, shaped both by elite reformers and by working-class immigrants. Here, the attitude toward play and recreation molded by Progressive-era social reform and consumer culture became part of the expressive life of the immigrant community. Revere Beach reflected the transition among first- and second-generation immigrants to American-style pleasure seeking and mass entertainment. In claiming Revere Beach as "their" fun zone, immigrants turned it into an extension of their neighborhoods and created a new sphere for ethnic assimilation. At Revere Beach, entertainments and crowds also reflected a consciousness of racial boundaries between white ethnic and non-white racial outsiders. These boundaries emerged as the tensions and hierarchies among European immigrants subsumed themselves in a new collective experience of leisure and recreation.

Herlihy's account examines how immigrant community culture, initially located on a social periphery, gradually reshaped the mainstream and became part of it. The presence of ethnic "succession" at the beach was an overspill of ethnic succession in the nearby communities. Immigrant Americans may have alternately embraced and resisted assimilation into mainstream American culture, but there was a further stage of synthesis in which they reconstituted the components of the mainstream. The "popular culture" content of this recreational public sphere—changing trends in dress, hair-dos, food, music, games—absorbed ethnic and working-class styles of self-expression, helping them move from marginal to acceptable in the popular mainstream.

From the 1860s to the 1990s, immigrant Massachusetts had taken on a new form. Over the course of several generations, immigrant groups had adapted themselves to the commonwealth at the same time that they turned their new homeland in new directions. The process continues today, and will as long as immigrant groups find new homes in Massachusetts.

No collection of essays can hope to address a subject as comprehensively as a monograph, and this volume is no exception. The history of family life, education, and employment are examples of subjects that might have fit into this collection comfortably but receive only passing attention here for want of space or an appropriate contribution. By the same token, a different selection of essays might reasonably have included contributions on many immigrant groups that receive little or no mention here—for example, Greeks, Armenians, and Germans as well as the many distinct Hispanic and Asian groups that have reshaped life in Massachusetts in recent decades. If this volume is not the final word on the history of immigrant Massachusetts, it will serve its purpose, nevertheless, if it advances our knowledge of the public dimension and civic significance of this fascinating subject and promotes further research on the topic.

Reed Ueda
Conrad Edick Wright

Notes

1. Mary Antin, *The Promised Land* (Boston and New York, 1912), xi.
2. Lawrence Fuchs, *The American Kaleidoscope* (Middletown, Conn., 1990), 20.
3. Oscar Handlin, *The Uprooted*, rev. ed. (Boston, 1973), 175.
4. Nathan Glazer and Daniel Patrick Moynihan, *Beyond the Melting Pot: The Negroes, Puerto Ricans, Jews, Italians, and Irish of New York City* (Cambridge, Mass., 1963).

ACKNOWLEDGMENTS

The essays that make up this collection were first presented at "Immigrant Massachusetts, 1840–2000," a conference at the Massachusetts Historical Society, May 18–20, 2000. Generous donations from Thomas Flatley and Citizens Bank helped to make that program and this volume possible. We are grateful to both for their support. We are also grateful to many others who took part in the program but whose work does not appear here. The conference featured a keynote address by Thomas H. O'Connor, the dean of active historians of Boston, and papers by Dexter Arnold, James F. Beauschesne, Aixa N. Cintrón, Peggy Levitt, Ellen Smith, and Michael M. Topp. Thanks also go to the commentators at the conference: Martin Blatt, Howard P. Chudacoff, Jay Dolan, Michael S. Dukakis, Lawrence Fuchs, Nathan Glazer, James Green, Robert L. Hall, Marilyn Halter, Michael Jones-Correa, Kathleen J. Mahoney, James O'Toole, and Bruce M. Stave. Finally, we owe a debt of gratitude to Director William M. Fowler, Jr., and to many members of the staff who worked so hard to make the conference a success: Oona E. Beauchard, Christopher A. Carberry, Sharon E. DeLeskey, Peter Drummey, James Foley, James P. Harrison III, Elizabeth J. Krimmel, Ondine E. Le Blanc, Erin Pipkin, Jennifer Smith, Seth M. Vose III, and Donald Yacovone.

Reed Ueda
Conrad Edick Wright

Faces of Community

Frameworks for Immigrant Inclusion

Civic Dimensions of Immigration,
Naturalization, and Pluralism in
Massachusetts, 1870–1965

REED UEDA

 HAT THE PEOPLE of Massachusetts should strive to constitute themselves as an ideal community had been a public creed since the founding of the Bay Colony. As industrialization attracted immigrants and enlarged cities, the search for an ideal community remained no less vigorous. The quest turned along pathways for discovering how the new, urban, immigrant enclaves could become full members of the local and national community. Massachusetts immigrants and natives embarked upon a course of mutual discovery that would provide lessons to the rest of the country on how to make intergroup relations work in the new immigrant America.

After the American Revolution, the commonwealth sought rigorous standards for membership in the local political and civic community. With the onset of mass immigration from Ireland and the far reaches of Europe in the course of the nineteenth century, questions arose over how successfully the newcomers would become American citizens and adopt an American national identity. Indeed, the Know-Nothing Party of the early 1850s pushed for tougher naturalization requirements for immigrants, although it ultimately failed to achieve these measures.[1] In the post-Civil War era, policymakers in Massachusetts approached these questions along pathways that led them into opposed camps of restrictionists and assimilationists.

Massachusetts advocates of immigration restriction such as Henry Cabot Lodge and Prescott F. Hall called for submission to a naturalistic and predetermined collective destiny. From their viewpoint, people were so tied to their heritage that ultimately only ancestry and cultural essentialism mattered for national identity.[2] They did not believe that a citizenship based on active reason of the common person was always possible where immigrants were concerned. The ascriptive deficiencies of immigrants limited their participation in a voluntary community defined by the rational exercise of consent and choice. Nonetheless, in the face of these restrictionists, who urged programs and public philosophies excluding immigrants and setting them apart, an influential and multigenerational network of Massachusetts opinionmakers advocated inclusionary frameworks of liberal nationalism and civic pluralism.

Liberal nationalist ideology defined a societal position for immigrants "above" ethnic origins that sprang from the possibility of assimilation under the aegis of unitary and voluntary citizenship. Under its terms, immigration informed American nationhood, as the assimilation of ethnic minorities became a core process of nation building.[3] The United States, explained one nineteenth-century congressman, was "destined to expand by assimilating." By receiving new inhabitants, America offered to newcomers the possibility of assimilation by a civic inclusion that elevated those who had been "misgoverned" and "oppressed."[4] Theodore Roosevelt expressed this assimilative, transformative concept when he endorsed a homogeneous national identity for immigrants and inveighed against "hyphenated Americanism." He announced an unequivocal faith in the civic capacity of immigrants to become American, saying if an immigrant is "heartily and singly loyal to this republic, then no matter where he was born, he is just as good an American as anyone else."[5]

Adherents to the civic traditions of American liberal nationalism like Theodore Roosevelt assumed the possibility of creating an American national identity on the basis of a politics of reason. Rooted in Enlightenment rationalist philosophy and expounded by Thomas Jefferson, this premise conceived of the United States as an idea, "an idea to which everyone could be assimilated for the very reason that it was a universal idea," according to the historian of nationalist ideology, Hans Kohn. As a country formed out of popular ideological allegiance, the United States could become a "universal nation" that was "valid for the whole of mankind."[6]

The Civic Boundaries of Immigration Policy

The problem of maintaining American citizenship while accepting immigrants reached a crisis over the admission of immigrants from China, and

Massachusetts public leaders took a strong interest in the national debate over the eligibility of the Chinese in particular. Although the Chinese population in Massachusetts was very small compared to the situation in California and the far west, Massachusetts leaders saw the issue as crystal-izing the relationship of American citizenship to immigration, a question that had absorbed the Know-Nothing Party of Massachusetts before the Civil War, and which promised to arise with renewed vigor as new waves of immigration arrived.

The Massachusetts congressional delegation produced some of the country's most influential spokesmen for liberal nationalist principles in immigration policy, and these delegates made some of their finest philosophical arguments for these principles in the congressional debates on Chinese immigration. Sen. Charles Sumner, who once championed the abolition of slavery, submitted an amendment to a naturalization bill before the U.S. Senate in 1870 intended to provide the right of naturaliza-tion to Chinese immigrants. This measure took aim at the original Con-gressional statute of 1790, which set a uniform rule for naturalization and stipulated that an applicant must be a "free white person." In his sponsoring statement, Sumner invoked the founding touchstone of civic universalism, the Declaration of Independence. "It is 'all men' and not a race or color," instructed Sumner, "that are placed under the protection of the Declaration, and such was the voice of our fathers on the fourth day of July, 1776."[7] Despite his eloquent pleas, the Senate rejected his mo-tion to include the Chinese in the new naturalization statute that made black immigrants eligible for American citizenship. A decade later, the passage of the Chinese Exclusion Act in 1882 that barred Chinese laborers made explicit the prohibition against naturalized citizenship for Chinese immigrants.

In 1886, U.S. Sen. George Frisbie Hoar of Massachusetts rose in the Senate to attack the discriminatory criteria used to exclude immigrants from China. Hoar denounced the exclusion of the Chinese on the basis of their racial identity as a violation of the principle of individual quali-ties.[8] In 1902, Hoar reiterated this point as the Senate renewed Chinese exclusion. Assailing the tactic of "striking at any class of human beings merely because of race" without regard to "personal and individual worth," Hoar affirmed that "all nationalities contain persons entitled to be recognized everywhere they go on the face of the earth as the equals of every other man."[9]

During World War II, Rep. John McCormack of Massachusetts tapped the liberal nationalist tradition, once invoked by Charles Sumner and George Frisbie Hoar, in his support of the repeal of Chinese exclusion. In the congressional debates over this issue, he argued that opening the gates of the country to Chinese immigrants would provide "a denial of the false doctrine of racism and a reiteration of the American principles of equality of opportunity for life, liberty, and happiness for all mankind."[10] McCormack portrayed the Chinese as heroic freedom fighters against the Japanese invaders of China. Moreover, he argued that in their armed resistance the Chinese people had shown their incipient Americanism:

China is more to America than an ally. She is our friend, united in her sentiment of friendship for the people of the United States. Our constitution has been her governmental inspiration. Her children quote with pride our constitutional guarantees of liberty and equality. They are taught to believe that America believes that all men are created equal, with rights and privileges which the State did not create, but which the State is bound to safeguard and protect. The Stars and Stripes to the Children of China is the flag of a generous nation protecting human rights from tyrannical intolerance.[11]

Much to Representative McCormack's satisfaction, Congress abolished Chinese exclusion in 1943. But this step was mainly taken out of urgent realpolitik, the instrumental usage of immigration policy to strengthen the wartime alliance with China, not McCormack's idealistic principles. Nevertheless, McCormack's words signified a turning point in congressional treatment of the Chinese immigration issue, arguing for admission of the Chinese not just according to constitutional principle, but also because of their demonstrated civic capacity.

From the era of Reconstruction, prominent federal legislators from Massachusetts supported the admission of Chinese immigrants by arguing that American nationality was based on an individual's allegiance to the institutions of democracy, not on ancestry. These legislators grounded their advocacy in liberal nationalist values that prescribed the treatment of Chinese immigrants as potential American citizens. Their principled logic formed the central and indispensable tactical mechanism in the long congressional campaign to establish the rights of the Chinese to admission to and naturalization in the United States.

With the official recognition of the civic assimilability of Chinese immigrants, the United States took a major step toward liberalizing the immigration and naturalization system, starting a trend to make it fully consistent with founding constitutional principles. One key member of the Massachusetts congressional delegation in the postwar years, John F. Kennedy, had a leading role in spearheading this drive. Active in immigration policymaking during his terms as a U.S. representative and senator from Massachusetts, Kennedy came to regard restrictionist policy as an anachronism, satisfying neither a national nor an international purpose. As president, Kennedy called for a reformed immigration policy that recognized the equal capacity of all immigrants for American citizenship, a goal finally achieved in 1965 with the passage of the Hart-Celler immigration act.[12]

Naturalization as a Civic Sphere of Assimilation

In the era of immigration restriction, federal policy barred from entry laborers from China and other Asian countries and also classed all permanently resident foreign-born Asians as "aliens ineligible for citizenship." In other words, federal naturalization policy separated Asian immigrants from the national community as a permanent class of aliens. Conversely, it operated toward European and other immigrants to overcome rather than reinforce ethnic status differences.

Judicial decisions, interpreting the statutory requirement that an applicant for citizenship be a "free white person," held that aliens from southern and eastern Europe and the Middle East were racially qualified for naturalization. Jews, Armenians, Turks, and Arabs were judged to be "white" with respect to the right of naturalization.[13] *In re Halladjian* (1909) marked this course of naturalization policy. In this case, the United States Attorney's office in Boston sought a ruling to deny naturalization to a group of Armenian applicants on the grounds that they were Asiatics who were racially ineligible. The federal district judge in Boston, however, found otherwise and upheld their right to apply for citizenship. Louis Marshall and Max Kohler, who represented the American Jewish Committee, acted as amici curiae to affirm that "white" was an all-inclusive term denoting the eligibility for naturalized citizenship of all persons not designated as members of any other distinct racial category.[14]

Although naturalization policies fell under the domain of the federal government, its ramifications for a state with high levels of immigration such as Massachusetts were too important to leave unattended by local officials. It was necessary for the state government of Massachusetts to address the problem of how immigrant aliens would become American citizens. The Massachusetts Commission on Immigration, empaneled to investigate the local impact of immigration, gathered information on the naturalization of immigrants. The Massachusetts Department of Education monitored how adult immigrants prepared themselves for the naturalization exam by studying English, civics, and American history in special night classes.

The homogeneous sphere of civic identity entered through the naturalization process provided an individual with the rights, opportunities, and duties that paved the way to assimilationist experiences. In this way, naturalization policy softened the dividing line between "old" immigrants and "new" immigrants from Europe, which figured prominently in admissions policy, and it created a common ground of shared civic identity and civic activity. As a social process, naturalization became a voluntary mass movement sensitively reflecting the changing ethnic structure of the alien population in the United States and transforming the social foundations of American nationality and citizenship.[15]

Besides securing allegiance, naturalization was a means of securing the residential and civil status of immigrants in the United States, both as individuals and as family members. Immigrants established an absolute right to residency when naturalized, and their immediate relatives received enhanced immigration and naturalization rights. The minor children of naturalized male immigrants became derivative citizens and so did their wives until 1922. After 1924, spouses and minor children of naturalized immigrants who lived in the home country enjoyed the right to admission to the United States without limitation by restrictionist nationality quotas. For many Italian immigrant laborers, for example, who had spouses or minor children in homeland communities whom they wished to bring to the United States, this right for family reunification made naturalization highly desirable. Furthermore, before a spouse and children joined him, any naturalized immigrant could return for long visitations, assured, because he was a citizen, that he would be able to return to America without fear of exclusion.[16] In the drawn-out process of "chain" migration, naturalized citizenship helped immigrants to maintain their family ties and reunite with family members.

By deciding to naturalize, an immigrant made the crucial move toward building a permanent public identity in the United States. In a 1913 letter to the Massachusetts Commission on Immigration, a Polish immigrant appealed for assistance to help him improve his situation. In his view, achieving naturalized citizenship was intertwined with the pursuit of economic opportunity, learning English, and embracing an official American identity. He described the necessity to escape from an ethnic enclave that cut off contact with "american people." "I work in the shoes-shop with polish people—I stay all the time with them—at home—in shop—anywhere," he explained. "In this way," he continued, "I can live in your country many years—like my [Polish] friends—and never speak—write well english—and never be good american citizen." This anonymous immigrant asked the Immigration Commission to put him in touch with someone who could give him "another job between american people," and allow him to "live with them and lern english." He mentioned Polish friends who "live here 10 or moore years, and they are not citizens, they don't speak well english, they don't know geography and history of this country, they don't know constitution of America." Declaring "I don't like be like them," this Polish immigrant wished to move out of a transnational locality "between" his home society and the host society, a limbo state where he had limited agency, into an American civic sphere that could give him access to the public mainstream where assimilation was possible.[17]

The path to successful naturalization took at least five years and the applicant had to fulfill several requirements along the way. The federal Naturalization Act of 1906 systematized the qualifying process for American citizenship, requiring the applicant to file a Declaration of Intention to become a naturalized citizen, fulfill residency and character requirements, demonstrate the ability to speak English, show a basic knowledge of American civics and history, and, finally, submit an acceptable petition for citizenship to a law court of record. Applicants who fulfilled all these requirements in a timely manner then took an oath of citizenship and finally received certificates of naturalization.[18]

The Massachusetts Commission on Immigration conducted interviews with over a thousand adult male immigrants to determine how they were making preparations to apply for American citizenship. The commission stated in 1915, "So far as the interests of the State are concerned, proper preparation for naturalization is a highly important consideration." The commission recognized that these immigrants had to overcome many difficulties to ready themselves for naturalization. They were "wearied by long hours of work." Many did not have the ability to communicate in spoken English, which was a basic naturalization requirement, and remained "unaccustomed to study" and unfamiliar with the "customs of the country." Sadly, the commission judged that the state had not been doing enough to provide more opportunities for potential applicants to gain the skills required to pass the naturalization exam. Thus the immigrant was thrown back upon his own efforts at self-preparation, attending outreach programs started by private agencies such as the North American Civic League, the YMCA, and the Daughters of the American Revolution. Immigrants also attended the "public evening school," night classes held at public schools which became increasingly available in immigrant neighborhoods.[19]

The Massachusetts Department of Education conducted interviews with men and women taking night classes in English and civics to determine how they educated themselves for citizenship. Their extraordinary efforts, described as "both inspiring and pathetic," involved sacrificing meals, family time, and sleep to attend courses in English, civics, and American history after long and arduous workdays. Because the courses ran for months at a time, the students made substantial time commitments. The department reported some admirable rates of attendance despite these challenging circumstances. The City of Cambridge, for example, revealed that in one year 220 students in its night citizenship classes had perfect attendance records. Other towns such as Marlboro, Lowell, Watertown, and Lynn also recorded impressive attendance records.[20]

Groups of immigrant aliens made creative organized efforts to prepare for American citizenship. The Massachusetts Commission on Immigration reported in 1915 that Poles, Italians, and Lithuanians had started "naturalization clubs." It described typical examples of these organizations and their operations, drawn from the City of Lynn. This North Shore city had an Italian Naturalization Society that was incorporated and had seventy-eight members, twenty of whom had completed naturalization. The society had a clubhouse in the downtown section that provided a venue for lectures on citizenship. Lynn also had an incorporated Polish Naturalization Society, with ninety-eight members, over half of whom were successfully naturalized. That society's clubhouse offered lectures in both Polish and English and English lessons. The Polish club also had a fund for the naturalization hearing to pay for witness fees, loss of wages, and transportation for needy members.[21]

As immigrants prepared in organized study groups and classes for the naturalization exam, they learned how to use the vocabulary of official Americanism to exhibit the knowledge and attitudes expected of "new Americans." The City of Cambridge published "uncorrected attempts at English of men and women in the foreign classes," the majority of whom "had come to the United States within a year" to illustrate their progress in Americanization:

> I like my teacher very good—he explains fine the English language.
> . . . I like the country of American, becose it is a liberty contry.
>
> SOPHIE SOPOLOWSKY

> I am in this country eleven months. I was attending this evening school three times every week. I learned here to read, write and speak the english language. Then I learned the life story of the famous Americans as Abraham Lincoln, George Washington and Thomas Edison. Beside that I learned the constitution. This evening school helps to me a good deal.
>
> CHARLES PREEDIN

> Let us gives thanks to god, because he favored us with his son and sent us great many brave people. Look at George Washington the president of the U.S.A. And than Abraham Lincoln and many others gave their lifes for this country. . . . We must be come good citizens of America. . . . Hurra America and hurrah American flag. We wish you float in the earth forever.
>
> ARAKEL MARKARIAN[22]

British immigrant Horace J. Bridges noted in his autobiography that naturalization was a "privilege" that offered "participation in American sovereignty," and moral and civic equality with "fellow citizens." In short, naturalized citizenship acted as a force for equalizing the status of immigrants and natives. The experience of successfully going through naturalization functioned as a proxy for—indeed, as a reenactment of—the civic act of volitional allegiance in which the American people participated at the national founding. Through the act of naturalization, immigrants publicly legalized their allegiance and their claim to full acceptance as Americans.²³

For nearly all immigrant populations in the early twentieth century, relative time of arrival consistently determined naturalization rates. Thus, the groups with the largest share of naturalized citizens had been in the country longer than groups with smaller proportions of citizens. As the latter stayed on, they increased their share of naturalized citizens much as the former groups had. Since married female immigrants did not have naturalization rights independent of their spouses until the Cable Act of 1922, the annual numbers of female naturalizations initially lagged behind those for males. By World War II, however, they equaled the annual totals of male naturalizations.²⁴ Naturalization occurred in a one-by-one process of individual qualification that accumulated into a mass social movement of civic assimilation.

Toward a Civic Sphere of Pluralistic Assimilation

The immigrants of Massachusetts brought to the experience of becoming American in the civic sphere their own interpretations of this complex process. The views of immigrants were colored by the need to find an accommodation between their ethnic identity and American national identity. They sought to establish a public meeting area—a creative laboratory for exploring the possibility of positive intergroup relations—where they could work out the intermeshing of particularistic group characteristics, with a wider Bostonian and American public culture.

At the core of Massachusetts community life lay patterns of acculturation that promoted the immigrant's capacity to accept inner tension and ambiguity. In a study of the Jewish community of Boston, historian Ellen Smith noted the "struggle to define a working balance between being Jewish and being a Bostonian, between being a part of, and distinct from their American communities." It was an adaptive strategy, requiring the ability to live with degrees of contradiction that afforded balanced cultural options.²⁵

The leaders of Boston's mid-nineteenth-century Jewish community of immigrants from central Europe played a key role in formulating this sophisticated style of cultural adjustment and conveying its practical possibilities to later waves of Jewish immigrants from eastern Europe. Smith described how Boston's central European Jews "attempted to pass on . . .

their model for living a consciously Jewish life in new ways, adapted to the advantages of Boston and America, and creative with the ambiguities that such a conjoined existence could bring."

Immigrant leaders generally worked to project a positive civic image for their community and contended for control of group representation in the public media with journalists, politicians, and scholars from the world outside the ethnic enclave. Irish, Italian, Jewish, Greek, and Armenian communities produced elites who wrote in newspapers, organized community politics, and became influential in the field of intergroup public relations, challenging invidious preconceptions and stereotypes. They were able to show the external world that immigrants were adapting successfully and absorbing American ways while remaining respectful of their heritages. Many immigrants supported leaders who sought to establish their expanding participatory role in American life on their own terms.[26]

During World War I, the Carnegie Corporation commissioned an eleven-volume set of explorations in assimilation called the "Americanization Studies" series. These volumes included a prefatory note that defined *Americanization* as a form of reciprocal assimilation, as "the uniting of new with native-born Americans in fuller common understanding and appreciation to secure by means of individual and collective self-direction the highest welfare of all." The preface urged that "Americanization should perpetuate . . . a growing and broadening national life, inclusive of the best wherever found," and predicted that, "With all our rich heritages, Americanism will develop best through a mutual giving and taking of contributions from both newer and older Americans in the interest of commonweal."[27]

The directors of the series optimistically espoused Americanization as a mutual-exchange process for creating a new American community. This conception of Americanization was inherently inspirational and positive. It counteracted the group tensions and suspicions produced by World War I, labor conflict, and the acrimonious national debate over immigration restriction. Their advocacy of a mutual-assimilation agenda intermeshed with the stance of public Americanization "on ethnic terms" supported by immigrant leaders and their constituencies. A pluralist and reciprocal assimilation ethic corresponded to the immigrants' sense of how they were becoming American by contributing a part of their ethnic selves to the collective life of their native hosts.

In his study of the emergence of the Jewish community of Boston, William A. Braverman described a public event in 1915 that seemed to project the pluralist assimilation model of progressive Americanizers and liberal immigrant leaders. Boston's reception of a week-long conference of eight Zionist organizations, according to Braverman, reflected the Hub's acceptance of "the compatibility of Americanism, Zionism, and strong Jewish identity": "Mayor James Michael Curley offered the Zionists the key to the city, and American and Zionist flags decked the streets. In the Public Garden, a large floral display featured a Star of David at its center." Braverman interpreted this official response as expressive of a public mood that no longer responded to "unpatriotic images" of Zionism and American Judaism. Evincing this new spirit of civic acceptance, an editorial in the *Boston Post* concluded at the end of the conference that "it was in a notable sense a popular gathering, representative not of class politics but essentially and collectively of American citizenship."[28]

From the Progressive era to the post-World War II era, community leaders and those who represented immigrants to the wider society through politics, journalism, and public activities defined assimilation as the reciprocal linkage of American citizenship and collective legacies. Their primary emphasis lay on the inherent Americanism and patriotism of their respective groups. Asserting that the values of their particular heritages corresponded to the official values of American tradition, ethnic Americans pointed out that the love of democracy, the work ethic, the education ethic, or the family ethic held great significance in their traditional subcultures, as well. In this manner, immigrants and their leaders made a public claim that their heritage reinforced American national identity, rather than detracted from it, as anxious Americanizers and nativists feared.

This formula of intercultural match-making appeared in early-twentieth-century American history textbooks used in Massachusetts parochial schools. A Catholic textbook author pointed out that the church's teachings had provided the most effective means to build a nation based on liberty and unity. "There can be no true, permanent union and liberty," the author stated, "except where the spirit and the faith are dominating forces [as found in the Catholic Church]." *A History of the United States for Catholic Schools* announced, "The great share that Catholics have played in the founding of America should thrill with respectful joy the heart of every Catholic student, and cause him to love more sincerely and serve more loyally the chosen country of God."[29]

Ordinary immigrants in their personal life-worlds were quick to make the connection between ethnic heritages and American traditions. Elgy Toury, who grew up in Lowell, Massachusetts, recalled that her Greek-born mother considered "Greekism" and "Americanism" as directly related and equivalent in cultural importance. Electra Parigian, another daughter of Greek immigrants from Lowell, felt that her teachers in public school treated Greek Americans with "respect" because they "knew that the Greek philosophy of life was in every history, astronomy, science, and math book in America."[30]

Asserting the compatibility of Americanism and ethnicity allowed one to define assimilation as mutualist and pluralist, a pathway to a democratic pluralism rather than Anglo-conformity. The proponents of this model of ethnic Americanization called for a civic sphere that mediated in an egalitarian way between the universal and the particular and that legitimized the overlapping areas between national and ethnic identity.[31] They echoed the sentiment of Jane Addams who once hoped that "American citizenship might be built without disturbing these [ethnic] foundations which were laid of old time."[32]

Immigrants spoke of their ability, because of their foreign origins and experiences, to appreciate and feel loyalty to a civic tradition of liberty and voluntarism. Mary Antin's autobiography, *The Promised Land* (1912), describes her path as a young Russian immigrant toward participation in this civic tradition.[33] In her view, the Boston Public Library symbolized the opportunities afforded by American citizenship, even to the newest arrivals in the United States. Almost breathlessly, Antin confessed, "It was my habit to go very slowly up the low, broad steps to the palace entrance, pleasing my eyes with the majestic lines of the building, and lingering to read again the carved inscriptions: Public Library—Built by the People—Free to All." Free educational opportunity signified that "in America a child of the slums owns the land and all that is good in it." In America, all citizens—including immigrants—enjoyed the same opportunities for self-improvement. Mary Antin could rhapsodize, "All the beautiful things I saw belonged to me, if I wanted to use them; all the beautiful things I desired approached me."[34] As an immigrant from Russia, who knew first-hand the restricted place of Jewish minorities in that land, Antin had the double-vision to appreciate the gifts of American freedom.[35] Her autobiography expressed a loving sense of gratitude for democratic traditions that provided individuals with opportunity regardless of their station in life. The opportunity to be educated became the cornerstone of her deeply felt civic patriotism, her intense pride in being a citizen of the United States.

The connection between the immigrant experience and the liberating domain of American democracy was explored in the post-World War II years by Harvard historian Oscar Handlin, whose parents were Jewish immigrants from Russia. In *The Uprooted* (1951), Handlin wrote an evocative social history in which immigrants assumed a central role in the shaping of American national identity. This complex essay demonstrated that the immigrants "were American history," and its subtitle, "The Epic Story of the Great Migration That Made the American People," indicated that the history of the immigrant was nothing less than the saga of the making of a new nation.[36] The archetypal American immigrant in *The Uprooted* faced life as an unfettered individual, moving through a new world without the security of the "nest," driven to face personally the unknown, always ready to push ahead into new realms of action under the uncertain conditions of liberty.

Handlin once noted that Mary Antin, too, had pondered the connection between the American immigrant and the expansion of liberty. In his introduction to the Princeton University Press edition of *The Promised Land* published in 1969, Handlin commented that Antin affirmed "America is liberating," by supplying "opportunities" and making "possible what had been out of reach earlier by cutting the individual away from the past and allowing his own personality to flower."[37] Exploring the relation of the immigrant to the unsecured and open life under modern democracy, *The Uprooted*, like *The Promised Land*, recognized the immigrant's key role in expanding the sphere of American liberty.

The Uprooted also demonstrated how the immigrant's exposure to free conditions did not result in a homogenizing and linear assimilation process. Instead, adjustment to the new environment brought the immigrant "ever deeper within a separate existence." Paradoxically, as immigrants adapted and changed, they found themselves "more often and more completely operating inside the limits" of "cultural and social enclaves." This developmental path sprang from the conditions of liberty that allowed "social concerns" to be addressed through "the function of voluntary, autonomous combinations, free of the State and all on an equal footing." In this "realm of spontaneous organization," which encompassed native groups as well, immigrant groups discovered "distinctive similarities within themselves" and built an associational life on "the distinctive differences" that "cut them off from the whole society." Under the general conditions of civil society, immigrants created the framework for an ethnic-American cultural pluralism that enlarged the dimensions of liberty and strengthened the voluntary impulse underlying democratic life.[38]

In *A Nation of Immigrants*, first published in 1957 and then republished in expanded form in 1964, John F. Kennedy, a later-generation descendant of Irish immigrants, provided a high-profile, celebratory account of the historic connection among immigration, American freedom, and democratic pluralism. In his panoramic survey, which cited the insights of *The Uprooted*, President Kennedy referred to the "American idea": the historic pattern of a voluntary society based on achieved identity and an accommodation to cultural pluralism. Immigrants built a nation by the contribution of inherited cultural legacies that lived on. Kennedy noted that although the "melting pot" idea symbolized how "many strains" blended "into a single nationality," Americans "have come to realize in modern times" that the "melting pot" did not "mean the end of particular ethnic identities or traditions." As exemplars of the American idea, by furthering American pluralism, immigrants helped to broaden and strengthen the voluntary foundations of modern democratic nationhood.[39]

Massachusetts Architects of Inclusive Nationalism and Civic Pluralism

Intellectually connected to eighteenth-century Enlightenment rationalism and early-nineteenth-century liberalism, pro-immigration federal lawmakers from Massachusetts publicly portrayed the United States as an "immigration country" whose national ideology supported immigration and civic assimilation for all. They argued for acceptance of the incipient republican civic identity of Chinese immigrants and thus for ending the exclusion of the Chinese from admission and naturalized citizenship. Naturalization formed a vital part of the liberal nationalist framework, recruiting immigrants from Europe into a mass movement of civic assimilation. In the words of Mary Antin, immigrants who naturalized became part of a democratic community, "relatives" of George Washington.[40]

The establishment of a positive civic pluralism had to await new social developments and did not emerge as a defining agenda of public policy until the twentieth century. Out of group interaction in the robust civil society of urban-industrial Massachusetts, a popular conception emerged of a mutual balance between the ethnic "parts" and the national "whole." In this way, a new style of democratic pluralism began to overtake the liberal nationalist assimilation model that focused on individual identity and devalued collective identity.

Immigrant communities evolved in a public sphere that allowed them to develop voluntary and creative initiatives for expanding social communication within groups and among groups. Progressive reformers and Americanizers encouraged the expansion of group horizons to stimulate a wider civic consciousness. Concurrently, ethnic leaderships reached outward to public sites for intergroup contact. In the process, they won for their constituents broader acceptance of their rightful place in a community of fellow citizens. Developing public relations with the host society under the assimilationist ethos of Progressive reformers and Americanizers, immigrant leaders met the latter halfway, by stressing the readiness of their ethnic cohorts to contribute to American citizenship and democracy. Mary Antin was a public representative of the proud immigrant community who clarified the special capacity of immigrants to improve American citizenship and to participate in expanding American liberty.

In the postwar era, other Massachusetts descendants of immigrants shaped a vision of the American experience as a saga of freedom, inclusive of immigrants in a fundamental way. Oscar Handlin's archetypal immigrant was also the archetypal modern American facing a life defined by changes and choices. *The Uprooted* placed immigrants at the center of America's saga of nation-building, demonstrating the fundamental connection between immigrants and a civil society giving rise to cultural pluralism. Moving along the interpretive pathway of the *The Uprooted*, John F. Kennedy's *A Nation of Immigrants* supplied a parallel popular account of the immigrant's contribution to the building of a modern pluralist democracy.

Massachusetts was a creative laboratory for finding a more inclusive national identity and new modes of civic relations that could bring together immigrant and native communities. From the Civil War and Reconstruction era to the Cold War, Massachusetts opinionmakers, policymakers, and ordinary immigrants built a civic life that guided the nation toward a unifying democratic pluralism.

Notes

1. Tyler Anbinder, *Nativism and Slavery: The Northern Know Nothings and the Politics of the 1850s* (New York, 1992), 121-122, 137-138; Oscar Handlin, *Boston's Immigrants, 1790-1880: A Study in Acculturation*, rev. ed. (Cambridge, Mass., 1959), 203.

2. Barbara Miller Solomon, *Ancestors and Immigrants: A Changing New England Tradition* (Cambridge, Mass., 1956), 101-102, 114-116, 147-151.

3. Hans Kohn, *American Nationalism: An Interpretative Essay* (New York, 1957), 150-151; Solomon, *Ancestors and Immigrants*, 3-6; Arthur Mann, *The One and the Many: Reflections on the American Identity* (Chicago, 1979), 127-128; Yehoshua Arieli, *Individualism and Nationalism in American Ideology* (Cambridge, Mass., 1964), 87-89.

4. Albert K. Weinberg, *Manifest Destiny: A Study of Nationalist Expansionism in American History* (Baltimore, 1935), 361; Mann, *The One and the Many*, 127.

5. Theodore Roosevelt, "Americanism," in *Immigrants in American Life*, ed. Arthur Mann, rev. ed. (Boston, 1974), 180.

6. Kohn, *American Nationalism*, 138.

7. Alexander Saxton, *The Indispensable Enemy: Labor and the Anti-Chinese Movement in California* (Berkeley, 1971), 36.

8. *Congressional Record*, 49th Cong., 1st sess., May 26, 1886, 4958.

9. *Congressional Record*, 57th Cong., 1st sess., Apr. 16, 1902, 4252.

10. *Congressional Record*, 78th Cong., 1st sess., Oct. 20, 1943, 8579.

11. *Congressional Record*, 78th Cong., 8580.

12. E. Hutchinson, *Legislative History of American Immigration Policy, 1798-1965* (Philadelphia, 1981), 340-342; David M. Reimers, *Still the Golden Door: The Third World Comes to America* (New York, 1985), 65.

13. Eric J. Hooglund, ed., *Crossing the Waters: Arabic-Speaking Immigrants to the United States before 1940* (Washington, D.C., 1987), 44; Paul S. Rundquist, "A Uniform Rule: Congress and the Courts in American Naturalization, 1865-1952" (Ph.D. diss., Univ. of Chicago, 1975), 194-205.

14. *In re Halladjian*, 174 F. 834 (1909) 835-836.

15. James H. Kettner, "The Development of American Citizenship in the Revolutionary Era: The Idea of Volitional Allegiance," *American Journal of Legal History* 18(1974):208-242; Mann, *The One and the Many*, 55-60.

16. Reed Ueda, "Naturalization and Citizenship," in *The Harvard Encyclopedia of American Ethnic Groups*, ed. Stephen Thernstrom (Cambridge, Mass., 1980); Reed Ueda, *Postwar Immigrant America: A Social History* (New York, 1994), 127-128.

17. *Report of the Commission on Immigration on the Problem of Immigration in Massachusetts* (Boston, 1914), 134.

18. Naturalization Act of June 29, 1906 (34 Statutes-at-Large 596). Also see Nathaniel C. Fowler, Jr., *How to Obtain Citizenship* (New York, 1913); R. K. O'Neil and G. K. Estes, *Naturalization Made Easy: What to Do and What to Know*, 6th ed. (San Francisco, 1917).

19. *Report of the Commission on Immigration*, 158-159.

20. Massachusetts, Department of Education, Bulletin No. 50, Charles M. Herlihy, "The Massachusetts Problem of Immigrant Education in 1921-22," in *Immigration: Select Documents and Case Records*, ed. Edith Abbot (Chicago, 1924), 568-570; John Higham, *Strangers in the Land: Patterns of American Nativism, 1860-1925* (New Brunswick, 1955), 379; Massachusetts, Division of University Extension, *Courses for Americanization*, Bulletins 1-14 (Boston, Mass., 1916-1929).

21. *Report of the Commission on Immigration*, 159.

22. City of Cambridge, *Annual Reports, 1913* (Boston, 1913), 479-481, cited by W. Dean Eastman, "The Influence of Immigration on the Development of Civic Education in the United States from 1880-1925" (master's thesis, Harvard Univ., 1999), 29.

23. Horace J. Bridges, *On Becoming an American: Some Meditations of a Newly Naturalized Immigrant* (Boston, 1919), 5-8, 13-23.

24. Ueda, "Naturalization and Citizenship"; Ueda, *Postwar Immigrant America*, 128; Luella Gettys, *The Law of Citizenship in the United States* (Chicago, 1934), 129-141; Sophonisba Breckenridge, *Marriage and the Civic Rights of Women* (Chicago, 1931), passim; Nancy F. Cott, "Marriage and Women's Citizenship in the United States, 1830-1934," *American Historical Review* 103(1998):1440-1474.

25. Ellen Smith, "Strangers and Sojourners: The Jews of Colonial Boston" and "'Israelites in Boston,' 1840-1880," in *The Jews of Boston: Essays on the Occasion of the Centenary (1895-1995) of the Combined Jewish Philanthropies of Greater Boston*, ed. Jonathan D. Sarna and Ellen Smith (Boston, 1995), 44, 65.

26. John Bodnar, *Remaking America: Public Memory, Commemoration, and Patriotism in the Twentieth Century* (Princeton, 1992), 83-84.

27. See "Publisher's Note" in Frank V. Thompson, *Schooling of the Immigrant* (New York, 1920).

28. William A. Braverman, "The Emergence of a Unified Community, 1880-1917," in *The Jews of Boston*, 88.

29. Ethan Hoblitzelle, speaking at a Tufts University History Department Roundtable, April 1999, cited these and similar statements from Sadlier's *Excelsior Studies in the History of the United States for Schools* (New York, 1910); The Franciscan Sisters of the Perpetual Adoration, *A History of the United States for Catholic Schools* (New York, 1914); The Franciscan Sisters of the Perpetual Adoration, *The Cathedral History of the United States* (New York, 1920); William Kennedy and Sister Mary Joseph, *A History of the United States for Upper Grades of Catholic Schools* (New York, 1926).

30. Colleen M. Knight, "Education, Americanization, and Acculturation in an Immigrant Community: Lowell, Massachusetts and its Greek Americans, 1910-1930" (master's thesis, Tufts Univ., 1999), 60-61, 67.

31. Lawrence H. Fuchs, *The American Kaleidoscope: Race, Ethnicity, and the Civic Culture* (Hanover, N.H., 1990), 5.

32. Jane Addams, *Twenty Years at Hull House* (1910; New York, 1960), 185.

33. Mary Antin, *The Promised Land* (Boston, 1912).

34. Antin, *The Promised Land*, 341, 357-358.

35. Werner Sollors, introduction to *The Promised Land*, by Mary Antin (1912; New York, 1997), xxix.

36. Oscar Handlin, *The Uprooted: The Epic Story of the Great Migration That Made the American People* (Boston, 1951), 3.

37. Oscar Handlin, foreword to *The Promised Land*, by Mary Antin (1912; Princeton, 1969), xii.

38. Handlin, *The Uprooted*, 185-186.

39. John F. Kennedy, *A Nation of Immigrants* (New York, 1964), 67.

40. Antin, *The Promised Land*, 224-225.

Southern Black Migration and Community Building in the Era of the Civil War

Worcester County as a Case Study

JANETTE THOMAS GREENWOOD

N JUNE 1862, amidst news from the Civil War battle-front, the *Worcester Spy* announced the "arrival of a 'Contraband'"—a slave who had absconded to the safety of Union lines in search of freedom. The refugee had just come from New Bern, North Carolina, where he had "rendered important services to Gen. Burnside, in the capacity of pilot." In return for his aid, "he was sent north with his wife and child," bearing "recommendations from officers high in rank." The newspaper editor appealed to readers to consider hiring him, as "such a man certainly deserves immediate employment here—a chance for honest labor, which is all he wants."[1]

The arrival of the escaped bondsman and his family in Worcester marked the beginning of a small but steady stream of "contrabands" and then emancipated slaves to Worcester County, Massachusetts, during and immediately following the Civil War. Their story contains several clues about the origin and nature of this development. Southern black migration to central Massachusetts from the 1860s on was rooted in the experience of the Civil War, first and foremost in relationships built between Northern white soldiers and Southern blacks during the conflict. Some fugitives and Northern white soldiers, sharing the experience of the war, forged strong personal bonds that led former slaves to accompany the veterans North to their homes. Missionary teachers from Worcester, following in the paths of county units, reinforced military networks of migration, bringing additional freedpeople North with them after their service in the South. Personal and highly localized, this wartime journey established Southern black migration networks to Worcester County evident through the turn of the century.

As the contraband's story suggests, Civil War-era migration was profoundly different from the massive Great Migration of the twentieth century, with its own unique context, internal dynamic, and networks. Yet this process has rarely been studied on its own terms. The Great Migration dominates the literature and consequently our understanding of black migration. Great Migration studies also generally treat the Civil War-era movements in a cursory way, as mere prologue to the Great Migration.[2]

Worcester County, Massachusetts, provides an outstanding context for tracing Civil War-era black migration to the North and the intricate connections created among Southern blacks, Northern white soldiers and missionaries, and their home communities. In the first two years of the war, Worcester County raised several regiments made up of white men from the county. Among the most prominent were the Massachusetts Twenty-fifth Volunteer Infantry and the Massachusetts Fifteenth. The Twenty-fifth, a three-year regiment, was part of the Burnside Expedition that successfully invaded and controlled much of northeastern North Carolina, including New Bern, in the spring of 1862. The Massachusetts Fifteenth Volunteer Infantry, another three-year Worcester County unit, spent most of the war engaged in the bloody, protracted campaigns fought in Virginia and Maryland.

Missionary teachers from Worcester County enthusiastically followed in the paths of local units serving in the South. Because of the presence of the Massachusetts Twenty-fifth in New Bern, young men and women eager to teach former slaves flocked to eastern North Carolina. Others established and taught in freedpeople's schools in southeastern Virginia, also in proximity to Worcester County soldiers.

Black migration networks to Worcester County mirrored the specific paths its troops and missionaries trod. Runaway slaves from northern Virginia and from northeastern North Carolina all sought refuge and freedom with the county's units during the war. Like the "contraband" family in 1862, they made their way North during and immediately following the war in the company of local soldiers, paving the way for future migrants from these specific Southern locales. Between 1862 and 1870, approximately 370 Southern blacks—the overwhelming number from North Carolina and Virginia—migrated to the county, significantly augmenting its African American population (from approximately 769 to

1,136) and nearly doubling the city's black community (from approximately 264 to 513). Civil War-era journeyers established patterns of chain migration in which they rapidly facilitated the arrival of additional family members and friends. Moreover, they helped to create a migration tradition of men and women from Virginia and eastern North Carolina that lasted at least through the end of the century. By 1900, North Carolinians and Virginians helped quadruple the city's "colored" population, giving it a decidedly Southern cast.[3]

Notably, a handful of Louisianans also moved to northern Worcester County with the Massachusetts Fifty-third, a nine-months unit raised largely from northern county towns, after their service in the Teche and Port Hudson Expeditions in 1863. But unlike the North Carolinians and Virginians, the Louisianans never managed to establish patterns of chain migration to central Massachusetts. Louisiana may simply have been too distant to make such a migration feasible. Moreover, Worcesterites never established a missionary presence in Louisiana—because of the short service of the Fifty-third and its distance—which would have provided another network of association and migration. The contrasting experiences of North Carolina and Virginia migrants with their Louisiana counterparts suggest not only that a Yankee presence of several years in the South was crucial in establishing and supporting migration networks, but also that a critical mass of migrants from a specific locale was necessary to create and sustain long-term movement from South to North.[4]

An examination of Civil War-era migration not only sheds light on the bonds of war created between Southern blacks and Northern white soldiers and teachers but also demonstrates how their interactions profoundly shaped each group. Wartime relationships left deep and lasting impressions that went far beyond the exigencies of war and reflect another dimension of wartime bonding.

In addition, Worcester County's Civil War-era black migration affords a rare glimpse into the lives and strategies of "contrabands of war," of black men, women, and children on the cusp of freedom. Their stories not only reveal significant contributions that African Americans made to the Union war effort but also show how former slaves negotiated a new world of wartime freedom, the strategies they employed, and the decisions they made to ensure their liberty and that of family and friends whom they subsequently brought North.

Black migration to Worcester in this period also provides a rich case study of a tiny but highly organized and politically active Northern black community that played a crucial role in settling Southern migrants. Black Worcesterites, in many cases former slaves themselves who had sought refuge in the city before the Civil War, found migrants housing and employment and helped integrate them into a supportive community. Complemented by a solid infrastructure of antislavery and freedman's relief organizations, the support of patrons—both black and white—eased the transition of former slaves to a more complete freedom in the North.

While white sympathy for refugees from the South soon faded and blacks faced discrimination in industrial employment, they nonetheless continued to move to Worcester and by the 1870s built and nourished their own cultural enclave within the city's small African American community. Drawn together by common experience and a shared Southern culture, they established a distinctive neighborhood, centered on their own church, and cultivated an identity apart from the older established community. While much smaller and poorer than the ethnic enclaves established at the same time by French Canadians, who were welcomed by Worcester's burgeoning industries, Southern blacks nonetheless managed to establish and maintain a distinctive identity on Northern soil.

The "contraband" family, whose arrival the *Worcester Spy* heralded in June 1862, blazed the trail from eastern North Carolina to Worcester, a path black Carolinians continuously trod during and after the Civil War. The escaped slaves were probably William and Mary Bryant and their child. The Bryants wed in Worcester in January 1863. Not only did their marriage record list their places of birth as New Bern, but a city official also carefully wrote "contraband" after their names in the registry.[5]

The Bryants were among thousands of eastern North Carolina slaves who sought refuge with the Union army early in the war as the massive Burnside Expedition seized northeastern North Carolina and placed it under federal control. In February 1862 Burnside's armada, consisting of naval vessels, gunboats, and transports holding 13,000 soldiers—among them Worcester County's Massachusetts Twenty-fifth Infantry—bore down on the Carolina coast. The Union forces first took Roanoke Island in February, and then in March, with only minimal resistance, seized New Bern, the second-largest city on the North Carolina coast. As the Yankees moved onto North Carolina's shores, terrified white residents fled the area, seeking refuge in the interior.[6]

Immediately slave men, women, and children took advantage of the chaos and confusion to liberate themselves. Only a few days after taking New Bern, Gen. Ambrose Burnside reported that the city was "being over-run with fugitives from the surrounding towns and plantations." Within several months, approximately 10,000 eastern North Carolina blacks had escaped to Union strongholds in the area, with 7,500 settling in New Bern alone.[7]

East Carolina blacks worked their way to the Union encampments by hiding in the woods and swamps in the day and traveling at night. Although the Civil War, as defined by the Lincoln administration, was not yet about the abolition of slavery but rather the preservation of the Union, slaves themselves cared little about official policy. In their minds, the war had always been about their freedom. They were sure that the Yankees had come to liberate them.

The slaves who ran away to the Union army complicated official policy for the Lincoln administration and their status remained ambiguous. In May 1861, when a Virginia master demanded the return of his slaves who had escaped to the Union army at Fortress Monroe, Gen. Benjamin Butler refused. In a highly publicized reply, the general explained that since Virginia had left the Union, the fugitive slave law no longer applied. Butler employed the runaways and referred to them as "contrabands of war," a term henceforth widely used to describe slaves who absconded to the Union army. While the Lincoln administration, with ambivalence, allowed Butler's policy, Congress passed the Confiscation Act in August 1861, six months before the Burnside Expedition, permitting federal troops to seize all property used in aiding the rebellion. Notably, the law affected only slaves directly employed by the Confederacy. Therefore, New Bern's contrabands, like those who had sought refuge elsewhere behind Yankee lines, possessed a tenuous freedom; they were free only as long as Union soldiers agreed to protect them—in violation of federal law.[8]

Soon after arriving in New Bern and its environs, the soldiers of Worcester County's Massachusetts Twenty-fifth Regiment had their first direct contact with runaway slaves, an experience that, for many, served as a defining event. Popularly referred to as "The Worcester County Regiment," as all ten of its companies had been recruited from the city of Worcester and three county towns, the Twenty-fifth attracted many well-educated sons of the local middle class. As the unit formed, the *Worcester Spy* constantly commented on the "well appointed" composition of the regiment, made up of "young men of merit and intelligence," many of whom left behind "large business interests," abandoning "permanent and valuable situations in banks and elsewhere."[9]

As middle-class Worcesterites, these recruits were well acquainted with the county's abolitionist tradition. Antislavery sentiment ran deep in Worcester County. The town made its feelings clear as early as 1765 when it charged its representative to the General Court to do what he could "to put an end to that unchristian and impolitic practice of making slaves of the human species." In 1781, a Worcester County slave named Quock Walker successfully sued for his freedom and ultimately helped win emancipation for all slaves in Massachusetts. In the 1830s, when William Lloyd Garrison helped ignite abolitionist sentiment in the North, antislavery societies mushroomed throughout Worcester County, sponsoring lectures, debates, and public meetings all aimed at raising public consciousness about the evils of slavery.[10]

From the 1830s on, Worcester played a leading role in nearly every major antislavery endeavor of the era. In many ways, Worcester initiated more groundbreaking and radical antislavery activity than its more glamorous counterpart, Boston. Underground Railroad activity was rampant throughout the county, and Worcester served as the destination for numerous fugitive slaves. The city was the birthplace of the Free Soil Party in 1848 and local Free Soil leaders helped found the Republican Party in 1854. That year, Worcesterites Thomas Wentworth Higginson, a radical minister, and Martin Stowell, a local farmer, led a group of abolitionists attempting to free Anthony Burns, held in a Boston prison under the Fugitive Slave Act. A contingent of ten Worcester citizens, armed with axes, provided much of the muscle for the unsuccessful rescue of Burns. Also in 1854, after the passage of the Kansas-Nebraska Act, Eli Thayer's New England Emigrant Aid Company recruited the first party of settlers intent on securing Kansas as a free state and contributed several groups of colonizers—as well as guns—to battle the "slave power" in the West. When John Brown and his revolutionary band attempted to instigate a slave rebellion at Harpers Ferry in October 1859, Worcester's Higginson aided them with arms, while Charles Plummer Tidd of Clinton, in Worcester County, served as one of Brown's "captains." On the day of Brown's execution in Virginia, several city churches tolled their bells, businesses closed, and citizens held memorial services throughout the county.[11]

While Worcester was the home of several nationally known abolitionists, including Higginson and Stephen and Abby Kelley Foster, many other less renowned citizens, especially members of the city's tiny but highly activist African American community, devoted themselves to the cause of abolition in the decades preceding the Civil War. In response to the notorious Fugitive Slave Act of 1850, black and white residents organized the Worcester Freedom Club and a local Vigilance Committee and stood watch for slavecatchers and U.S. marshals in pursuit of runaway slaves. Numerous city and county churches and citizens also regularly donated funds to the Boston Vigilance Committee—in charge of housing, feeding, and transporting fugitive slaves to safe locations. In October 1854, when Deputy U.S. Marshal Asa Butman appeared in Worcester after the Burns trial, black citizens, fearing that he was seeking fugitives, allied with white abolitionists to run the officer out of the city. The hostile response that the marshal met in Worcester, known as the Butman Riot, guaranteed that no one ever attempted to recapture runaway slaves in the city.[12]

Although antislavery sentiment predominated in the county, Worcester's volunteers nonetheless held differing opinions about the Civil War's meaning. Like young men who volunteer to fight in any armed conflict, some simply had yet to make up their minds about the war's purpose. The antislavery culture of their community may have predisposed most of them ultimately to commit to abolitionism, but letters written home by members of the Twenty-fifth reveal that at least some did not become abolitionists until they witnessed slavery firsthand, particularly through their interactions with the "contrabands of war." Personal encounters with refugees recast slavery from a distant, abstract institution to a system with a human face.

Worcester County soldiers were startled to find themselves engulfed in a wave of refugee slaves who viewed them as their God-sent liberators, the long-awaited answer to their prayers. "Tank God, massa," a refugee greeted Worcester's Maj. Josiah Pickett, "now I *do* 'bleve de Lord is come *for sure!* ... We've ben praying and praying dis long time dat de Lord *come*, and I *knowed* he would." Runaways spoke openly with the Yankee troops about the horrors of slavery, discussed their understanding of the war as a war to end the institution, and demonstrated their passion for freedom. In the process, they "educated up" many Worcester soldiers, in the words of one. Capt. J. Waldo Denny described many such encounters and transformations in his letters home, remarking that "conservative men"—even some who voted for Southern Democrat John Breckinridge in the 1860 presidential election—now embraced abolition as a war aim.[13]

Not only were Worcester County soldiers in New Bern deeply impressed with the slaves' understanding of the war and their deep desire for freedom, but the devotion of runaways to the Union also genuinely moved them. In eastern North Carolina, where Northern soldiers resided among resentful, openly defiant whites and seemed particularly vulnerable to Confederate attack, blacks appeared to be their only true friends. Worcester soldiers repeatedly contrasted the fidelity of African Americans with the disloyalty of white North Carolinians, contending that blacks "are the only Union men we have here."[14]

Runaway slaves proved the depth of their loyalty to the Union by providing invaluable and highly dangerous service. Almost immediately after seizing control of New Bern, General Burnside, like General Butler before him, put contrabands to work for the Union army, paying men $10 a month to work as laborers and women $4 a month as servants. Men built fortifications, unloaded and loaded government ships, and labored as crew members aboard steamers. Women and children eased the lives of white soldiers by washing and ironing, cooking, and baking pies and cakes. Skilled contrabands also lent their expertise to the Union cause, working as blacksmiths, coopers, ship-joiners, and even bridge-builders.[15]

In addition, a group of about fifty "of the best and most courageous" contraband men worked continually for the Union army as spies, scouts, and guides—among them William Bryant. Spies ventured as far as several hundred miles behind Confederate lines to bring back valuable information to Federal forces. Some were chased by bloodhounds and barely escaped with their lives. Others were captured and shot. Boat pilots like William Bryant provided indispensable assistance to Union officers through their knowledge of eastern North Carolina's intricate waterways. An officer wrote from New Bern that having observed "large numbers of 'contraband' negroes . . . my respect for the black race has been greatly increased thereby," since "they obtained important information when white men could not; they have acted as spies when white men could not be hired to risk their necks."[16]

William Bryant's service to General Burnside must have been especially exemplary to warrant the attention and reward that he received. While it remains a mystery whether the idea to move North as payment for his service originated with Bryant or Burnside and his staff, it seems clear that runaway slaves and later freedpeople strongly identified New England, and especially Massachusetts, with liberty. As the home of abolitionism and their liberators, "old Massachusetts," in the words of one post-Civil War Southern migrant to Boston, represented "liberty in the full sense of the word." Although far from perfect in its treatment of blacks, Massachusetts nonetheless was a land of fresh beginnings for those who sought to leave the South and its weighty legacy of slavery behind.[17]

The Bryants' decision to seek a more secure freedom in the North in June 1862 was likely prompted by political developments that illuminated the fragile nature of the contrabands' liberty and threw New Bern into near chaos. In May 1862, President Lincoln, still defining the conflict as a war to preserve the nation, appointed native Unionist Edward Stanly as military governor of North Carolina, hoping that like-minded Tarheels would rally behind him and end the rebellion in that state. Wanting to retain slavery in a Unionist North Carolina, Stanly demanded that runaway slaves be returned to masters who took an oath of allegiance.[18]

Governor Stanly's policies filled the contrabands with terror. A reporter in New Bern observed "a stampede in all directions" as "many [contrabands] took themselves to the woods" to hide from returning masters. A Northern reporter in New Bern noted that "a perfect panic prevails among them," with some hiding in swamps and other "out-of-the-way places," many declaring that "they would rather die" than return to slavery.[19]

Possessing an uncertain freedom in North Carolina, William Bryant opted to leave his master far behind and to secure his liberty in the North. Arriving in Worcester with "recommendations from officers high in rank," Bryant likely got to Worcester through the influence of the Reverend Horace James, chaplain of the Massachusetts Twenty-fifth, who emerged soon after the unit's arrival in New Bern as an advocate for contrabands. Pastor of the Old South Congregational Church when he volunteered to serve as chaplain of the Twenty-fifth in the fall of 1861, James was an abolitionist committed to radical social change. Preparing the contrabands for their freedom became the focus of James's chaplaincy, and his high profile attracted attention from commanding officers. Immediately after the successful invasion of New Bern James enlisted approximately thirty young men of the Twenty-fifth to serve as volunteer teachers, setting up evening schools for the fugitives. Beginning in the spring of 1862, he played an especially crucial role in forging strong links between Worcester and eastern North Carolina that provided the underpinning for migration networks from New Bern to Worcester County.[20]

The schools that James and Worcester County soldiers opened soon became casualties of the Stanly administration as well. Just as the governor demanded a return to the *status quo* in regard to runaway slaves, Stanly insisted that according to state law, schools for blacks were a criminal offense in North Carolina and closed them. The Northern press widely publicized Stanly's actions regarding both schools and runaway slaves. In Worcester, the governor's deeds seemed like a personal affront as Horace James and the county's sons played a key role in New Bern's contraband schools. John Denison Baldwin, the fiery editor of the abolitionist *Worcester Spy*, vociferously criticized Stanly preceding the Bryant family's arrival in the city. Through numerous newspaper reports, editorials, and soldiers' letters home, Worcester County citizens became well aware of the explosive situation in New Bern and the plight of the city's contrabands.

By the time that the Bryants arrived in Worcester, many citizens sympathized with the predicament of New Bern's contrabands and the plight of black refugees from the South. As early as December 1861, Worcester women had organized the Ladies Committee, soon renamed the Association for the Relief of Liberated Slaves, to gather books, clothing, and other supplies for refugee slaves who had fled to the Union army in Port Royal, South Carolina. Nearly every Worcester County town boasted a similar organization. After the Burnside invasion, New Bern's refugee slave population became a favorite focus for relief efforts. The highly publicized efforts of freedman's relief organizations coupled with numerous newspaper reports and personal letters from local soldiers, some of which were reproduced in the *Spy*, generated a great deal of compassion in Worcester for the contrabands of war.[21]

Similar to refugees of twentieth-century wars, as described by Cheryl Benard, the contrabands served as political symbols, who "by their mere existence" personified "a profound criticism of the state they have fled." Worcester, with its strong abolitionist tradition, stood ready to embrace the refugees of slavery. By making their way North during and after the Civil War, the contrabands anticipated the experiences of twentieth-century refugees, particularly Jews and "displaced persons" in the aftermath of World War II and Vietnamese refugees in the 1970s. Like their twentieth-century counterparts, Civil War refugees benefited from the aid of advocates such as the *Worcester Spy* and the numerous freedman's relief organizations that dotted the county, all of which publicized their hardships, generated public support for their presence, and encouraged sponsorship.[22]

When the *Spy* announced the arrival of the contraband family and appealed to Worcesterites to give William Bryant "a chance for honest labor," the newspaper urged potential employers to contact "R. H. Johnson, truckman." Johnson's involvement in settling the Bryant family reveals the crucial role that Worcester's black community played in facilitating the Civil War-era migration of Southern blacks from its earliest days. While white military officers served as the Bryants' initial patrons, Worcester's black community subsequently settled the "contraband" family in the community, providing shelter and employment.[23]

Robert H. Johnson belonged to a tiny community of blacks consisting of approximately 264 people in 1860 in a city of 25,000 residents. Approximately 500 additional African Americans resided in the county, making its black residents less than .5 percent of its total population. Unlike Boston, the overwhelming majority—approximately 80 percent—of Worcester's black residents in 1860 were born in the North, a full 60 percent Massachusetts-born. Many were "Black Yankees," with deep roots in the area extending to colonial times. Only about 17 percent were Southern-born, with an overwhelming majority of these, like Johnson and his wife, Mary, born into slavery in Maryland.[24]

Johnson was one of a number of former slaves who had found refuge in Worcester before the Civil War. Indeed, in the 1850s, Worcester had become, in Thomas Wentworth Higginson's words, "Canada to the Slave," as evidenced in the city's open defiance of the Fugitive Slave Law in the 1854 Butman Riot. Along with barbers Gilbert and Allen Walker and William Jankins, and cleaner Isaac Mason, Johnson was an ex-slave from the Upper South who had become a well-known personage in the city. Arriving in Worcester in 1856, Johnson established a family and business in Worcester as a job truckman. Perhaps remembering his own migration North from Maryland and his transition from slavery to freedom, Johnson assumed the role of employment agent for the Bryants.[25]

For former slaves such as Johnson, who had arrived in Worcester in the years before the Civil War, securing freedom in the North did not absolve them of responsibility to their brothers and sisters still in chains in the

South. Through the 1850s and early '60s they fought boldly to end their subjugation and to aid ex-slaves seeking a new start in the North. As members of the city's Vigilance Committee and Freedom Club, they built alliances with Black Yankee families, such as the William Browns, as well as with radical whites, such as T. W. Higginson and Martin Stowell, by participating in Underground Railroad activities, guarding their community from slavecatchers, and answering the call to aid captive Anthony Burns in Boston. They contributed to the New England Emigrant Aid Society to settle Kansas, sent a representative to the New England Colored Citizens' Convention, and offered food, shelter, and employment to fugitive slaves.[26]

The "contraband" Bryant family—and subsequent Civil War-era migrants—greatly benefited from Worcester's tightly organized black community and well-established interracial networks of aid and support. By 1863, through the efforts of Robert H. Johnson and other members of Worcester's African American community, William Bryant obtained work as a laborer and resided with his wife, Mary, at 62 Union Street, a house Johnson had previously occupied. Their residence placed them on the outskirts of the city's largest black residential cluster and reveals an intricate web of support provided by Worcester's Southern-born blacks to migrants.[27]

Isaac and Anna Mason owned the house at 62 Union Street. The Masons played a central role in assisting the Bryants and other Southern migrants in the era of the Civil War. Like the Bryants, the Masons knew what it was like to elude a grasping master. Born a slave in Kent County, Maryland, Isaac Mason escaped with several companions to Philadelphia around 1848. After a close brush with his master's son, who attempted to recapture him in 1850, Isaac Mason fled to Boston, where he resided with black abolitionist Lewis Hayden for several weeks. Despite its reputation as a safe haven for fugitive slaves, Boston offered few jobs and Mason struggled to find employment. Radical abolitionist Martin Stowell, hearing of the arrival of several fugitives in Boston, found work for Mason and two fellow fugitives in Worcester. Mason's wife, Anna, eventually joined him.[28]

Isaac Mason, along with many other fugitive slaves, chose to make Worcester his permanent home. The city proffered two key benefits for fugitives: in Mason's words, "plenty of good employment and benevolent sympathizers." Isaac Mason soon established himself as a carpet and window cleaner. In 1856, the Masons purchased what would become 62 and 64 Union Street.[29]

That Mason, a fugitive slave, and his wife became property owners within six years of their arrival in Worcester was highly unusual. Only about 20 percent of all Worcesterites owned any real property. That they managed this acquisition attests to their work ethic and reputation, as well as the support of the city's "benevolent sympathizers." In his first years in Worcester, Mason established a reputation for industry and "an honest and truthful life," according to Worcester lawyer and politician George Frisbie Hoar, one of several prominent white antislavery advocates who befriended Mason when he came to the city. Two other white sympathizers, industrialists George T. Rice and George Barton, and a black citizen, Delaware-born Robert Wilson, who worked in a city crockery shop, enabled the Masons to purchase the Union Street properties by capitalizing a mortgage.[30]

As Isaac Mason had received aid from Worcester's "benevolent sympathizers" in the decade before the Civil War, he, in turn, became a benefactor to Southern migrants who made their way to Worcester during and after the war. According to his friend Hoar, Mason "did his best always for his race." Residing at 64 Union Street, the Masons rented the house next door at 62 Union to former slaves, including Robert H. Johnson, the Bryants' "employment agent," who lived there with his family in 1861. Johnson likely directed the Bryants to this house.[31]

William Bryant's choice of employment also attests to Isaac Mason's role as patron. In 1864, like Mason, William Bryant listed his occupation as "carpet cleaner," a job that included house and window cleaning as well. Isaac Mason likely gave William Bryant his start in this business. Bryant may have been working for Mason and learning the trade when he first listed his occupation as "laborer" in the 1863 city directory.

By 1865, only three years after arriving in Worcester, Bryant established his own cleaning business. In 1866 he was successful enough to pay for a listing in the Worcester city directory. A year later—unlike Isaac Mason, the only other carpet cleaner in the directory—Bryant listed a separate business address: a prime location at 248 Main Street. By 1869, Bryant was successful enough to advertise in the *Spy*, promising "Windows Washed, Carpets Cleaned, and General Housework Done in the Best Manner."

Another testament to his achievement was that William's business was successful enough to support the Bryant family without Mary working outside the home.[32]

While Isaac Mason and other members of the city's black community provided invaluable support in establishing the Bryant family, Worcester's blacks were too few in number to secure William Bryant's success in the cleaning business. In 1866, the first year that Bryant listed his business in the city directory, three other black Worcesterites listed themselves as carpet cleaners. By the next year, only Mason and Bryant remained. To establish his own business on Main Street, Bryant needed to develop a large and dependable white clientele. Sympathetic whites, aware of Bryant's story, may have patronized him and helped him establish a successful business in the city.

Well before establishing his own business, but only months after finding work and a home, William and Mary Bryant married in Worcester, on January 25, 1863. Legalizing their marriage, a right denied them in slavery, was another important step the Bryants took to define, secure, and celebrate their status as free people. Like countless former slaves before and after them, the Bryants sought legal sanction for a relationship unrecognized by the slave regime. The Reverend Joseph G. Smith, pastor of the A.M.E. Zion Church, the city's single black church, founded in 1848, performed the ceremony.[33]

Financially secure by the time the Civil War ended, the Bryants leased a home at 24 Wilmot Street. The move to Wilmot Street reflected the family's improving economic status. While Union Street provided supportive Southern neighbors, the street was hemmed in by a railroad yard, a lumber yard, and machine shops. On Wilmot Street, the Bryants situated themselves in a more bucolic setting, their house backing up to hospital grounds and a reservoir. Moreover, they now lived only several streets away from prominent community leaders such as Gilbert Walker.[34]

The family's growing prominence and financial stability is also evident in the fact that Bryant became a moneylender. In 1867 William loaned $150 to Lacy and Ruth Liel to purchase a house and property near the Adriatic Mills. Lacy Liel, like Bryant, was a Southern migrant, a Virginian who came to Worcester during or immediately after the war and worked as a waiter in the city. As Isaac Mason had done before him, William Bryant perpetuated a tradition of aid to Southern migrants. His role as a moneylender in the black community proved especially crucial to a young migrant couple such as the Liels who might have otherwise had difficulty financing a house.[35]

William and Mary Bryant also served as patrons in another crucial way. As soon as they fashioned a foothold in Worcester County, they assisted additional family members in coming north, helping craft the first links of chain migration from New Bern to Worcester. A second North Carolina Bryant family, Christopher, Harriet, and Eliza Bryant, appears in the 1865 state census, residing near William and Mary Bryant. In addition, soon after the war, Julia Ann Bryant of New Bern, who was probably William's younger sister, resided in Worcester and in 1868 married a fellow Southern migrant, Henry Johnson of Mississippi. Bryant employed his brother-in-law in his cleaning business.[36]

That other Bryant family members joined William and Mary in the North attests to the Bryants' success in Worcester. Family ties, a sympathetic community, and economic opportunity combined to pull additional New Bern Bryants north to Worcester. Political instability, with the resurgence of white Conservative rule at the end of 1865, and postwar economic problems likely provided a push from North Carolina. New Bern, a magnet for east Carolina freedpeople since the Yankee invasion in 1862, offered little economically for black workers. An excess of unskilled laborers and a dearth of jobs made steady employment almost impossible.[37]

Against this backdrop, William and Mary Bryant's success in Worcester must have stood out in sharp relief to their Carolina kin. By 1870, an extended Bryant family of about ten people made Worcester their home. The city would become the long-term home of Julia Ann Bryant Johnson and her family, which blossomed to four children by 1880, as well as Christopher and Harriet Bryant and their growing family.

William and Mary Bryant, however, left the city under a cloud of scandal. In 1869 William's neighbor Lunsford Lane, a fellow migrant from North Carolina, accused him of setting his house on fire. Ultimately, the municipal court found William Bryant not guilty for lack of evidence. Because the court records no longer exist, it is impossible to know the nature of Lane's accusations against Bryant and whether they represented more than personal tensions between the two families.[38]

Despite the unceremonious departure of Worcester's pioneer "contraband" family, they had nonetheless broken new paths of migration from eastern North Carolina to Worcester in the era of the Civil War. By the time the Bryants left Worcester, the city and county had attracted well over 250 Southern migrants since 1862, the overwhelming majority from eastern North Carolina and Virginia, reflecting the Southern service of Worcester County's volunteer regiments. Many came through the same military networks that had brought the original contrabands to Worcester. Their stories are variations on the themes revealed in the tale of the Bryant family: contrabands and former slaves, many of these migrants found their freedom with sympathetic Worcester County units. Some forged close personal bonds with white soldiers—most often officers— through outstanding wartime service. Exchanging that service for a new beginning in the North, they accompanied these officers back to Worcester County at the end of the war. Soldiers, their families, and sometimes whole communities—many with a tradition of abolitionist activity— served as patrons to migrants. For some, as in the case of William Bryant, their wartime service provided a fund of goodwill upon which they drew to establish themselves in the North.

Overall, between 1860 and 1870, Worcester County's black population more than doubled, augmented significantly by the migration of Southerners. Within five years of the end of the war, black Southern migrants lived throughout the county, often in the households of Civil War veterans. Jane Waples, a New Bern contraband like the Bryants, was among them. During the war she worked as a servant for Col. A. B. R. Sprague— an organizer and commanding officer of the Massachusetts Twenty-fifth —and his wife, who joined him during the war in New Bern. At the end of the war, Waples accompanied the Sprague family to Worcester, where she worked in their household for several years. Similarly, when Lt. Andrew Fuller of Clinton, an officer in the Massachusetts Fifteenth, resigned from the army in 1861 because of ill health, Thomas Clinton, a twenty-two-year-old Virginian, accompanied him home. Fuller, a skirt manufacturer, employed Clinton—who may have taken his surname from his adopted town—as an operative in his mill. In 1865, Henry Jones, a seventeen year old from New Bern, lived and worked on the Harrington farm in Paxton. Samuel Harrington had been stationed in New Bern during the war as an officer of the Massachusetts Twenty-fifth. A twelve-year-old boy with the unlikely name of Spencer Contraband returned with Dr. Samuel Hartwell of Southbridge, a surgeon with the Thirty-eighth Massachusetts.[39]

By 1870, Worcester County missionary teachers to the South broadened and deepened military networks of migration. Following in the wake of local units, young men and women from Worcester County went South during and after the war to teach contrabands and former slaves. The Reverend Horace James played an especially crucial role in building missionary networks between Worcester and New Bern on the foundation of the military networks. Because of his work in establishing schools for New Bern's contrabands, in early 1863 James received an appointment from General Foster as Superintendent of Negro Affairs in North Carolina, placing him in charge of the well-being of approximately 15,000 African Americans who now made their home in the federally occupied parts of eastern North Carolina. To support his schools and communities, James, along with his wife, Helen, who joined him in New Bern to assist in this work, continually appealed to friends and organizations back in Worcester. Horace and Helen James also inspired many civilian Worcesterites to follow in their footsteps; they practically inundated eastern North Carolina from 1863 on. So many Worcesterites—soldiers, missionary teachers, and the occasional businessman—converged in New Bern that a soldier remarked in a letter home that "Newbern abounds with Worcester faces." Responding enthusiastically to James's appeals for missionary teachers in New Bern, they fanned out to teach freedpeople in Washington, Plymouth, Beaufort, and Elizabeth City.[40]

Some of these white Worcesterites, like the soldiers before them, developed personal relationships with their black students as they shared similar goals and common hardships. And like the soldiers, missionary teachers came to symbolize Massachusetts in the eyes of freedpeople, serving as ambassadors for the Bay State. One Massachusetts teacher in New Bern related the "creed," as she put it, of her students there: "1st, they believe in 'de good Lord,' who has heard their prayers; 2d, in Abraham Lincoln, who has broken their chains; 3d in Massachusetts, and everything that comes from it."[41]

Seeking the promise of Massachusetts, some freedpeople received aid from their teachers in migrating North and accompanied them back to Worcester County at the end of their service in the South. The missionary teachers also fostered sponsorship of former slaves in New England. Veteran Yankee missionary teacher Sarah Chase became a patron to several black Virginia couples who migrated to Worcester with her when she completed her service. With her sister, Lucy, Chase taught for three years in the Norfolk area. In 1866, suffering from ill health, she returned to Worcester with several black Virginians. According to family oral tradition, George and Elizabeth Wilson were one of several couples who accompanied Chase back to Worcester. The Wilsons named their first child, born in Worcester in 1873, after Sarah. Sarah Chase cultivated a long and fruitful relationship with her namesake, Sarah Ella Wilson, and served as her mentor. Sarah Ella Wilson became a beloved teacher in the city's public schools as well as an officer in the New England Branch of the Federation of Colored Women's Clubs. Similarly, schoolteacher Mary A. Kimball, who taught in eastern North Carolina and Virginia under the auspices of the New England Freedmen's Society, helped bring Virginian Alexander Boomer to her parent's household in Brookfield, where he labored on the Kimball farm.[42]

As it had done for the Bryants, Worcester's black community also embraced wartime migrants, sheltering many of them and finding them employment. Robert H. Johnson, who guided the Bryants' entry into Worcester in 1862, housed three young men of Southern birth. Similarly, Isaac and Anna Mason continued to aid former slaves as they had aided the Bryants, finding room in their large, extended household for numerous migrants. Black activist Gilbert Walker and his wife, Sarah, also opened their home to numerous Southern newcomers, including Laura Edwards of New Bern, Edward Allen of North Carolina, and Edward Stokes of Virginia. Allen, a barber, and Stokes, a barber's apprentice, probably worked in Walker's barbershop. Similarly, J. G. and Elizabeth Mowbray, born in Maryland like Johnson and the Walkers and residents of Worcester since the 1850s, hosted a house full of seven Southern migrants in 1865. Long involved in antislavery activities in Worcester, Elizabeth Mowbray served as president of the Colored Freedmen's Aid Society, formed in Worcester in 1864.[43]

Worcester's white abolitionists also housed and employed black migrants, demonstrating an ongoing commitment to Southern blacks that went beyond emancipation. Abby Kelley and Stephen Foster, nationally known abolitionists, employed and housed George Wiggins, a young migrant from New Bern. Wiggins worked as a farm laborer on the Foster farm and ultimately settled in Worcester, where he married a fellow Southern migrant and raised a family. Once a stop on the Underground Railroad, the farm, after emancipation, continued to serve as a passage to a new life in the North.[44]

Several Worcester County towns with a strong abolitionist tradition embraced "contrabands of war." North Brookfield showed its gratitude to several former slaves for their personal service to the town's soldiers. A nearly all-white community at the time of the Civil War, North Brookfield sent many sons to the Massachusetts Fifteenth, a unit that participated in some of the war's bloodiest fighting, including Antietam and Gettysburg.

David Porter Allen earned the indebtedness of the North Brookfield community for his aid to Col. Francis Walker, originally a sergeant in the Fifteenth. A slave from Harrison's Landing, Virginia, Allen secured his freedom in 1862 during the Peninsula Campaign by running away to the Massachusetts Fifteenth where he found employment as Walker's personal servant. When Confederates captured Walker in the summer of 1864, Allen dutifully gathered up all of the officer's belongings and made his way to the Walker family home in North Brookfield. "Feeling a lively interest in one who had served their friend so faithfully," Walker's parents and neighbors took Allen into their homes, employed him as a servant, "taught him his letters," and sent him to the town's school.[45]

Residents of North Brookfield also welcomed Robert Morse, another former slave from Virginia. Morse served as the personal attendant of Dr. Warren Tyler, a surgeon in the Thirty-sixth Massachusetts during the war. According to Morse's obituary, Dr. Tyler became "so attached to him that he brought him to North Brookfield when the war was over." Morse initially lived and worked as a servant in Tyler's household for several years.[46]

That Allen, Morse, and many other wartime migrants worked as servants in the homes of their white patrons suggests that their white benefactors had mixed motives in bringing them North. White patrons may have merely wanted to continue the personal service that they had become used to in wartime. Moreover, they may have simply been seeking cheap household help. The fact that most migrants continued working as servants may also reflect the racialist notions of some of their white benefactors, who may have believed that personal service fit black "characteristics" of devotion and humility.[47]

A groundswell of interest among Worcester's white citizens in employing "colored help" after the Civil War also suggests complicated motives for migrant sponsorship and employment. In September 1867, the *Spy* announced "in accordance with the desire of a number of citizens," a movement "to establish in this city a freedman's home and intelligence office, where colored help can be furnished." It seems almost certain that local citizens worked in conjunction with the Freedman's Intelligence and Employment Agency, formed by the Freedman's Bureau to reduce the number of dependent freedpeople in the Washington area by finding them employment and relocating them to other parts of the country. By April 1868, the Freedman's Home and Intelligence Office had been established on Boyden Street. An ad in the *Spy* appealed for positions for three freedmen, "first-class men," seeking jobs in the city "attending to horses, taking charge of a gentleman's place, or to act as a Porter in a Wholesale Store, delivering goods, &tc." While no further mention of the office can be found in the *Spy* or other local records, privately owned employment agencies, at the same time, also began publicizing the availability of "colored help." Freedman's Bureau records indicate that the bureau worked directly with private agents as well, supplying them with a seemingly endless supply of freedpeople seeking jobs in the North.[48]

Northerners in general, and Worcesterites in particular, seemed to have an insatiable appetite for black domestic workers, in the aftermath of the Civil War. Freedman's Bureau records brim with requests from Northern employment agents for "colored servants," especially women. A Philadelphia agent asked the bureau "to send me a number of women and girls (freedwomen), as I have constant demand for them." Mrs. E. J. Browne's employment agency in Worcester regularly advertised "Situations Wanted—For Colored Help," and guaranteed in 1869 that she "was now prepared to furnish at short notice" African Americans to fill positions as "coachmen, cooks, second girls, and for general housework." She also regularly advertised "colored men for waiting or teaming." Irwin's Employ Office also appealed to local white families seeking to employ "the olive-cheeked daughters of our own sunny South." In addition, from 1868 to 1872 especially, numerous individuals advertised specifically for "colored help" in the want ads of the local press. Typical ads sought "colored women" as housekeepers or cooks.[49]

Whether selfish and racialist sentiments figured prominently in decisions to sponsor black migrants is simply unclear. While some local citizens appear to have established the Freedman's Home and Intelligence Office from benevolent motives to aid freedpeople in finding economic independence after the war, private employment agents may have simply hoped to profit from the desperation of unemployed freedpeople. The many white families seeking "colored help" could have merely been seeking cheap labor in their homes. In addition, employing black servants may have seemed more exotic, and perhaps represented more prestige, than hiring an Irish maid. At the same time, given the legacies of slavery and the troubled climate of Reconstruction, liberal white Worcesterites could also have viewed black migrants as refugees of a despotic regime who deserved their help. Like the many Americans who felt a moral responsibility to resettle refugees in the aftermath of World War II and the Vietnam War, white Worcesterites may have acted from a deep-seated sense of obligation. As living symbols of the South's repression, Southern blacks granted a fresh start in Worcester may have symbolized the commitment of its citizenry to the concurrent battle for equal rights.

Although motivations for sponsorship and employment may have been complex and even ambiguous, it is clear that at least some Civil War-era migrants did not continue in subservient positions for very long. And those who did remain as servants or unskilled laborers nevertheless managed to use their situation to establish a separate household and life independent of white patrons. Whenever possible, wartime migrants seized upon the opportunities available in the North to establish themselves on their own. David Porter Allen translated his position as an in-house, personal servant in North Brookfield into a professional career. While he worked as a servant in the homes of several white families, Allen also attended public school, where he "made very rapid progress in his studies." Through "his own exertion," in the words of one observer, Allen convinced his patrons that he was capable of advanced education. He entered Westfield Normal School in western Massachusetts, where he earned a teaching certificate in 1871 and pursued advanced study in languages and science. With his teaching certificate in hand, Allen departed for North Carolina in 1872 to educate freedpeople and their children, feted by his North Brookfield benefactors, who provided him with a "purse" to pay his expenses and aid him in establishing his new profession.[50]

Robert Morse also managed to build an independent life for himself after his initial years of service in the household of Dr. Tyler. Like William Bryant in Worcester, Morse used his Civil War service and connections as a springboard to standing in his adopted town. What is most notable about Morse is that he rose to distinction in North Brookfield, a nearly all-white town with no separate black community or institutions. Leaving Tyler's household in the late 1860s, Morse found work as a fireman in one of the town's many shoe factories and established his own home after marrying a fellow Virginian, Fanny Williams, in North Brookfield. The Morses raised three children and played an integral part in community life. Morse served as a deacon in the Union Congregational Church; when the church became an Episcopal parish, he was elected a vestryman. In addition, the town's Civil War veterans bestowed on Morse a highly unusual tribute. Although he never served in a Union uniform, the town's G.A.R. Post 51 inducted him as an honorary member. The veterans and the North Brookfield community not only commemorated his Civil War service but also recognized it throughout his life. When Morse died in 1912, the North Brookfield paper emphasized his service in the war and his Civil War connections with Dr. Tyler.[51]

While Jane Waples remained a servant in Worcester, she nonetheless used that position to establish a home for herself and an extended New Bern family in Worcester. After working for several years in the Sprague household, she married Charles Mero, a native of Vermont and veteran of the renowned Massachusetts Fifty-fourth Colored Infantry. Following his death due to war-related injuries, Waples Mero—probably through her connections to Sprague—worked as a domestic servant for some of Worcester's most prominent families. In 1874, she managed to purchase a house for her growing family, which included her son, Charles Sumner—whose name reflected Waples Mero's reverence for the abolitionist senator from Massachusetts—as well as family members she helped bring to Worcester from New Bern such as her elderly mother, her daughter, and her son-in-law. Her brother and sister-in-law, also of New Bern, moved nearby. Moreover, Waples Mero played an active part in the black community's organizational life as a member of the city's A.M.E. Zion Church.[52] Like William Bryant, Jane Waples Mero successfully negotiated two communities: sympathetic white patrons and the city's black community. While she continued to work in the homes of prominent whites, she nonetheless established her own independence and took a prominent place in Worcester's growing black community.

Like the original Bryant family, wartime migrants helped additional kinfolk join them in Worcester. Civil War-era migration generated an ongoing relocation of eastern North Carolinians and Virginians to Worcester County, evident in censuses, local records, and community institutions. By 1900, North Carolina- and Virginia-born migrants made up 61 percent of Worcester's Southern-born population, up from approximately 11 percent in 1860. Birth, marriage, and death records, specifying the birthplaces of many Southern migrants who came to Worcester through the end of the nineteenth century, reflect the towns and cities

Worcester soldiers and missionary teachers traversed. New Bern appears frequently, along with Kinston, Washington, and Williamston—all within the orbit of the Massachusetts Twenty-fifth and Worcester's missionary teachers in the era of the Civil War. Likewise, Richmond, Culpeper, Norfolk, and Leesburg replicate the trail of the Massachusetts Fifteenth.[53]

While the first generation of Southern migrants enjoyed the patronage of influential, sympathetic whites, later generations, brought North through family connections, did not benefit from the same networks forged in the crucible of the Civil War. Indeed, white sympathy and patronage dramatically faded with the memory of slavery and the war and as the abolitionist generation—the "benevolent sympathizers," in Isaac Mason's words—passed from the scene. Franklin Rice, summing up the condition of Worcester's "colored population" in 1893, noted the city's worsening racial climate and its noticeable decline from its abolitionist past. "Negroes," he commented, "are not treated with the consideration they were before the war, when Worcester was thought a paradise for the fugitive from oppression."[54]

Industrial employment was one crucial area where blacks sorely felt a lack of consideration. Even though African Americans migrated just as Worcester evolved into a major manufacturing center, local industrialists preferred to hire European immigrants who were then flocking to the city. By 1870 Worcester emerged as the second largest city in the state and boasted hundreds of manufacturing establishments and over 10,000 workers. By 1900, nearly 25,000 workers labored in the city's numerous and diverse factories. Yankee industrialists desperately seeking laborers often complained of shortages. But most Worcester firms limited their hiring to whites. In an era when employers constructed a hierarchy of the most desirable industrial workers among those of European descent— with the Protestant Swedes at the top of the list, followed by the French Canadians, and then the Irish at the bottom—African Americans had little chance.[55]

Lack of access to industrial jobs had significant ramifications for social mobility and the wealth and well-being of the city's black community. Any advantages gained by the first generation of Southern migrants through Civil War-era patronage networks were no longer evident by the turn of the century. A comparison with French Canadian immigrants is especially revealing. Arriving at the same time as the Southern blacks, beginning in the Civil War years, with their numbers increasing dramatically in the 1870s, French Canadians, like their black counterparts, came from a rural, nonindustrial background. While Southern migrants generated some sympathy as refugees of the Civil War and victims of slavery, many local citizens held French Canadians in contempt, viewing them with a great deal of suspicion, as they seemed unusually clannish and unwilling to assimilate. French Canadians worked for low wages, insisted on maintaining their language, and immediately set up their own separate schools and Catholic parishes as the cornerstones of their separate ethnic communities. Carroll D. Wright, chief of the Massachusetts Bureau of Statistics of Labor, labeled the French Canadians "the Chinese of the East" in a highly publicized report. But as people of European descent, with the doors of Worcester's industries open wide to them, they managed to advance rapidly from unskilled to skilled positions, particularly as operatives in boot and shoe factories, as iron- and steelworkers, and as machinists in the city's many manufactories. Over 66 percent of French Canadian workers in 1900 were engaged in manufacturing and mechanical occupations, and only 9.5 percent labored in unskilled jobs. Skilled jobs could be handed down to sons and daughters, ensuring economic security and a better chance at upward social mobility.[56]

By contrast, Worcester's black population remained mired in the same domestic service and unskilled occupations that they held years before. While two-thirds of French Canadians worked in manufacturing enterprises in 1900, less than 20 percent of blacks held such jobs—in a city where over half the workforce labored in manufacturing and mechanical pursuits. Instead, well over half of the city's black working population— 57.9 percent—toiled in domestic and personal service. Black women found Worcester's industries even less welcoming than their male counterparts. While 40 percent of the city's working women labored in the manufacturing sector, less than 10 percent of black women did so. The city's corset-making industry, boot and shoe factories, and textile mills, which employed thousands of white women, many of them French Canadian and Irish, did not employ a single black woman. Instead, black women toiled overwhelmingly as domestic workers: 165 of the city's 195 black working females (84.6 percent) served as domestics. Summing up the state of Worcester's "colored population," in 1893, Franklin P. Rice noted that "there are a few well-to-do colored men here, but the majority are not prosperous."[57]

Even Irish workers, who complained about job discrimination by Worcester's manufacturers, far outstripped blacks in employment opportunities. Only 20 percent labored in unskilled positions and Irish men and women found work in all of the city's manufactories. Irish men were concentrated in machine shops, iron- and steelworks, and wireworks; and even though 38 percent of Irish women worked as domestics, Worcester's clothing manufacturers, corset makers, textile mills, and other industries provided them opportunities unavailable to black women.[58]

Access to skilled jobs in manufacturing provided the economic grounding for a prosperous and rapidly growing French Canadian community in Worcester in contrast to that of the city's blacks. As one local French resident noted, "In 1869 we had nothing to speak of" but by 1882 the community had built "a French convent and a French church," constructed at a cost of $80,000. The city's French community boasted a benevolent society as well as several other clubs and even a French-language newspaper. A walk through Worcester revealed "French grocers on every street" and "three French doctors" as well as "French clerks in every first-class store." The community's leaders seemed well aware of the value of their whiteness. In response to Wright's negative portrayal of the French, a local leader demanded a meeting with Wright to "show him that we are white people, and that we have been well brought up." Possibilities for advancement seemed so certain for the French in Worcester that, by 1900, they were the city's second-largest foreign population, consisting of over 14,000 people.[59]

By contrast, Southern blacks trickled into the city of Worcester, to a community that had grown to roughly 1,100 in 1900 and which lacked both the wealth and the population to sustain the numerous cultural institutions the French Canadians managed to establish in a short period of time. Like their counterparts in other Northern cities, African Americans in Worcester found their chances for economic security—and those of their children—significantly diminished due to racialist hiring practices, especially in comparison to European immigrants. In their study of Pittsburgh, which compared the experiences of black and Polish workers from 1900 to 1930, John Bodnar, Michael Weber, and Roger Simon found that Southern migrants faced especially harsh discrimination as they were "particularly unwanted because they were thought to be 'inefficient,' 'unstable,' and unsuitable for the heavy pace of mill work." Worcester's blacks seem to have faced the same "urban racism and structural inequality" that severely limited the upward mobility of blacks in Pittsburgh, finding that like their Pennsylvania brethren they were "unable to overcome racial hostility and pass job skills on to their children."[60]

While facing a color bar that severely limited economic advancement, especially compared to European immigrants, Southern blacks nonetheless continued to migrate in numbers that would change the texture of the city's black community. Despite its limitations, Worcester at least promised jobs with higher wages than those in the South, education for children in integrated schools, and an escape from the legacies of slavery that continued to cast shadows across much of the "New" South. Through ongoing migration, based on the highly localized networks established in the era of the Civil War, Southerners consistently made up nearly half of Worcester's adult black population from 1870 to 1900.[61]

The small but steady migration of Southern blacks in the last quarter of the nineteenth century transformed local black culture in several obvious ways, particularly in the city of Worcester, where most settled. Beginning in the 1870s, Virginians and North Carolinians created their own residential pocket off of Highland Street. Previously, Worcester's black population had clustered in two areas, both on the city's east side: around Pine Street and on the south side of Belmont Street roughly bounded by Liberty and Laurel streets. While never exclusive to the Southern-born alone, a separate residential pocket of North Carolinians and Virginians on the west side of Worcester suggests that Southerners made a conscious effort to live together.[62]

Whether Southern migrants voluntarily chose to live in close proximity or were unwelcome in older African American residential clusters is not clear. The black community's embrace of the early contrabands and the presence of Southern migrants, such as the Bryants, in older neighborhoods suggest that newcomers in the Civil War years did not experience animosity from older residents. But by 1870 so many Southern blacks had come to Worcester that they made up well over a third of the city's black population. Perhaps established Black Yankee families resented the arrival of large numbers of their poorer, less educated Southern cousins. E. Franklin Frazier noted that in the subsequent Great Migration "the Negroes who had been North for quite some time met their fellowmen with disgust and aloofness." Similarly, in the late nineteenth century, well-established German Jews resented the massive influx of impoverished, less sophisticated Russian Jews.[63]

At the same time, the older residential areas may have not had adequate housing to contain the Southern influx. It is also likely that Virginians and North Carolinians simply felt more comfortable living near each other— like the Irish, French Canadians, and Swedes who immigrated to Worcester in the same period and created their own ethnic enclaves. Especially given the fact that the migrants came from the same parts of the South, and often shared family ties and a common culture, they would have voluntarily gravitated toward one another. In any case, Southern migrants established their own community in Worcester. While it was never exclusive, it was clearly recognizable as a distinctive entity.

By 1885, Southern migrants further cemented a separate identity when they established their own church in the midst of the Southern residential enclave. Just as the immigrant church served as the cornerstone for ethnic community life in the late nineteenth and early twentieth centuries, the John Street Church represented a sense of common identity and purpose in sustaining the culture of the migrant's "homeland." Self-consciously Southern in its membership, leadership, and worship style, the John Street Baptist Church began as a prayer meeting in 1878, organized by "a little band of Southern Negroes," all former slaves. This "little band," described by a local Baptist as "poor and little burdened by worldly effects," held meetings in private homes and halls under the auspices of the predominately white Pleasant Street Baptist Church. While Worcester had two black churches at this time, the A.M.E. Zion Church and the Bethel A.M.E. Church, these Southerners sought denominational continuity, preferring to worship as Baptists. At the same time, they wished to worship separately from the city's white Baptist churches and missions. By establishing their own church, the Southern migrants could perpetuate their own style of worship and transplant and sustain a key element of Southern black culture in their new home in the North. Their own church also allowed them to exercise self-determination as well as bolster a sense of community among Southern migrants.[64]

The choice Southern black Baptists made to create their own church generated controversy in Worcester. According to a white Baptist leader, "Some of their friends in the other churches considered the movement rather questionable." Indeed, in a city with a black population of only 750, two well-established black churches, and four Baptist churches and several missions already in existence, the decision of the Southerners to establish their own church must have appeared imprudent. Also, given the fact that most black Worcesterites—and especially recent migrants—labored in low paying, unskilled jobs, ongoing support of another black institution would have seemed tenuous at best.[65]

Despite the doubts and concerns of others, the black Southern Baptists went forward with their plans. Originally a mission, the group received recognition from the Worcester Baptist Association as the Mount Olive (colored) Baptist Church in 1885. A year later, the congregation called a fellow Southern migrant to pastor the church. The Reverend Hiram Conway, a native of Northumberland County, Virginia, who had migrated to Massachusetts before the Civil War, guided the church from 1886 until his death in 1920. Under Conway's leadership, the congregation purchased land on John Street, in the midst of the black Southern residential enclave, and in 1891 dedicated its new church building, subsequently known as the John Street Baptist Church. At the dedication of the new church, Isaac Mason, who as a former slave had aided many Civil War-era Southern migrants, gave an address. A member of the Bethel A.M.E. Church, Mason's participation as "a warm friend" of the new church linked the new institution with older, established community institutions, providing an imprimatur for the endeavor. In five years, the congregation grew to over one hundred members from the original band of twelve. Early clubs in the church, such as the Sons and Daughters of North Carolina, reflected the origins of its members and the importance of nurturing Southern identity in the North.[66]

The exponential growth of the John Street congregation suggests a deep thirst on the part of Worcester's Southern black migrants for their own culture and institutions and their determination to sustain their own separate institutions, even in a very small black community. Even though the church's early years would be marked with struggle, when the congregation felt that "they could hardly maintain themselves," John Street Church managed to survive. Although Southerners played an active role in other key community organizations in Worcester's black community, such as the North Star Lodge of the Odd Fellows and the Women's Progressive Club, they nonetheless—at the same time—made a point of celebrating and perpetuating Southern black culture through the John Street Church. In the process, Southern migrants contributed cultural complexity to Worcester's small black community and recast some of its most fundamental institutions.[67]

* * *

Emanating from the specific context of the Civil War, Southern black migration to Worcester County reflects a type of migration to the North very different from the Great Migration that would follow. Built on personal bonds constructed amidst the chaos and upheaval of war and impending emancipation, the migration not only tells us about the close relationships forged between some white Northerners and black Southerners in the crucible of war, but also about steps that Southern blacks took to guarantee their freedom and improve opportunities for themselves and their families. Moreover, it reveals a tightly organized and activist black community that helped situate Southerners in the North. Those Southerners, in turn, facilitated the transplantation of additional friends and family members from the South, perpetuating an ongoing Southern migration in the last quarter of the century, through the same channels established during the Civil War. Subsequent generations forged a collective Southern identity within Worcester's small black community, as North Carolinians and Virginians fashioned their own distinctive neighborhood and institutions. Paths of migration created in wartime widened and deepened by the end of the century, augmenting Worcester County's black community and giving it a decidedly Southern cast.

A summer stipend from the National Endowment for Humanities supported research that appears in this essay.

Notes

1. "Arrival of a Contraband,'" *Worcester Spy*, June 28, 1862.
2. See, for example, Florette Henri, *Black Migration: Movement North, 1900-1920* (Garden City, 1975); Gilbert Osofsky, *Harlem: The Making of a Ghetto, Negro New York, 1890-1930* (New York, 1966), 18, 24, 29-30, 32. Clyde Vernon Kiser's *Sea Island to City: A Study of St. Helena Islanders in Harlem and Other Urban Centers* (New York, 1932), 95-97, briefly examines the post-Civil War migration of a small number of Sea Islanders to the North. One of the few studies of Civil War-era migration to the North is Elizabeth Pleck's *Black Migration and Poverty: Boston, 1865-1900* (New York, 1979). While examining the role of the Freedmen's Bureau in facilitating the migration of Tidewater Virginia blacks to Boston after the Civil War, Pleck's study is less interested in networks of migration than in comparing urban poverty among blacks and immigrants and the impact of poverty and discrimination on the city's blacks.
3. U.S. Bureau of the Census, Manuscript census schedules, Worcester County, Massachusetts, 1860, 1870, 1880, and 1900; Massachusetts Census, Worcester County, 1865, Massachusetts Archives, Boston, Mass. Using census data to reveal the racial composi-

tion of a town or county is fraught with problems, but it is one of the few sources available for this kind of documentation. Census takers received few or no guidelines for determining racial classification and definitions changed significantly from 1860 to 1900, making data comparisons problematic. Moreover, many Worcester County residents of African descent intermarried with Native Americans before the Civil War; some of these individuals are classified as black, some as mulatto, and still others as Indian, and some are classified differently in various census years. At best, for people of color, the census paints a community portrait with a broad brush. For more on the problems inherent in using the census to study Northern blacks, see James Oliver Horton, *Free People of Color: Inside the African American Community* (Washington, 1993), 28. In his study of Finnish migrants to North America, Reiro Kero makes a distinction between chain migration and a migration tradition. Chain migration refers to original immigrants, the "first to arrive in a particular locality," who "drew after them relatives, friends, and acquaintances." A migration tradition is "the existence of migration between two specific areas . . . extending over a prolonged period of time." See Reiro Kero, "Migration Tradition from Finland to North America," in *A Century of European Migrations, 1830-1930*, ed. Rudolph J. Vecoli and Suzanne M. Sinke (Urbana, 1991), 119.

4. According to both the 1865 state census and the federal manuscript census for 1870, 10 young black Louisianans migrated to Worcester County; most of them accompanied soldiers from the Massachusetts Fifty-third. For more on the Fifty-third and its service in Louisiana, which includes numerous references to "contrabands" who were "adopted" by the unit, see Henry A. Willis, *The Fifty-third Regiment, Massachusetts Volunteers* (Fitchburg, 1889).

5. Vital Statistics for the City of Worcester, Marriage Records, January 1863, Worcester Public Library.

6. John G. Barrett, *The Civil War in North Carolina* (Chapel Hill, 1963), 74-75, 91.

7. A. E. Burnside to E. M. Stanton, Mar. 21, 1862, in *The War of the Rebellion: A Compilation of the Official Records of the Union and Confederate Armies*, ed. U.S. War Department (Washington, D.C., 1883), ser. 1, 9:199; Joe A. Mobley, *James City: A Black Community in North Carolina, 1863-1900* (Raleigh, 1981), 5; Vincent Colyer, *Report of the Services Rendered by the Freed People to the United States Army in North Carolina in the Spring of 1862, after the Battle of Newbern* (New York, 1864), 6.

8. James McPherson, *Battle Cry of Freedom: The Civil War Era* (New York, 1988), 355-356.

9. *Worcester Spy*, Oct. 8, Sept. 19, 1861.

10. James Eugene Mooney, "Antislavery in Worcester County, Massachusetts: A Case Study" (Ph.D. diss., Clark Univ., 1971), 3; opinion quoted in John D. Cushing, "The Cushing Court and the Abolition of Slavery in Massachusetts: More Notes on the 'Quock Walker Case,'" *The American Journal of Legal History* 5(1961):133; Mooney, "Antislavery in Worcester County," 10-15.

11. Albert von Frank argues that Worcester's uncommon antislavery activism was rooted in the identification of slavery as a labor problem, tied to free labor, free soil, and white advancement: "One of the reasons why Worcester was so forward in the Burns matter and in antislavery in general was the presence there of a vital culture of artisans, mill workers, and shopkeepers. From the moment of Burns's arrest it was understood that help was to be looked for not from fashionable Boston, where capital and corporations

held sway, but from 'the country,' particularly Worcester" (158). Higginson was one of the "Secret Six" who backed Brown's raid at Harpers Ferry. For more on Higginson and Stowell, see Albert J. von Frank, *The Trials of Anthony Burns: Freedom and Slavery in Emerson's Boston* (Cambridge, Mass., 1998). For more on Worcester's role in Kansas emigration, see Eli Thayer, *The New England Emigrant Aid Company* (Worcester, Mass., 1887), and Eli Thayer, *A History of the Kansas Crusade: Its Friends and Its Foes* (New York, 1889); Mooney, "Antislavery in Worcester County," 264; and "The Execution of John Brown, Commemoration of the Event in Worcester & Vicinity," *Massachusetts Spy*, Dec. 7, 1859.

12. The Worcester Freedom Club made a dramatic appearance at the Court House during Anthony Burns's trial in Boston. They bore a silk banner inscribed with the words "Warm Hearts and Fearless Souls—True to the Union and the Constitution," written above a picture of Liberty. See von Frank, *Trials of Anthony Burns*, 138; Account Book of Francis Jackson, Treasurer, The Vigilance Committee of Boston, American Antiquarian Society, Worcester, Mass. While Butman most likely came to Worcester seeking witnesses for the Burns trials in Boston, many antislavery activists, especially the city's blacks, were convinced that he was seeking fugitive slaves, despite Thomas Wentworth Higginson's assurances at the time that Butman had no such purpose. In an article written almost a quarter-century after the event, the Reverend Albert Tyler claimed that Butman came to Worcester in pursuit of William H. Jankins, a local barber, who had escaped from his Virginia master in the 1840s. See Tyler, "The Butman Riot," *Worcester Society of Antiquity Publications* 1(1873):85-89. For contemporary accounts of the Butman Riot, see "Great Excitement in Worcester," *Worcester Spy*, Oct. 21, 1854, and "More Excitement in Worcester," *National Aegis*, Nov. 1, 1854.

13. "What a Soldier Thinks," *Worcester Spy*, June 15, 1862; "Letter from Newbern," *Worcester Spy*, Apr. 26, 1862.

14. "Extracts from a Soldier's Letter," *Worcester Spy*, July 7, 1862; "From the Fifty-first Regiment," *Worcester Spy*, Feb. 19, 1863. W. P. Derby of the Massachusetts Twenty-seventh, also stationed in eastern North Carolina, recalled the enthusiastic greeting conferred on the Union troops by runaways after the Battle of New Bern. By contrast, he noted, "there was not the least demonstration of loyalty or Union sentiment with the whites, but a sullen moroseness, indicative of intense disloyalty." W. P. Derby, *Bearing Arms in the Twenty-Seventh Massachusetts Regiment of Volunteers Infantry during the Civil War, 1861-65* (Boston, 1883), 96.

15. Colyer, *Report of the Services Rendered by the Freed People*, 6, 33.

16. Colyer, *Report of the Services Rendered by the Freed People*, 9, 33. Official correspondence of Union officers in eastern North Carolina contains numerous references to the contributions of contrabands. See, for example, *Official Records*, ser. 1, 9:208, 286, 354, 369-370, 373-374; and "Contrabands and Their Services," *The Liberator*, July 11, 1862.

17. Susie King Taylor, *A Black Woman's Civil War Memoirs: Reminiscences of My Life in Camp With the 33rd U.S. Colored Troops, Late 1st South Carolina Volunteers*, ed. Patricia Romero (New York, 1988), 137.

18. Barrett, *Civil War in North Carolina*, 126-127. Nicholas Bray was among the masters who appealed to Stanly for the return of his property, a young slave girl who had escaped to the Union army in New Bern. Although a number of soldiers appealed to

General Burnside to intercede on her behalf, Burnside refused. A group of soldiers, including some from Worcester County, angrily entered Bray's home, and in the words of one witness, "held a pistol at the head of Bray and his wife—put the girl into a carriage and left—one of the houses was burned down." The soldiers recreated, in a new context, New England's famous fugitive slave rescues of the 1850s. Dr. R. R. Clarke to John G. Metcalfe, June 5, 1862, Civil War Collection, American Antiquarian Society.

19. Dr. R. R. Clarke to Dr. Metcalf, June 5, 1862, Civil War Collection, American Antiquarian Society; Elias Smith, *New York Times*, May 31, 1862, quoted in Colyer, *Report of the Services Rendered by the Freed People*, 48-51.

20. Colyer, *Report of the Services Rendered by the Freed People*, 41, 44; Horace James to the Old South Sabbath School, June 21, 1862, Horace James Papers, American Antiquarian Society; Mobley, *James City*, 23. For a thorough account of Horace James's vision of a new social order for the South, see Stephen Edward Reilly, "Reconstruction through Regeneration: Horace James' Work with the Blacks for Social Reform in North Carolina, 1862-1867" (Ph.D. diss., Duke Univ., 1983). James also enlisted soldier-teachers from the Massachusetts Twenty-third and Twenty-seventh as well as the Tenth Connecticut.

21. "The Contrabands," *Worcester Spy*, Dec. 27, 1861; "An Appeal," *Worcester Spy*, Nov. 22, 1862. For examples of the numerous published reports of freedman's relief activities in Worcester County, see "Freedman's Relief," *Worcester Spy*, Jan. 15, Oct. 10, 1863, Mar. 3, 1864.

22. See, for example, *Worcester Spy*, June 9, 1862; Cheryl Benard, "Politics and the Refugee Experience," *Political Science Quarterly* 101(1986):620; Gil Loescher and John A. Scanlon, *Calculated Kindness: Refugees and America's Half-Open Door: 1945 to the Present* (New York, 1986), xvii, 9-13, 112.

23. "Arrival of a 'Contraband,'" *Worcester Spy*, June 28, 1862.

24. U.S. Bureau of the Census, Manuscript census schedules, 1860. James Oliver Horton notes that in 1860, over 60 percent of Boston's black population had been born out of state. The city's reputation as the center of abolitionism likely attracted more migrants to Boston. See Horton, *Free People of Color*, 26-27. While the 1860 census undoubtedly undercounts Southern blacks, since runaway slaves would have avoided a census listing—especially after 1850—the census nonetheless confirms that most Worcester blacks were Northern-born and Southern blacks were small in number. Horton, *Free People of Color*, 28.

25. U.S. Bureau of the Census, Manuscript census schedules, Worcester County, 1870; *Worcester City Directory*, 1862. Speaking before Worcester's Free Church in the aftermath of the attempted Burns rescue, Higginson implored his congregation: "No longer conceal Fugitives and help them on, but show them and defend them. Let the Underground Railroad stop here! Say to the South that Worcester, though part of a Republic, shall be as free as if ruled by a Queen! *Hear, O Richmond! and give ear, O Carolina! henceforth Worcester is Canada to the Slave!*" Higginson, *Massachusetts in Mourning: A Sermon Preached in Worcester, June 4, 1854* (Boston, 1854), 14. Brothers Gilbert and Allen Walker and Isaac Mason had been born slaves in Maryland. William Jankins had been a slave in Virginia. See "The Late 'Prof.' Walker," *Worcester Evening*

Gazette, Dec. 17, 1890; "Death of Gilbert Walker," *Worcester Spy*, Dec. 17, 1890; and Isaac Mason, *Life of Isaac Mason as a Slave* (Worcester, 1893). In the 1865 Massachusetts Census, R. H. and Mary Johnson listed three Massachusetts-born children, the oldest 10 years old.

26. Gilbert Walker, for example, contributed to the New England Emigration Society in 1854 and later served as a recruiter for the Massachusetts Fifty-fourth Volunteer Infantry, the first Northern black regiment in the Civil War. For the role of black Worcesterites in the "Butman Riot," see "Great Excitement in Worcester," *Worcester Spy*, Oct. 31, 1854; and "More Excitement in Worcester," *National Aegis*, Nov. 1, 1854. For more on black Worcester's antebellum activism, see Nick Salvatore, *We All Got History: The Memory Books of Amos Webber* (New York, 1996), 107-109; and von Frank, *Trials of Anthony Burns*, 122.

27. *Worcester City Directory, 1863* (Worcester, 1864).

28. Mason, *Life of Isaac Mason*, 1-2, 49-52. Mason gave this account of his coming to Worcester at his 75th birthday party, reported in "Isaac Mason's Celebration," *Worcester Telegram*, May 15, 1897. The reporter recorded Mason as referring to "a man named Store" who helped bring him to Worcester, "one of the most uncompromising anti-slavery and freesoil men in all this vicinity." Mason later remarked that "Store" emigrated to Kansas and died there. He then recounted that he had recently visited with "Store's" widow, a Mrs. Kimball, who had remarried and lived in New Hampshire. Mason's discussion of Mrs. Kimball confirms that "Store" was indeed Martin Stowell, who died not in Kansas but in Tennessee during the Civil War. According to Civil War pension records, Stowell's widow remarried a man named Kimball and resided in New Hampshire. (Thanks to Robert Cormier for sharing pension information with me.)

In his autobiography, Mason gave a slightly different—but not contradictory—account of his arrival in Worcester, claiming that Hayden (a close abolitionist associate of Stowell) sent him to Worcester with a letter of introduction to William Brown, a prominent black upholsterer, and Brown helped him secure housing with another black Worcesterite, Ebenezer Hemenway. See Mason, *Life of Isaac Mason*, 55-56. Mason's freedom proved tenuous even in Worcester. In 1852, he recalled in his autobiography, the "hunting slave fever got so high" as a result of the Fugitive Slave Law "that our sympathizing friends advised me to leave at once to go to Canada." After a brief sojourn to Montreal and then Toronto, Mason returned to Worcester—walking from Rochester, New York, for lack of train fare.

29. Worcester County Registry of Deeds, Book 562/538, Book 562/539, Book 571/370, Worcester County Court House.

30. Joshua Chasan, "Civilizing Worcester: The Creation of Industrial and Cultural Order, Worcester, Massachusetts, 1848-1876" (Ph.D diss., Univ. of Pittsburgh, 1974); "Isaac Mason's Funeral: Senator George F. Hoar Pays a Tribute to His Character," *Worcester Spy*, Aug. 30, 1898. Chasan estimates that in 1860, 82 percent of city residents did not own real property. In 1863, the Masons deeded the property at 62 Union to Rice, Barton, and Faler (see Worcester County Registry of Deeds, Book 683/503), apparently unable to pay their mortgage on the property, although they did pay off their loan to Wilson.

31. *Worcester City Directory, 1861* (Worcester, 1862); "Isaac Mason's Funeral," *Worcester Spy*, Aug. 8, 1898.

32. *Worcester City Directory, 1866* (Worcester, 1867); *Worcester City Directory, 1867* (Worcester, 1868); *Worcester Spy*, Oct. 28, 1869. In both the 1865 Massachusetts census and the 1870 federal census, Mary Bryant is listed as "keeping house."

33. Worcester Vital Statistics, Marriages, January 1863, Worcester Public Library.

34. *Worcester City Directory, 1865* (Worcester, 1866).

35. Worcester County Registry of Deeds, Book 709/22; Book 746/444, Worcester County Court House.

36. Massachusetts Census, Worcester County, 1865; U.S. Bureau of the Census, Manuscript census schedules, Worcester County, 1870; Thomas Doughton, *Births, Deaths, Marriages of People of Color* (Worcester, 1990), 49. Julia Ann Bryant listed her birthplace as New Bern and her parents as William and Hager Bryant in her marriage record. William Bryant listed Henry Johnson as a partner in the ad published in the *Worcester Spy* on Oct. 28, 1869.

37. Alan D. Watson, *A History of New Bern and Craven County* (New Bern, 1987), 428, 433, 442, 446-447.

38. *Worcester Spy*, Apr. 27, 29, 1869; *Worcester Evening Gazette*, Apr. 27, 1869. The last listing for William Bryant in the city directory was 1870.

39. Willis, *Fifty-third Regiment*, 99-100; Massachusetts Census, Worcester County, 1865; "Clinton," *Worcester Spy*, Feb. 2, 1864.

40. "From the Twenty-fifth," *Worcester Spy*, May 11, 1863. James addressed a large crowd at Mechanics Hall in Worcester in July 1863, in which he sketched out a plan to colonize Roanoke Island and establish a model community there and appealed for funds to expedite his plan. "City and County," *Worcester Spy*, July 18, 1863. Also see, for example, *Worcester Spy*, Aug. 14, 1863, and Jan. 5, 1864, and "Letter From Mrs. James to the Colored People of Worcester," *Worcester Spy*, Apr. 27, 1864. Among the many local residents inspired by the Jameses to teach in eastern North Carolina were Anne P. Merriam and Emily Piper of Worcester; the H. S. Beals family, who taught in Beaufort; and fellow Worcester County Congregational ministers William T. Briggs and Clarendon Waite, who joined James in 1864 to assist him in his educational efforts. Due to the Beals' efforts, Worcester industrialist and veteran abolitionist Ichabod Washburn donated $300 toward the establishment of a freedpeople's school, named Washburn Seminary, in Beaufort. "From the Fifty-first Regiment," Dec. 10, 1862.

41. *The Liberator*, Oct. 9, 1863. Similarly, Nell Irvin Painter points out that Southern black migrants to Kansas in the late 1870s identified the state with John Brown and his fight for black emancipation, a connection that enhanced the appeal of Kansas as a land of freedom. See *Exodusters: Black Migration to Kansas after Reconstruction* (New York, 1976), 159.

42. Corrine Bostic, *Go Onward and Upward!: An Interpretive Biography of the Life of Miss Sarah Ella Wilson* (Worcester, n.d.), 42; American Missionary Association, North Carolina Letters, Reel 2; Massachusetts Census, Worcester County, 1865.

43. Massachusetts Census, Worcester County, 1865; "Letter from Mrs. James to the Colored People of Worcester," *Worcester Spy*, Apr. 27, 1864.

44. U.S. Bureau of the Census, Manuscript census schedules, Worcester County, 1870.

45. *Abstract of the Census of Massachusetts, 1865* (Boston, 1867), 232. North Brookfield listed one black resident in 1860. "North Brookfield," *Worcester Spy*, Jan. 10, 1872; Massachusetts Census, Worcester County, 1865; U.S. Bureau of the Census, Manuscript census schedules, Worcester County, Massachusetts, 1870.

46. "Robert Morse Goes to Answer Last Call," *Worcester Evening Telegram*, May 31, 1912; "Death of Robert Morse," *North Brookfield Journal*, May 31, 1912; U.S. Bureau of the Census, Manuscript Census Schedules, Worcester County, Massachusetts, 1870.

47. George M. Fredrickson argues that this racial notion, which he calls romantic racialism, was "a doctrine which acknowledged permanent racial differences," while rejecting "a clearly defined racial hierarchy." This notion of racial difference, epitomized by Harriet Beecher Stowe's Uncle Tom and especially prevalent among the Northern white middle class, attributed "childlike" characteristics to blacks, such as emotionalism, spirituality, and servility, while whites embodied rationality and dominance. See George M. Fredrickson, *The Black Image in the White Mind: The Debate on African-American Character and Destiny* (New York, 1971), 107, 110.

48. *Worcester Spy*, Sept. 27, 1867, Apr. 6, 1868; Lois Elaine Horton, "The Development of Federal Social Policy for Blacks in Washington, D.C. after Emancipation"(Ph.D diss., Brandeis Univ., 1977), 93-95. Freedman's Bureau Records reveal only a handful of freedpeople who got to Worcester directly through the aid of the bureau. However, the records document numerous employment agents in New England, especially in Providence and Boston, who worked with the Freedman's Bureau to place freedpeople in jobs. Worcester's employment agencies may have worked directly with these agencies. See, for example, Employment Records, Local Superintendent, District of Columbia, Vol. 1, Records of the Bureau of Refugees, Freedmen, and Abandoned Lands, Record Group 105; and Records of Transportation Requests Approved by the Assistant Commissioner, District of Columbia, Records of the Bureau of Refugees, Freedmen, and Abandoned Lands, Record Group 105, National Archives.

49. *Worcester Spy*, Mar. 29, 1869, Nov. 25, 1872, Dec. 15, 1869; Bureau of District of Columbia, Office of Local Superintendent, Description Lists of Freedpeople Granted Transportation, Bureau of Refugees, Freedmen, and Abandoned Land, Record Group 105. For more of Mrs. Browne's advertisements concerning "colored help," see *Worcester Spy*, Apr. 20, 1869, Mar. 17, 1870.

50. "North Brookfield," *Worcester Spy*, Jan. 30, 1872; letter to the author from Prof. Robert T. Brown, Westfield State College, June 19, 1996; "Death of S. S. Edmands," *North Brookfield Journal*, Sept. 13, 1901.

51. U.S. Bureau of the Census, Manuscript census schedules, Worcester County, Massachusetts, 1870 and 1880; "Death of Robert Morse," *North Brookfield Journal*, May 31, 1912.

52. Worcester County Registry of Deeds, Book 923/266; *Worcester City Directory*, 1865-1880; "Worcester Whittlings," *Boston Guardian*, Feb. 14, 1903 (obituary).

53. The 1860 U.S. manuscript census, while almost certainly underestimating Worcester's black population in the aftermath of the Fugitive Slave Law, lists only one Virginian and four North Carolinians living in the city before the Civil War (three additional Virginians lived in the county, and one North Carolinian); by 1900, approximately 80 North Carolinians and 71 Virginians lived in the City of Worcester. Based on the vital

58 JANETTE THOMAS GREENWOOD

records of the City of Worcester in *Births, Deaths, Marriages of People of Color: Worcester 1849-1890*, Thomas Doughton has compiled a list of 54 North Carolinians who died or were married in Worcester, from 1865 to 1890, 42 of whom listed a specific town or county birthplace in the vital records or other sources. A total of 31 listed New Bern as their birthplace; two hailed from Craven County (of which New Bern is the county seat); and five others were born in other eastern North Carolina towns or counties (Kinston, Goffstown, and Williamston). Thanks to Thomas Doughton for this information.

54. Franklin P. Rice, *Dictionary of Worcester and Its Vicinity*, 2d ed. (Worcester, 1893), 24.

55. Roy Rosenzweig, *Eight Hours for What We Will: Workers and Leisure in an Industrial City, 1870-1920* (New York, 1983), 12; *Twelfth Census of the United States, Special Reports: Occupations* (Washington, 1904), 760-763. For more on the ethnic segmentation in Worcester's industries in the late 19th century, see Rosenzweig, *Eight Hours,* 9-32. On Worcester's labor shortages from the 1860s on, see Rose Zeller, "Changes in Ethnic Composition and Character of Worcester's Population" (Ph.D. diss., Clark Univ., 1940), 142. For more on Worcester's industrial hiring practices, see Timothy J. Meagher, "The Lord Is Not Dead: Culture and Social Change among the Irish in Worcester, Massachusetts" (Ph.D. diss., Brown Univ., 1982), 174-175; and *Twelfth Census, Special Reports: Occupations,* 760-763.

56. *Report of Massachusetts Bureau of Statistics of Labor, Twelfth Annual Report* (Boston, 1881), 469; Meagher, "The Lord Is Not Dead," 160

57. *Twelfth Census, Special Reports: Occupations,* 760-763; Rice, *Dictionary of Worcester,* 24.

58. Meagher, "The Lord Is Not Dead," 161; *Twelfth Census, Special Reports: Occupations,* 760-763.

59. *Report of the Massachusetts Bureau of Statistics of Labor, Thirteenth Annual Report* (Boston, 1882), 79-80, 81; Meagher, "The Lord Is Not Dead," 376.

60. See John Bodnar, Michael Weber, and Roger Simon, "Migration, Kinship, and Urban Adjustment: Blacks and Poles in Pittsburgh, 1900-1930," *Journal of American History* 66(1979):554, 549.

61. U.S. Bureau of the Census, Manuscript census schedules, Worcester, Massachusetts, 1870, 1880, 1900.

62. Salvatore, *We All Got History,* 98; *Worcester City Directory,* 1860, 1870, and 1880.

63. E. Franklin Frazier quoted in Farah Jasmine Griffin, *"Who Set You Flowin'?": The African American Migration Narrative* (New York, 1995), 107. Griffin describes the campaign of Chicago's Urban League to assimilate Southern migrants, whom they found embarrassing, going so far as to distribute a pamphlet that encouraged migrants to pay attention to their personal appearance, to "refrain from wearing dust caps . . . house clothing and bedroom shoes for out doors" and "to reject their Southern mannerisms." See *"Who Set You Flowin'?",* 104.

64. "A New Baptist Church," *Worcester Evening Gazette,* Feb. 25, 1885; *Minutes of the Worcester Baptist Association* (Worcester, 1885), 78. Historians have written extensively on the role of the immigrant church in sustaining ethnic culture. See, for example, Robert C. Ostergren, *A Community Transplanted: The Trans-Atlantic Experience of a Swedish Immigrant Settlement in the Upper Middle West, 1835-1915* (Madison, Wisc., 1988), 211-212.

65. "Mt. Olive Corner Stone Laid," *Worcester Telegram*, June 23, 1891; *Worcester City Directory, 1880*; U.S. Bureau of the Census, Manuscript census schedules, Worcester County, 1880.

66. "A New Baptist Church," *Worcester Evening Gazette*, Feb. 25, 1885; "Obituary Report, Hiram Conway," *1921 Massachusetts Baptist Year Book*, 151-152; "In New House of Worship," *Worcester Telegram*, Oct. 24, 1891.

67. "Tenth Year of Pastor's Work," *Worcester Daily Telegram*, Sept. 11, 1896.

Un Dimsdale Canadien

Curé and Community in Late-Nineteenth-Century Worcester

John F. McClymer

N Tuesday evening, January 17, 1882, the people of *Notre-Dame-Des-Canadiens* gathered to bid farewell to their *curé*. The atmosphere in the church, according to *Le Travailleur*, Worcester's French-language newspaper, was "literally like a tomb."[1] All of the parish societies had prepared formal testimonials; all had gifts, tokens of their respect for the priest who had founded the parish twelve years earlier. Many believed that Father Jean-Baptiste Primeau had, in creating *Notre-Dame*, created the French Canadian community in Worcester. Not only had he given them a church, said midnight mass on every Christmas Eve, and baptized their children, he had set up the school where their children could learn proper French along with Canadian history. He had nurtured their clubs and associations, helped them become naturalized citizens, and served as their principal spokesman to an often suspicious, sometimes hostile English-speaking world. It was he, for example, who had made clear that the "assassin Gateau [*sic*]," who had murdered President Garfield less than a year before, was not a Canadian.

One measure of the parishioners' sense of loss lies in the elaborateness of the ceremony they planned. A meeting of the men of the parish had unanimously voted to bid a "solemn farewell" to their "well-loved *curé*." They would meet in the church at 7:00. There would be speeches from representatives of all the clubs. Then Father Primeau would give his farewell address. Next would come the presents. After that, the whole parish would march with the priest to Union Station, where he would take the 9:30 train to Boston. This parade, they expected, would stretch out for a mile or more. Once at the station, the parishioners would form two lines along the corridor for "the final handshaking and 'au revoir.'" Nor would this be the end. The members of the parish's executive committee, a uniformed contingent from the *Garde Lafayette*, the pastor's two brothers, his mother, and several other local notables would accompany him to Boston, where he would change trains.[2]

At 7:00 the church was full. The organ played a "plaintive air." But Father Primeau did not appear. Instead, his newly appointed successor, Reverend Firmin Vignon, S. J., walked to the altar. "This old one," as *Le Travailleur* phrased it, "with the venerable appearance and with an emotional tone," said first in Latin and then in French: "'We do not live forever, but we look to the life to come which will be eternal.'" The meaning of the prayer, he explained, was that Father Primeau would not be attending the ceremony. He was exhausted with all of the last-minute details. More importantly, he did not think he could withstand emotionally "the solemn moment of farewells." He had written them a letter instead. In it, among other "beautiful sentiments," he told his people that he was "offering the sacrifice of my absence to the greater good of the parish." Many in the pews found the letter so moving they wept. Father Vignon assured them that he would forward their testimonials and gifts. The congregation slowly filed out.[3]

As they did, some encountered a reporter for Worcester's morning paper, the *Daily Spy*. What did they think of the charge lodged against Father Primeau? Was he guilty? And, if not, why had he left town just one jump ahead of the sheriff?

Historians have begun to pay attention to such questions. They have learned, as Charles Joyner put it, that history happens *somewhere*. There was no abstraction called slavery, he pointed out. There were rice plantations and sugar and cotton plantations, some large and some small. Slavery happened to particular people at particular times and places. So too with immigration. Immigrants faced generic challenges, such as building a community and constructing a public identity in specific places at specific times. The story of Father Primeau and his flock is not, therefore, the story of all immigrants. That story does not exist. Yet, because his story catches people in a moment of crisis, it reveals some of the dynamics of the immigrant experience.[4]

If the methodology sometimes called "micro-history" is currently fashionable, its application in this case requires us to employ a category of analysis more familiar to the contemporaries of Nathaniel Hawthorne than to ourselves. That category is sin. Like the Reverend Arthur Dimmesdale in *The Scarlet Letter,* the Reverend Jean-Baptiste Primeau was a sinner. He too fathered an illegitimate child. He too could not bring himself publicly to acknowledge his sin. Further, like Dimmesdale, his greatest sin was not his sexual misdeed. Both committed the sin of scandal. In common speech, *scandal* refers to any notorious act. In theology, however, it has a more restricted meaning. An act is scandalous if, and only if, it threatens the faith of others. This was Dimmesdale's real sin, and Primeau's as well.[5]

On the morning after the abortive farewell the *Spy* carried a single paragraph about the *curé.* Entitled "A Bad Case," it recounted how "a warrant was sworn out against him for bastardy by Mary Cote [*sic,* perhaps Marie Côte], a girl of about 19 years of age, who formerly lived in his house as a domestic." The child, a daughter, had been born in November "and is still living." An officer had attempted to serve the warrant on Father Primeau just before the ceremony but found him already gone. "Large numbers" of parishioners, the paper continued, "openly assert their belief in the innocence of the man, and charge that the girl was induced to make the complaint by parties who have grievances against the pastor." Some, however, "do not hesitate to state their belief in the charge."[6]

The Evening Telegram, the city's other English-language daily, added a few details on Wednesday. The baby had been born on November 3. The mother named her own father and two local physicians as able to corroborate her charge against the priest. Finally, "a careful search of the records at the City Clerk's office fails to disclose a return of birth by the attending physician," a fact which suggests that the mother had left Worcester before the birth and had only recently returned. Like the *Spy* the paper declined to speculate on the veracity of the charge. Instead it pointed out that the pastor's devotion to his people had won him admirers outside, as well as inside, the *Canadien* community.[7]

Despite their initial disbelief, even Primeau's greatest admirers quickly became convinced Marie Côte was telling the truth. *Le Travailleur* editor Ferdinand Gagnon initially left the question open. So did a meeting of the "heads of families" of the parish.[8] Had there been grounds for challenging the young woman's story—had Primeau denied it, had he stayed to confront his accuser—this all-male gathering would likely have rallied to his cause. But he made no denial and apparently fled to avoid being served with the warrant. What was more, the charge explained much about the *curé's* recent behavior that otherwise seemed inexplicable.

L'Abbé Jean-Baptiste Primeau had announced his decision to leave *Notre-Dame* after Sunday Mass the week before Christmas. He needed a rest, he explained. He would travel for several months and then return to Canada. His decision, he added, was "irrevocable." Parishioners, Ferdinand Gagnon reported, were "devastated."[9] Several decided that, if the pastor would not listen to their appeals, perhaps they might persuade the bishop in Springfield to intervene. The bishop heard the delegation out but told them "without going any farther . . . it is not possible." Father Primeau "has been wanting to leave you for a number of years now. Whenever he gets a chance he reiterates his request. So what more can you ask of me? I certainly can't refuse him what he has been asking for so long."[10]

With the bishop's decision there was no longer any hope the *curé* would remain. Indeed, he was leaving almost immediately. Because New England suffered a serious shortage of French Canadian clergy, Father Primeau's insistence on leaving so abruptly exposed his parishioners to the risk that they might go without a full-time priest for an indefinite period. This fear vanished when *Le Travailleur* reported in its January 4 issue that Father Vignon, the superior of the Jesuit residence in Montreal, would be the new pastor. Still the *curé* had made his "irrevocable" decision, and had fixed the date of his departure, before there was any assurance about a successor. The reason he gave, that he was tired, did not satisfy. He was only forty-five and in apparently excellent health. His parishioners worked ten to twelve hours a day. They knew what it meant to be tired.

Ferdinand Gagnon thought that he knew why their pastor was abandoning them. He blamed the "obstinacy" of a handful of "malcontents" who were dissatisfied with the way Primeau managed parish finances.[11] Gagnon intimated that the pastor himself was the source for his story.

The editor did not doubt that this was the real reason Primeau was leaving, but "we cannot approve his decision. It is not in the middle of an undertaking like this, with schools, a convent, etc., etc., that the *curé* of the French Canadians of Worcester ought to leave his post over an issue where simple common sense and justice agree in sanctioning the decision of almost the whole of the faithful of the parish." It was not as one of the faithful that Gagnon dared to criticize. "It is as a French-Canadian journalist," as "a friend of the great religious endeavors of our compatriots," he wrote in an open letter to the pastor: ". . . in abandoning the struggle, you compromise the future of your parish."[12]

Marie Côte's accusation provided a compelling explanation for the priest's decision but an explanation too painful to bear. What was more, the public airing of her charges constituted a scandal which brought "dishonor" upon "the good name of the parish." So said a group of male parishioners in calling for an "indignation meeting" to "avenge the honor of the parish."[13]

What did they understand the "scandal" to be? Upon whom would they avenge themselves? And how? There was no consideration whatever of targeting the *curé*. He might have deceived them about the reasons for his leaving; he might have behaved with monumental hypocrisy in permitting them to organize the elaborate series of tributes that marked the two weeks leading up to what was to have been the climactic farewell on January 17.[14] Doubtless many, perhaps most, of the men gathered at the meeting thought their pastor had played them for fools. Yet, in public, the parishioners would not criticize their *curé*.

Marie Côte might seem a suitable target. She was a "fallen" woman, no matter who fathered the child. Further, she had sworn the warrant, thereby implicating the entire community in her disgrace. How sympathetic to her were the men of the parish, gathered to "avenge" its "honor," likely to prove? Yet no one said a word in public against her.

Who was she? Finding traces of obscure people, especially women and more especially those with common names, in the U.S. Census and other sources is often a hopeless task. In the case of Marie Côte the records lead nowhere.[15] In all probability she was a newcomer to the city in 1880 and went to work in the rectory some time after June; thus she was not recorded in the census. Assuming she carried the baby to full term, she had become pregnant sometime around the beginning of February 1881. From Gagnon's open letter to the *curé* asking him to remain, we know there were no rumors about her.[16] If Côte left Worcester in May or June, before her pregnancy began to show and less than a year after her arrival, her departure would have excited little attention, and her return on January 17, 1882, would then have come as a bolt out of the blue, as indeed it did.

Why not blame her? Her age may serve as part of the explanation. She was only eighteen, perhaps seventeen, when she went to live in the rectory. Father Primeau was forty-four. Furthermore, his habitual air of dignity would have made suggestions of her seducing the priest difficult to credit. But gossip often ignores probabilistic considerations. Perhaps, in private, parishioners did talk of her as a temptress.

In public, however, they charged that a small group inside the parish prompted the young woman to swear out the warrant. These traitors acted with the express purpose of bringing disgrace upon the *curé* and upon *Canadiens* generally. This explanation surfaced immediately. The *Daily Spy* noted it in its January 18, 1882, story. Ferdinand Gagnon, who might have been the *Spy's* source, aggressively pushed it in *Le Travailleur*. He began by misreporting the facts about the warrant. "Certain Canadians" had sworn it out, he wrote, when it had been Côte herself who had obtained it.[17] These conspirators sought to spoil the pastor's solemn leave-taking. "The authors of this shameful escapade ... have brought dishonor to the parish. . . . Poor Canadians of Notre-Dame, you who have been imposed upon by two or three spiteful ones, arouse yourselves and reflect upon the shame that their idiotic and mean-spirited vengeance has showered upon you."[18]

Gagnon played a leading part in the "indignation meeting," held a week to the day after the disastrous farewell. One can see the influence of his editorial in the remarks of Hermenegilde M. Couture, a clerk at a Main Street Dry Goods store. "As a Canadian, a Catholic, and an American citizen," he protested "the act of 4 or 5 [grown from the 2 or 3 mentioned initially by Gagnon] people who, like poisonous snakes, had wanted to inject their venom into the whole parish." Speech after speech followed. Then the meeting unanimously adopted a series of resolutions. They enumerated Father Primeau's many services; accused the "4 or 5" of conspiring to use the farewell ceremony as an occasion for expressing their personal grievances and for making a public scandal; claimed that members of other ethnic groups and Yankees, whether they spoke for or against "the victim of these accusations, were unanimous in condemning the actions of the accusers"; and declined to speak to the issue of the *curé's* guilt because, even if guilty, "well-brought-up children never take legal action against their father." Instead the parish, they resolved, "deeply regrets his departure" and

> protests energetically and solemnly against the anti-Christian, disloyal, and shameful action of several (4 or 5) Canadians who desired to involve the law in the farewells of the parish to her first pastor. The

parish stigmatizes this conduct. . . . In her indignation and outraged honor, cries: Shame! . . . Shame on these accusers who have dishonored the Canadians. Shame on these accusers who have wished to scandalize *Notre-Dame* parish. Shame on these accusers who have brought discredit to our Canadian parishes for the simple pleasure of avenging themselves for a personal grievance.[19]

There was no need to blame Marie Côte.

Who were the "4 or 5"? According to Gagnon, "charity" kept the speakers at the "indignation meeting" from mentioning the names of "the guilty parties." It was enough, he editorialized, to denounce "the act itself."[20] Presumably the audience already knew who the conspirators were. Their grievance, to judge from Gagnon's earlier editorial, had to do with the pew rental system Primeau had initiated and which had become a matter of bitter debate. But complaints, however vocal, do not constitute a conspiracy, much less a scandal.

Speaker after speaker had reiterated Gagnon's main contention. The timing of the warrant coincided so exactly with the farewell ceremony that it could not have been chance. The "4 or 5" knew, like everyone else, the exact date of Primeau's departure. Clearly they had planned to embarrass the priest and his supporters. No one at the meeting pointed out that they would also have had to know that Marie Côte gave birth to the priest's child. The speakers conveniently overlooked the fact that Côte and her father, not "certain Canadians," obtained the warrant. No one mentioned the father at the indignation meeting, perhaps because his personal grievance was all too clear and all too clearly had nothing to do with intraparish squabbles.

No one at the meeting even mentioned, much less tried to deny, the explanation Marie Côte herself gave when she obtained the warrant—that she sought to prevent the father of her child from disappearing without a trace. Yet this is the simplest explanation, and one that fits all the facts.

We do not know exactly when she left Worcester after confirming her pregnancy. Nor do we know where she went. No existing records can tell us whether Primeau made any promises to her when she left Worcester in the spring or early summer of 1881 or whether she left at his urging.[21] She could easily have learned of his intention to leave in the French-language press in either New England or Quebec since papers throughout the region tracked the clergy's comings and goings in great detail.[22]

Le Travailleur's December 20, 1881, story would have appeared in other papers throughout New England and Quebec anywhere from a week to several weeks later. Marie Côte might well have learned of Primeau's decision only days before it was to take place, which would explain why she did not seek the warrant before January 17.

Her father's presence suggests another, not incompatible, explanation. We do not know when he learned the identity of his daughter's seducer, but the timing suggests that it was not until just before the seventeenth. Had he known earlier, he would presumably have acted. Or, at the least, he would have sought assurances from the pastor. Had he and his daughter shown up at the rectory prior to going to the sheriff on that day? We cannot know, but somehow Father Primeau knew about the warrant in time to skip town.

There is no way to verify either of these suggestions. But we can rule out the conspiracy. The pastor had highly vocal critics who were happy to see him leave. They had no motive to do anything more terrible than boycott the "solemn farewell." Apparently not all of them did: several parishioners told the *Daily Spy* reporter that evening that they believed the charge. These statements constituted disloyalty of a very real kind and formed the kernel of truth in the denunciations of the otherwise mythic "4 or 5." Here lies the real mystery of *l'affaire Primeau*. Why was criticism of the *curé* to an outsider, no matter how casually or anonymously offered, a greater betrayal than the priest fathering an illegitimate child? If we can understand some of the reasons, we will have taken a long stride toward understanding some of the inner dynamics of their community.[23]

We will start where Ferdinand Gagnon did, with the reasons why a *Canadien* must never criticize a priest.[24] The priesthood, he began, is the most noble, benevolent, and respectable calling. The priest is the moral superior of any king, emperor, or governor. He is "powerful" too in that he alone can transform bread and wine into the body and blood of Jesus Christ. The priest is "self-sacrificing." He gives up family, friends, homeland. He takes vows of poverty and obedience and "renounces the pleasures of the world." He vows to be celibate. He administers the sacraments. He "preaches tenderness to parents, docility to children, fidelity to spouses, and kindness, charity, and brotherhood to all." From this idealized portrait Gagnon moved to the conclusion that the priest "must be respected," not only for whatever merits he might possess as an individual but "principally because of the sacred character imprinted on his person by the sacrament of Holy Orders."

All of this was ordinary Catholic teaching, as was Gagnon's conviction that "when you believe you have discovered some fault in the priest, remember he is flesh and bone like you," and put up with his failing in silence. You would thereby gain an indulgence.

Gagnon's argument was specifically French Canadian in its insistence that the *curé* actually served as a "father" to his parishioners. Just as children leap to defend the good name of their natural fathers, so too should a parish behave with respect to its pastor. "Instead of divulging his shortcomings," which are "most often imaginary" or seem glaring only because of "appearances imposed by uncontrollable circumstances," the "good parish will cover" these failings "with the mantle of charity, and, by this means, often prevent the unjust condemnation of a crowd of innocents because the public is all too ready to conclude from the particular to the general and is already prejudiced." We are surrounded, Gagnon reminded his readers, by people "who ask nothing better than to mock at everything Catholic."

This sense of living amidst Protestants eager to hold their religion up to ridicule drew upon a century and more of experience, first in Quebec, and then in New England. Gagnon reminded his readers further that they were living in "a time when the future of the *Canadien* missions rests on a volcano." At such a moment, "all of our congregations must crowd round their pastors and crowd out all who are critics." "Brothers in religion," Gagnon concluded, "show now enough public spirit and faith not to make a public scandal against a priest, guilty or not of the sins with which you reproach him." Instead "blast . . . the bad Catholics who have shamed themselves by maliciously doing a serious wrong to their religion by publicly denouncing their pastor."

It did seem to Gagnon and his contemporaries that they were perched upon a volcano. Just a year before, Carroll D. Wright, commissioner of the Massachusetts Bureau of the Statistics of Labor, branded them in his annual *Report* as the "Chinese of the Eastern States." His remarks triggered outrage among French Canadians, and their protests led Wright to hold a public hearing in October 1881 on the "Canadian French in New England," the transcript of which was published less than a week before Father Primeau's departure.[25] Canadians, led by Gagnon, had devoted much of 1881 to defending themselves.

Wright's remarks were, Gagnon editorialized, typical of the abuse heaped upon *Canadiens* and other immigrants. "Every day we read in the newspapers: Wanted an American servant. . . . No Irish need apply. Or, again: To let, an apartment to an American family, no foreigners." English-language newspapers never mentioned the nationality of an American-born murderer, "but, if the murderer is not an American, even when he is a naturalized citizen, they will say: the murderer is Irish or French Canadian."[26]

Acceptance as Americans, on the other hand, posed even greater dangers since the price, Gagnon and other Canadian patriots believed, was renunciation of their religion, their language, and the traditions of their homeland. Gagnon and his peers may have found it even more menacing that some Canadians willingly paid the price.[27] By 1880 an American-born generation, who often spoke English more fluently than French, was coming of age.[28]

For the first-generation immigrants, an historical tangle led to painful uncertainties about their own identity as French Canadians. They were, they knew only too well, excoriated in Quebec as deserters in the century-long struggle to resist English domination.[29] In their defense emigrés stressed their loyalty. Louis Honoré Fréchette, recently elected to the French Academy, made the case as eloquently as any. In his travels across the United States, he told a banquet audience in Holyoke, Massachusetts, he had encountered *Canadiens* "gathered around the bell-tower of the parish . . . faithfully preserving in the depths of their hearts, the religion, the traditions, and the memory of the fatherland they had left."[30] The logic of such loyalty required that the immigrant someday return, especially since the provincial government of Quebec established a repatriation program in the hopes of luring immigrants to settle on free land.

Repatriation became a subject of endless conversation, but few took up the province's offer and, by 1881, the policy had lapsed.[31] French Canadians, whether they could admit it to themselves or not, would find their future in the United States. This was Carroll D. Wright's conclusion after the hearing. What changed Wright's mind, what convinced him that they were "a steady stream of settlers" and not the "horde of industrial invaders" he had originally thought them, was the role of the church in their community. "The French Canadian," he wrote in his 1882 *Report*, "loves his church, and is loyal to it." The Canadian priest, taking "charge of the growing parish, soon found himself permanently established in New England, and his natural desire was to see his flock grow and prosper." With "strong French churches established . . . , repatriation is a failure."[32] With the churches came "the establishment of schools, societies, literary associations" and the like, including French-language newspapers such as *Le Travailleur*, with its dedication, emblazoned on its masthead, to "faith, language, and fatherland."[33]

Wright's conclusion that their "complete assimilation with the American people is but a question of time" stung worse than his gibe that the Canadian French were the "Chinese of the eastern states." *Le Messager* of Lewiston, Maine, fumed that "the Colonel [Wright] deceives himself. . . . No one assimilates less than a Frenchman." Gagnon chimed in that others "have offered" *Canadiens* "the kiss of peace in return for [them abandoning] their religious convictions or their fidelity to the traditions of their fathers," but history records that the Canadian "is never a traitor to his country." H. A. Dubuque, the attorney who chaired the hearing for the French Canadians, added that "if we can be loyal to the American Republic only on condition of renouncing all the sacred ties which unite us to France and to Canada, for my part, despite my love for our adopted land, I would blush with shame at the very idea of having so basely violated the holy law of memory."[34]

Wright had not demanded that French Canadians "abandon everything that is dear to them" or that "they forget Canada." He had done something worse. He had said they were in the process of doing these very things of their own volition, that assimilation was an inevitable consequence of their success in making a place for themselves in the United States. Far from assailing their Catholicism, he had said that the parish church served as the key to their assimilation—a point to which Gagnon, Dubuque, and other indignant *Canadiens* never turned. Instead they mispresented Wright's position and then denounced it.[35]

Wright's comment was such an affront because it challenged directly the French Canadians' own vision of themselves and used their own testimony at the hearing to do so. They viewed themselves, as *Le Messager* had it, as a people "detached, regarded as strangers, not speaking the language of the country" while "framing, in the United States, a new fatherland whose point of reference is the memory of the dear and venerable fatherland." *Canadiens* would be in, but not of, the United States. "Looked upon as strangers, they want to revive these memories and at the side of the Canadian church they will build the parochial school and the convent."

They would have their own mutual benefit organizations, just as "the Americans have their own secret societies." They would "cease work on the feast day of the Canadian nation [St. Jean-Baptiste Day], like the Irish, the English, and the Scots celebrate St. Patrick, St. George, and St. Andrew."[36]

Their task was to recreate Quebec in New England. The parishes, the parochial schools, the convents, the newspapers, the societies were all proof that they were succeeding. Wright's 1882 *Report* so exasperated because he offered an alternative reading. They really had abandoned Quebec, just as the priests back home had charged. Their patriotism to the fatherland was show, not substance. Their "Canadian" institutions revealed the depth of the roots they were sinking in New England. Wright gave voice to their own silent misgivings.

At the center of his interpretation of their experience, as well as that propounded by *Le Messager,* stood the church and the *curé,* institutions exemplified by *Notre-Dame-Des-Canadiens* and Father Primeau. In what sense, then, was the priest the "father" of the community? The perceptions of T. A. Chandonnet, who wrote the remarkable *Notre-Dame-Des-Canadiens,* an early history of the parish, can provide the answer. Chandonnet came as a missionary to Worcester in March 1872 after a year of preaching retreats throughout the northern states. He was impressed by the congregation and their pastor and eager to defend French Canadian emigrants from the charges that they "are deserters, men without a country!" When not preaching he spent his evenings talking with Father Primeau, who gave him free access to the church records. Chandonnet also interviewed many parishioners. Soon he knew "everything" about the community, "all its markings, under all its aspects."[37] In his history we come as close as we can to the voice of Father Primeau.

In 1869 Jean-Baptiste Primeau was superior of the College of Terrebonne. Before that he had taught philosophy at St. Teresa Seminary in Blainville, Quebec. Neither position satisfied him; he longed to be a pastor. When a fire destroyed the college he went to Montreal to ask for a parish. Before he saw the bishop, he ran into a priest just back from the American "mission" who told him of the great need for French Canadian priests in New England. Primeau decided on the spot to make this his life's work. Within a few days he had a summons from the bishop of Boston. Two days after that, on September 8, 1869, he found himself in Worcester, temporarily assigned as a curate in the parish of St. Paul's and charged with forming a separate French Canadian parish as soon as he could.[38]

As his first task, the young priest took a census of the French Canadian community. There were some 1,743 "souls," about 350 families, most headed by blue-collar workers. Shoe factory workers constituted the largest single group, followed by day laborers. Only a handful had white-collar positions: a doctor and a lawyer, a couple of grocers, and a few clerks. And, a few weeks after the census was complete, a twenty-year-old journalist named Ferdinand Gagnon arrived. About one male in six was a citizen; about the same proportion owned property in Worcester. An even smaller number, about one in ten, owned land in Quebec. Most were unable to read either French or English.[39] The average age of the heads of these families, by the time of the 1880 Census, was thirty-eight. They would have been even younger on average when Father Primeau first visited them in the fall of 1869. Virtually all had children living at home. Because the children were so young on average, most families made do with just the father's earnings.[40]

Living on one wage, particularly if the worker were unskilled, was precarious at best. If the father lost his job or, worse, were injured, the family would face destitution within weeks. Even when work was steady, families often made ends meet by cutting back on basic necessities, starting with food. They ate meat or fish only once a day; they did not eat fresh vegetables or fruits at all. For supper, the smallest meal of the day, they scraped along with bread and butter, washed down with tea. Breakfast was the main meal. Those who could afford it began the day with bread and butter, meat such as steak or pork chops, eggs, and cake or pie. To get by, families would substitute potatoes for the meat. Despite such limitations, even those most in need would try to dress respectably. Clothing was the last item they would cut back on.[41]

Such were the families Father Primeau met. He saw a people who "are neither rich nor poor. They enjoy a happy ease." "Ease" did not include luxury. Rather it meant a "happy mediocrity." Primeau prayed that his congregation be spared both riches and poverty. "Here, more than elsewhere, wealth . . . carries people closer to the Protestant or infidel class . . . ; it tends to make people enemies of their own faith; it pushes them toward contempt for their brothers." Poverty was just as dangerous. It led to crime and degradation. Primeau advocated mediocrity as the condition that "accomplishes prodigies, that builds churches, that maintains the sacred fire of the sanctuary."[42]

When Primeau undertook his census he knew that most of the poten-

tial parishioners were mired in the "Canadian sin." As Chandonnet para-
phrased him, "if Canadians in the United States don't have their own
church, with a French or Canadian priest at their head, then for that
reason they often consider themselves dispensed from going to church."
No more than forty had been attending weekly Mass even though the Irish
pastor set aside one service each Sunday especially for them at which he
read the Gospel and preached in French. The distance between this "sinful
abstention" and "the abyss where faith itself is fatally buffeted and ship-
wrecked" was all too short.[43] Only a separate national parish would avert
this calamity. Primeau called a meeting after Sunday Mass on September
12, 1869. He had been in Worcester less than a week. Should they form their
own parish? he asked. All agreed they should. Primeau would tell the Irish
pastor of their decision and attempt to arrange the use of the church basement until they could raise the money for a church of their own.

Father Power, whose efforts to reach the Canadians by preaching in
French and setting aside a special Mass for them had been rebuffed by the
community, refused to help. If they wanted to use the basement, any
money collected would belong to St. Anne's. So they were on their own.
Two weeks later Primeau celebrated Mass in Horticultural Hall, a large
building fronting the city Common.[44] About 450 individuals attended,
some ten times the number who had turned out at St. Anne's but less than
half of the Canadians in the city.

After Mass, Primeau turned to the congregation and

> in a voice filled with emotion, but strong and vibrant with energy, he
> raised his hand and pronounced these words of the prophet: "He
> swore to the Lord and this vow to the God of Jacob: I will not enter
> into the privacy of my home, I will not climb into the bed of my
> repose, I will not give sleep to my eyes, nor relaxation to my eyelids,
> until I have found a dwelling for the Lord, a tabernacle for the God
> of Jacob."

Would they take this same oath? He would circulate a subscription list
that evening after Vespers. Fifty families pledged $3,458 that night. By De-
cember, the pledges totaled $10,587. Six months later they reached $16,903.
The support represented, for families enjoying a "happy mediocrity," a
tremendous commitment.

The *curé*'s ability to initiate this shared dream—a church of their own—explains much of his role in the community. It helps explain why some thought of him as godlike while others regarded him as high-handed. He began by visiting their homes. He was not, he emphasized, asking for money. He wanted to get to know them. Still, he told Chandonnet, "no one could keep the great question from . . . finally taking over every conversation, in spite of everything." At one stop, a girl of five or six gave the priest the few pennies she had saved and gravely said: "Here, Father . . . to build your church." No doubt, Primeau told Chandonnet, her mother had coached her. Even so, the next week at Mass, "the pastor recounted the week's little scene," stressed the girl's "simple and naive confidence," and intoned: "I accept the sign. We will have our church. Only let us remember that we are called to be like this child." After this, he recalled, every child saved pennies, and he carefully recorded each little gift.[45]

Children faced extraordinary dangers in the United States, Primeau believed. For example, "the lack of leisure time . . . on the part of the parents" left them unsupervised for much of the day. They likewise suffered from the absence of Catholic schools where they might learn the fundamentals of faith and heritage. Worst of all, perhaps, were the "heretical or atheistic public schools," places of "dreadful Protestant propaganda." In response, he organized an informal school that met every Wednesday. In it "he had them read; even taught them their first words of their own language, since some of them did not speak French; and mixed in were singing, some small attempts at declamation, recitations, marching, etc." He also started a special children's Mass.[46]

Primeau reestablished several Canadian religious customs, such as Midnight Mass on Christmas Eve and the crêche, the wax figures representing the Holy Family in the manger at Bethlehem. At the same time, however, he made it clear from the outset that theirs would be an American parish, run on American principles. There would be a parish council, he said at that first meeting, but it would not, as in Canada, control the finances or set his salary. The bishop would have final say. Of course, given the far-flung nature of the diocese, the pastor would exercise full operational control. The council would advise. He would decide. On the other hand, he would make regular reports. The idea, according to Chandonnet, was to "banish the least vestiges of defiance . . . that might have existed in certain minds."[47]

Defiance, however, did not submit so readily. Some parishioners, "with a bit of that dark suspicion Canadians inherit from their ancestors, quickly imagined that this would be a responsible council, with the pastor presiding and each member having a voice equal to his at meeting." They wanted the Canadian system in which they would regulate everything by majority vote and in which the council, not the pastor, would report to the parish, which could then decide whether to keep them in office. Primeau stood firm. He would not "yield in any way his freedom of action."[48]

An early test came in May 1870. On the first Sunday of the month Primeau called a parish meeting. They needed to decide, he informed those in attendance, a crucial issue. Even before he stated the issue, he insisted that all must accept the decision and support it "without reservation, without hesitation, and without recriminations." Only after gaining this "solemn promise," did he tell them that they were to decide whether to build a church or buy an existing structure. Chandonnet reported: "Opinions differed, and the meeting was about to divide into two nearly equal parts." At this moment a member of the parish council suggested that "the whole thing" be left up to Primeau. "This proposition received a general and solemn 'Yes,' repeated several time. So they were unanimous."[49]

Primeau got to make the crucial decision but had not demanded this authority. Instead the parish had asked him to assume it. Two weeks later he told the congregation at Mass that, if they would look across the Common, they would see the site of the future *Notre-Dame*. It was the Park Street Methodist Church. They would take occupancy on the first Sunday in June. They would need even more money than they already had, however. He would lead the way. He would forego his salary for the next six months. He would not rent or buy a rectory. Instead he would live in the church basement until they were sure they could pay off the mortgage. He would ask them to do nothing he would not do himself. He was one of them.[50]

Locating *Notre-Dame* on the Common heightened the visibility of the community. On Sundays *Canadiens* joined Yankee members of the two Congregational and one Baptist churches, also located in the center of the city, in strolling across the Common. This was an unusual occurrence. Most Catholic churches were located in blue-collar neighborhoods, close to their parishioners' homes and far from downtown. *Notre-Dame*'s location, directly across from City Hall and right off Main Street, announced that the *Canadiens* intended to take their rightful place in Worcester's public life.[51]

They would take it, furthermore, as *Canadiens*. Chandonnet remarked on "the air of the homeland" which he found everywhere. None here, he reported proudly, blushed "to speak French." No one broke up their names or renounced "the blood that nourishes their veins! Nowhere is proud national feeling more at ease or better received" than in *Notre-Dame*. Patriotism was "lit in the bosom of the church; there under the wings of religion it grew and imposed itself upon the respect, esteem, and favor of the dominant population of strangers."[52]

Yet, even as Carroll Wright had recognized, the very process of building up the church led Father Primeau to Americanize his flock in crucial ways. An example is how the Canadians celebrated their national day, June 24, the feast of St. Jean-Baptiste, the patron saint of Quebec. Members of the community held meetings over several weeks in 1870 to plan the day. The *curé* also was making plans, plans he did not share until the Sunday before. His vision had "nothing in common with the ordinary merry-making of a national celebration" but called instead for those who did not work to gather at the church for Mass; those who did work should go off to the job with "the earnings of the day going to benefit" the parish. As for "banners, flags, insignias, music, wagons, caricatures or phantasmagoria" or "marshalls, commissioners," and the like, "there was to be none of that." No one would appear "in the streets, in procession, beneath the flags, at the picnic." Instead all would gather at the end of the day at a local music hall where they would sing, listen to music, and present "an offering . . . of the day's earnings."[53]

Primeau had his way. A gift of $1,403 augmented the parish fund. Each worker received a memorial card that had a cross in each of the upper corners and a beaver, symbolizing Canada, in the center. In gold letters the card proclaimed:

ABOVE ALL, LET US BE CANADIANS.
NOTRE DAME DES CANADIENS DE WORCESTER, MASS.
OUR RELIGION AND OUR HOMELAND WILL NEVER BE FORGOTTEN.
JUNE 24, 1870.

Then came a list of the contributors "with his day's earnings." At the bottom was the signature: J.B. Primeau, priest, pastor. It was a stunning display of authority. The pastor had overturned one local tradition and installed another. He had set aside the community's plans for perhaps the most important event of the year. He had gotten them to abandon the public celebration of their ethnicity, even though such "days" as St. Patrick's or St. Andrew's enabled nationality groups to commandeer, however briefly, the public life of the city and to bask in the flattery of politicians. He had done all this, and "at the eleventh hour."[54]

Primeau did not work only to serve his congregation's spiritual needs or to build up the parish, he also strove to build up the Canadian community in Worcester. Prior to his arrival in 1869, Worcester's French Canadians had tried and failed to create lasting organizations. The pastor proved to be the difference. He served as chaplain to the St. Jean-Baptiste Society, a mutual benefit association, and other secular associations. He promoted the Drama Club, which often held benefit performances for the church in return. He recruited a Canadian Band to play at High Mass. He urged *Canadiens* to subscribe to Ferdinand Gagnon's newspaper.[55]

He also adapted that most American of institutions, the Sunday School, to the community's purposes. Students competed to demonstrate mastery of the catechism. "There is a prize," Chandonnet recorded, "for anyone who undergoes a good examination. But the honor to which they are most sensitive . . . is to be chosen to pose the questions of a chapter of catechism, or to respond to them publicly, on Sunday after vespers in front of all the attentive people." This was a major event. "Mothers must dress their children well for the occasion. They must have new clothes. The little boys will have, for example, a black coat and white trousers; the little girls a white dress, a white veil and a crown."[56]

All of this tied people's lives to the church, making the parish and the community coextensive.[57] And the *curé* acted as though his word were law in both. Even Chandonnet admitted that some Canadians found this intolerable. They refused to contribute to the parish. In Canada everyone had been taxed to support the church, a system known as the twenty-sixth *minot*. In the United States, however, "a minority . . . rebels against the voice of religion, justice, equity, honor, and of its [own] spiritual and even temporal interest." These malcontents insisted upon their right, as Americans, to contribute as much or as little as each thought proper. Primeau, as his plan for St. Jean-Baptiste Day illustrated, believed he should determine how much each should give.

The issue came up over and over again, especially over payments for the sacraments and over pew rentals. Chandonnet defended the priest. All of the sacraments were free, save baptism and marriage, and there was a fee for marriage in Canada, albeit lower: "allowing for the fact that [marriage] generally presents itself once in each person's life, [the difference] is certainly not worth taking into account." As for pew rentals, an exasperated Chandonnet, no doubt echoing the exasperated Primeau, sputtered, "for heaven's sake, aren't pews paid for in Canada" in the form of the *minot*? "Is there really a difference? Not at all."[58]

Yet there was a difference. Pew rental was an American practice with roots in the congregational system of governance. A church's deacons or elders would set the fees for particular pews, and individual families would decide which pew to rent. By renting a particular pew, a family made a statement about its place in the local status hierarchy. Primeau gave this system a distinctive spin. He referred to it as the "salary days" system. Each family was to pay an amount equivalent to a set percentage of their income. Thomas Lachance, a bootmaker, for example, paid $100 to sit in the ninth row, right in the middle of the church. Alfred Chapleau, a blacksmith, paid $82 for space in the thirteenth row. The average charge was about $30. For families whose total income barely topped $600, this constituted a substantial sum.[59]

Any family who challenged the pastor's decision about which pew they should rent had to sit in one of the free pews, a position that advertised its refusal to support the parish. By the rented pews, of course, every parishioner could deduce almost to the dollar the annual income of every other. According to Gagnon, whose paper endorsed the system as "impartial, honorable, equitable and neither onerous nor vexatious," a full third of the parish boycotted the pew rentals.[60]

Feelings over the *curé* ran high. His supporters, such as Gagnon, initially believed when he announced his departure that the malcontents had succeeded in driving him out. Then came the scandal. Bad enough to have a minority of critics drive the pastor away. Far worse to have them proven right in challenging his leadership. Who was Primeau, after all, to say what others should do? An argument that had raged for more than a decade was settled in a single stroke. Such an outcome was intolerable, however, and the pastor's partisans insisted upon forcing the sorry tale of the *curé's* fall into the context of the battles over money and control. Gagnon and the priest's other supporters convinced themselves that a small cabal, the notorious "4 or 5," had caused all of this misery and disgrace.

The battle over control of the parish was also a struggle over how American, and how Canadian, the community was to be. All sides to the dispute combined Canadian and American ways of doing things. None was willing to admit to such a thing. All insisted that they were, as Father Primeau proclaimed when he ordered his parishioners to abandon their St. Jean-Baptiste celebration, "Above all, . . . Canadians."[61]

Notre-Dame's location and appearance illustrate the point. It looked out upon the Common, as did several prominent Protestant congregations. Further, it looked very much like those churches. A rectangular structure with two columns flanking three doors, it had a spire. Banks of large windows, with green shutters, ran along its sides. Dark red paint covered the rest of the building. It looked like the Methodist church it once had been.[62] In fact, it looked too Protestant for the pastor and the congregation. They added a statue of the Virgin to the church facade. More ambitiously, they commissioned a bell and bell tower. The bell figured in all their memories of village life in Quebec. With it their church would be truly Canadian.

So important was the bell that Father Primeau scheduled his departure for after its dedication, which took place on Sunday, January 15, 1882. Four thousand people, virtually every French Canadian in the region, crowded into Mechanics Hall on Main Street for the ceremony. The choir sang. The Cadet Band "in their brilliant uniforms" played. Father Primeau, "with his customary eloquence," spoke about the role of the bell in the religious lives of their parents and grandparents. Then he blessed it and rang it three times, first for the honor of Almighty God, then in honor of the Virgin, and then in the hope of peace for the parish. For a small donation parishioners got their chance to toll the bell. This took hours as hundreds queued up.[63]

The actual installation was the next day. The bell would ring for the first time in its tower on Tuesday, the seventeenth, to bid farewell to the pastor. But it remained silent that evening.

After leaving Worcester, Jean-Baptiste Primeau headed west. He briefly settled in Ohio and then became a missionary to the islanders of Montserrat in the Lesser Antilles. There he died, on June 3, 1899. He left his entire estate to his old parish. He had wished to live, he wrote in his will, as "a Catholic and a priest," and "if I have not lived as such, O God, forgive me." He had, he continued, a last request. "I state a desire, a need of my heart. Oh, how I have always wanted to be buried on the hill that was to become the cemetery of the Canadians of Worcester, not far from my dear Notre-Dame!" On his tombstone he wanted the words: POOR FATHER PRIMEAU. NOTRE-DAME-DES-CANADIENS. He wanted the dates SEPT. 10, 1869–

JAN. 17, 1882, the beginning and end of his pastorate, engraved on the stone rather than the dates of his birth and death.[64]

How would the people of the parish respond to this plea for forgiveness? They organized a "solemn" ceremony. Eight priests concelebrated a High Mass for his soul. The eulogy extolled his many contributions to *Notre-Dame*. Three months later, at the request of the parishioners, there was a second funeral service with his nephew Father Joachim Primeau as the celebrant. At the end of the Mass, the young Father Primeau read his uncle's will. People wept.

Would they honor his final wish, that "desire of the heart"? No. They would be the good children Ferdinand Gagnon had urged them to be. They would rally around their father's good name. But they would not forgive. Jean-Baptiste Primeau, in the words of *Le Worcester Canadien*, would sleep "his final sleep in that land populated by blacks, among whom he had voluntarily exiled himself to the end of his life."[65]

Father Primeau had wished to live his life "as a Christian" and "as a priest." Yet he was but "flesh and bone," as Ferdinand Gagnon put it, and thus a sinner.[66] His sin was not only of the flesh. Because he was a priest and because, like Hawthorne's Puritan divine, he attempted to carry on his public role despite his private guilt, he committed the sin of scandal. His flock, because of him, had to choose between their loyalty to their church, which they defined in terms of language and ethnicity as much as in terms of doctrine, and the truth.

Carroll Wright's report on "The Canadian French," in which he took back his characterization of them as "a horde of industrial invaders" and instead accepted their self-portrait as a "steady stream of settlers," posed the same moral dilemma. Loyalty required the pretense of repatriation. Someday they would return. In the meantime they would preserve intact "foi, langue, et patrie"—faith, language, and patriotic devotion to Quebec. Return was their fondest dream. Wright had initially taken them at their word. The Canadian French, he had written, "care nothing for our institutions." They work for any wages, he went on, seeking only to save up what they can so as to return to Quebec. The hearing made the truth clear. The *Canadiens* were rapidly assimilating. They were becoming naturalized, acquiring property, building schools and convents and churches, laying down roots in New England. The very institutions they pointed to as proof of their cultural loyalty were, in fact, evidence of their determination to make homes for themselves in their new land.

Their "complete assimilation" was merely a "matter of time," Wright concluded.[67]

So the twin mysteries this essay has explored—why the parishioners of *Notre-Dame-Des-Canadiens* regarded the casual expression of distrust in their pastor by their neighbors as a more heinous offense than his misconduct and why the French Canadians of Massachusetts regarded Carroll D. Wright's prediction of their "complete assimilation" as a worse insult than his earlier description of them as "the Chinese of the Eastern States"—turn out to have a single solution. Both posed a choice between faith and truth. It is small wonder that the French Canadians chose faith or that the choice proved painful or that they could never forgive those who forced the choice upon them.

NOTES

1. *Le Travailleur*, Jan. 20, 1882, provides the fullest account of the parish gathering. All translations from this and other newspapers are by the author.
2. The plans are detailed in *Le Travailleur*, Jan. 13, 1882, and the *Worcester Evening Gazette*, Jan. 17, 1882.
3. *Le Travailleur*, Jan. 13, 20, 1882.
4. Among the most acclaimed and accomplished of the so-called "micro-histories" are Laurel Thatcher Ulrich, *A Midwife's Tale: The Life of Martha Ballard, Based on Her Diary, 1785-1812* (New York, 1990); and Linda Gordon, *The Great Arizona Orphan Abduction* (Cambridge, Mass., 1999).
5. When Pope John Paul II publicly repented for the Roman Catholic Church's "sin" in condemning Galileo's advocacy of the heliocentric theory of the universe, it was for the sin of scandal. By condemning a theory that rested upon scientific experiment and mathematical measurement, the Church had forced believers to choose between faith and truth.
6. *Worcester Daily Spy*, Jan. 18, 1882. Côte was a common surname among French Canadians; no given name was more common than Marie. For example, in a congregation of nuns in Worcester, the Little Franciscans of Mary, founded in the 1890s, every single sister took the name Marie! This makes searching census and other records for Marie Côte an impossible task.
7. *Worcester Evening Gazette*, Jan. 18, 1882.
8. *Le Travailleur*, Jan. 20, 27, 1882.
9. *Le Travailleur*, Dec. 20, 1881.
10. The only account of this expedition to Springfield was published nearly 20 years after the fact as part of *Le Worcester Canadien*'s tribute to Primeau on the occasion of his death in 1900. *Le Worcester Canadien* was an annual directory of the city's French Canadians that included extensive information about their parishes, schools, organizations, and participation in politics along with advertisements and laudatory biogra-

phies of community members. Its account of this interview with the bishop has to be used with care. It contains a minor factual error concerning the time interval between Father Primeau's announcement and his actual departure. Further, it completely omits the charge of bastardy, since it was written to document the devotion of the parishioners and the bishop's high opinion of the *curé*. There is no reason to doubt, on the other hand, that some parishioners did ask the bishop to keep their pastor with them. Whether the bishop actually told the delegates that Primeau had been asking permission to leave "for years" is less clear. The evidence of Primeau's will, discussed below, calls into question the likelihood that he had made any such requests.

11. Ferdinand Gagnon, "The Event of the Day," *Le Travailleur*, Dec. 23, 1881.

12. Gagnon, "The Event of the Day."

13. The Call was published in *Le Travailleur*, Jan. 24, 1882. It was signed by 22 including Ferdinand Gagnon, whose names were published, plus "a great number of others" for whose names the paper had no space.

14. These included a ceremony after Sunday Mass on Jan. 8, at which the Ladies of the Holy Family gave the priest "a beautiful tobacco box ornamented with gold and silver and a satin handkerchief." On that same occasion the schoolchildren presented Primeau with "sympathetic and respectful" cards. Gagnon reported that "the pastor was very moved and he responded with his natural eloquence to these two manifestations of sympathy and sorrow on the occasion of his imminent departure." A few days later, the French Canadian clergy of the region gave Primeau a farewell dinner at which "Mr. L'Abbe Dumontier, *curé* at Marlboro, gave a toast to the Reverend *curé* in the most moving terms. Mr. L'Abbe Primeau responded with eloquence and emotion." *Le Travailleur*, Jan. 13, 17, 1882.

15. A search of the 1880 U.S. Census for Worcester yielded no Marie Côte of the correct age. The census is notoriously unreliable insofar as individual bits of information are concerned, especially with regard to ages and especially when the census taker did not speak the native language of the respondent. Usually, however, errors in ages occurred when respondents rounded them off to the nearest decade. For example, there are too many people who are exactly 20 or 40 in the census. The manuscript census listed four residents in the rectory: Primeau, a priest named Joseph Dupont, a 32-year-old housekeeper named Euphramia Girouz [*sic*, probably Giroux], and a 19-year-old male servant named Alexandre Lapointe. See Margo J. Anderson, *The American Census: A Social History* (New Haven, 1988), 83-115.

16. A zealous defender of the good name of French Canadians, Gagnon would never have urged Primeau to remain at *Notre-Dame* had he heard even a hint of sexual misconduct.

17. The warrant contained the name of one other Canadian, Côte's father. Neither of the two physicians mentioned was Canadian. One, Thomas O'Callahan, was Irish American. His office was near the rectory. The other, Merrick Bemis, was a Yankee who ran a private hospital in addition to maintaining an office in downtown Worcester. Gagnon made no mention of the physicians.

18. *Le Travailleur*, Jan. 20, 1882.

19. *Le Travailleur*, Jan. 27, 1882, carried the complete text of the resolutions, excerpts from Couture's speech, and a full account of the meeting.

84 &* JOHN F. MCCLYMER

20. *Le Travailleur*, Jan. 27, 1882.
21. The fact that the birth was not recorded in Worcester along with the absence of gossip makes it virtually certain she left the city. It is impossible to trace where she might have gone because her name was so common. She could have gone anywhere in New England or Quebec.
22. They routinely picked up and reprinted such announcements from one another.
23. Robert Darnton, in *The Great Cat Massacre and Other Episodes in French Cultural History* (New York, 1984), comments that one measure of whether we understand an historical era is whether we "get" the jokes. See especially pp. 4-5. One can make the same argument with respect to what the people of a specific time found scandalous.
24. This discussion is based upon Gagnon's editorial, "The Priest," written in the midst of the scandal. *Le Travailleur*, Jan. 24, 1882.
25. Carroll D. Wright, "Uniform Hours of Labor," *Twelfth Annual Report of the Massachusetts Bureau of the Statistics of Labor* (Boston, 1881), 150-151; Wright, "The Canadian French in New England," *Thirteenth Annual Report* (Boston, 1882). Gagnon's account of the hearings transcript and editorial reaction appeared the very day of Primeau's leaving. *Le Travailleur*, Jan. 17, 1882. For an account of Wright's charges, see John F. McClymer, "Carroll D. Wright, L'Abbé Jean-Baptiste Primeau, and French-Canadian Families," in *The Human Tradition in the Gilded Age and Progressive Era*, ed. Ballard C. Campbell (Wilmington, Del., 2000), 1-18.
26. "Denationalization," *Le Travailleur*, Feb. 21, 1882.
27. Gagnon began his discussion of "Denationalization" by reprinting a letter published in the *Marlboro Mirror*. Its author wrote that he no longer wanted to be known as French Canadian. He was an American. *Le Travailleur*, Feb. 7, 1882.
28. See, for example, the resolutions of the Third Convention of the French Canadians of Massachusetts and Rhode Island published in *Le Travailleur*, Oct. 11, 1881. One conceded the necessity of knowing some English but called upon all families to speak only French at home. Another called for the construction of more parochial schools to keep children from the Americanizing influence of the public schools.
29. A Canadian missionary, L'Abbé T. A. Chandonnet, wrote a highly detailed history, *Notre-Dame-Des-Canadiens and Les Canadiens aux Etats-Unis* (Montreal, 1872) (hereafter *NDDC*), to defend emigrants against these charges. Kenneth J. Moynihan of the Assumption College Community Studies program has translated this history into English. All references are to his translation, which is available at the French Institute, Assumption College.
30. *Le Travailleur*, Feb. 7, 1882. Similarly, Chandonnet began his defense of the parishioners of *Notre-Dame* by claiming that nowhere had he felt more at home than in Worcester. "It may not be the homeland, but in everything most noble and generous it is the sacred image of home." *NDDC*, i.
31. The Third Convention of French Canadians of Massachusetts and Rhode Island, quoted above, placed repatriation on its agenda, but "as the government of the province of Quebec does not appear to have enough patriotism to busy itself with the repatriation of our compatriots, the Convention awaits the action of the [provincial] government." *Le Travailleur*, Oct. 11, 1881. Carroll D. Wright questioned Ferdinand Gagnon and other witnesses closely at the hearing about repatriation, since it was the

main reason, Wright claimed, that the Canadian French were charged with "caring nothing for our [American] institutions." All, including Gagnon, who had been an agent for the province, assured him that the policy was a dead letter because so few wished to return. This candor, in turn, led other editors of French-language newspapers to charge Gagnon with lack of patriotism. In his own defense, Gagnon reasserted his devotion to repatriation and called upon the government of Quebec to renew its program. See "Denial!" *Le Travailleur*, Nov. 1, 1881. Among the papers that had attacked him were *L'Abeille* of Lowell and *L'Echo* of Manchester, New Hampshire.

32. Wright, "The Canadian French in New England," 89-90.

33. Wright, "The Canadian French in New England," 88-92.

34. "La Question Wright," as reprinted in *Le Travailleur*, Jan. 31, 1882; H. A. Dubuque, "Americans and Canadians," *Le Travailleur*, Jan. 17, 1882.

35. In Gagnon's case, at least, the misrepresentation was deliberate. His initial story and editorial on Wright's *Report* contain a detailed and highly accurate summary of the bureau chief's comments. *Le Travailler*, Jan. 17, 1882.

36. "La Question Wright." "Loyalty" to the United States, *Le Messager* continued, "does not consist of admiring the evil system of public education, or the narrow-minded ideas of people too puffed up over their origins and the success of their ancestors." Instead, it "consists of obeying the laws and respecting authority. Opposing prejudice, organizing self-help societies, teaching the French like the English language, professing one's religion, this is not disloyalty."

37. Chandonnet intended his book to honor Father Primeau and to celebrate the achievement of Worcester's French Canadians in building their congregation. "In Canada," there was "nothing original or remarkable" about setting up a parish. In the United States, however, "a parish is a creation: it is the joining together of free and isolated elements; it is a noble work of prudence, of planning, of zeal, and of enthusiasm." *NDDC*, iii.

38. Unless otherwise noted, all information about the founding of *Notre-Dame* comes from Chandonnet's work. *Le Worcester Canadien* for 1900 contains a biographical sketch of Primeau that provides the detail about the fire at Terrebonne.

39. The first census counted only "souls" and "communicants." I have used the much fuller 1872 census described in *NDDC*. The date of Gagnon's arrival is in Rosaire Dion-Levesque, *Silhouettes Franco-Americaines* (Manchester, N.H., 1957), 338.

40. A count using the 1880 manuscript census shows only 8.2 percent of French Canadian families had no children living at home; 64.4 percent of these families had only one wage-earner. In 1869 the percentage would have been even higher.

41. John F. McClymer, "Late Nineteenth-Century American Working-Class Living Standards," *Journal of Interdisciplinary History* 17(1986):379-398.

42. *NDDC*, 101. Did the parishioners agree with their *curé*? Chandonnet wrote: "All the people seemed impressed."

43. *NDDC*, 10.

44. "The chalice, the sacred vestments, and the essential altar linens" came not from St. Anne's but from "the good Sisters of Mercy." *NDDC*, 13.

45. *NDDC*, 15. Primeau also used other "signs" in his sermons. On the day of the meeting to discuss a separate parish, an 11-year-old boy, who had never been to confession,

drowned. A few weeks later, a man suddenly died from what had been thought a mild illness, also without benefit of the sacraments. Still another man, at the very moment Mass was beginning, accidentally shot himself while hunting. These were "warnings." *NDDC*, 13.

46. *NDDC*, 18. The Irish did not share this view of the public schools, largely because the superintendent hired so many Irish American teachers. As a result, the Irish parishes such as St. Anne's lagged far behind *Notre-Dame* in setting up parochial schools.

47. *NDDC*, 21. In 1870 Worcester became part of the new diocese of Springfield. Bishop O'Reilly commended Primeau's practice of reporting. Although "it is not allowed, without the bishop's permission, to grant laymen the least part in the management of church property, it is nevertheless good policy to acquaint the parishioners with the state of parish affairs at least once a year. This provides at one and the same time a very legitimate satisfaction and a strong encouragement to them, and to the bishop a protection against every suspicion of embezzlement, carelessness, or lack of foresight." *NDDC*, 22.

48. *NDDC*, 12.

49. *NDDC*, 23-24.

50. *NDDC*, 24. The purchase price was $22,750, which was about $5,000 more than they had in pledges. The terms called for $5,000 down, $1,000 a month for eight months, beginning with June, and then $1,500 a month for nine months. This would leave a lump sum of $8,250 due November 1, 1871.

51. See F. W. Beers et al., *Atlas of the City of Worcester* (1870; Rutland, Vt. 1971). For the Protestant dominance of downtown locations, see Carole Rifkind, *Main Street: The Face of Urban America* (New York, 1977).

52. *NDDC*, 25, 101. A case in point of the church fostering Canadian patriotism was the Seventh National Convention of Canadian Emigrants, which met in Worcester in September 1871. The 22-year-old editor, Ferdinand Gagnon, presided. Father Primeau opened the proceedings and also said a special Mass on Sunday at which he spoke of the "mission" of the Canadian people. The delegates elected him an honorary member of the convention's executive committee. *Etendard National* (*Etendard National* was the predecessor of *Le Travailleur*), Oct. 5, 1871.

53. *NDDC*, 28-29.

54. *NDDC*, 29-30.

55. *NDDC*, chap. 25. Perhaps the most important was the St. Jean-Baptiste Society. Blue-collar families could rarely afford insurance. In a mutual benefit society each member contributed a small sum each pay period. When a member became ill or was laid off, he received $5 or $6 a week for a specified period. There was also usually a death benefit, which amounted to enough to pay for a decent burial. The pastor also organized a number of parish societies, such as the Work of the Tabernacle for young women. Older women formed the Messengers of Providence who visited the sick and distributed alms to the indigent. Primeau set up an adoption agency in the parish for orphans and unwanted children, and he organized a parish library.

56. *NDDC*, 76.

57. W. I. Thomas and Florian Znaniecki, *The Polish Peasant in Europe and America* (New York, 1919), 2:1511-1574, provides the classic account of the role of the church in the cre-

ation of Polish American communities in the early 20th century. In general, historians of ethnicity have underemphasized, when they have not actually ignored, the role of the local parish and clergy.

58. *NDDC*, 56-57.

59. *Le Travailleur*, Mar. 29, 1881, contains the details about pew rentals. See McClymer, "Late Nineteenth-Century American Working-Class Living Standards," for a discussion of blue-collar family budgets.

60. *Le Travailleur*, Jan. 28, Mar. 29, 1881. Later, in his Dec. 23, 1881, editorial urging Primeau to stay the course, Gagnon claimed that 9 in 10 parishioners supported the system.

61. *NDDC*, 30.

62. When the structure was refurbished in 1880, Primeau hired Stephen C. Earle, who had designed some 20 churches, all Protestant, to oversee the work. Curtis Dahl, *Stephen C. Earle, Architect: Shaping Worcester's Image* (Worcester, 1987), 69, 28-38.

63. *Le Travailleur*, Jan. 17, 1882.

64. The full text of the will was printed in *Le Worcester Canadien* for 1900. The translation is by Professor Kenneth J. Moynihan of Assumption College.

65. *Le Worcester Canadien*, 1900.

66. *Le Travailleur*, Jan. 24, 1882.

67. Wright, "The Canadian French in New England," 88-92.

George Frisbie Hoar and Chinese Exclusion

The Political Construction of Race

JONATHAN CHU

> You may choose any of the following federally approved races.
>
> —DAVE BARRY[1]

N FEBRUARY 28, 1882, John Miller, Republican senator from California, opened the debates on the Chinese Exclusion Bill. Ostensibly intended to address the problems of Chinese competition with American labor, it proposed to suspend the entry of Chinese laborers into the United States for the next twenty years. Included in the bill was an amendment by Miller's Democratic colleague from California, James T. Farley, prohibiting the naturalization of Chinese. Miller's introductory speech and Farley's amendment demonstrated both men's belief in fundamental, intractable differences between Americans and Chinese that were rooted in race and history. "They remain," Miller argued, "Chinese always and everywhere; changeless, fixed, unalienable."[2] Writing his own speech as Miller addressed the Senate, George Frisbie Hoar, the junior senator from Massachusetts and also a Republican, cast his rejoinder as "broad as [Charles] Sumner himself would have made on the same subject," resting it upon America's traditional principles as articulated in the Declaration of Independence and the Constitution.[3]

While scholars have discussed the extent to which competition for jobs and racism led to the rise of the Chinese Exclusion Act,[4] the issues raised by Miller and Hoar reveal an internal tension borne in the application of history to the senatorial debates. Debates over Chinese Exclusion revealed the ways in which elements of new historical methods inspired by the work of Leopold von Ranke were brought to bear in matters of public policy. Prefiguring the work of Progressive historians such as Charles Beard, both sides sought authority for policy in the factual presentation of the past and revealed the extent to which prior assumptions shaped historical conclusions in determining policy outcomes. The assumptions about history, race, and culture redirected the outcome in Chinese Exclusion and revealed the precedence that racism, not competition for jobs, took in its passage. At the same time, the debates reconstructed hitherto diffuse multiple racial categories of whiteness into a single entity. In articulating their assumptions about the historic racial and cultural incompatibility of Chinese and Americans, the supporters of Exclusion also amalgamated what Matthew Jacobson has called whiteness of a different color.[5]

In his opening speech, Miller blurred distinctions between race and culture as he developed his argument in favor of Exclusion. In drawing upon what he saw to be lessons from the history of mankind, Miller noted that civilization—culture—emerged out of diverse racial traits that presumably were biologically innate. Thus, because Chinese cultural behavior had been unchanged for fifty centuries, they were products of a combination of evolutionary necessity and heredity. "They have been unable to change the habits and character that have been forced upon them and ground into them by necessity and a heredity as old as the records of man." Different races gave rise to diverse characteristics that in turn produced distinctive nations and civilizations. The recent history of Chinese settlement in California, he added, had demonstrated the incompatibility of the Chinese and Americans. The Chinese were different. They were incapable of assimilating western civilization, modern thought, and Christian teaching. Far from being the product of an unjust or illiberal mind, his argument, he averred, was "supported by incontrovertible fact and passionless reasoning and enforced by the logic of events."[6]

According to Miller, the past Chinese assimilation of Tibet and Manchuria provided harbingers of their abilities to transform American culture and race. After only a quarter of a century, Californians had demonstrated their susceptibility to the impact of "the stoical Chinese" in their moral and social conditions. White Californians had been forced into migrant labor—becoming "blanket men" who lived on farms during the harvest season only to move on when it was over—and they had witnessed a rise of a hoodlum element, loathsome diseases, and opium addiction. The past provided evidence of the future: like Hawai'i, America would be overrun, and the American people would "merge into a mongrel race, half Chinese and half Caucasian, as to produce a civilization half pagan, half Christian, semi-Oriental, altogether mixed and very bad."[7]

Central to Hoar's valiant, but doomed opposition to Exclusion was his reliance upon two interwoven historical arguments: the record of the Founders' reliance upon abstract principles of equality and the Chinese history of civilized accomplishment. In the charged context of late-nineteenth-century America both sides blended culture and race into fixed, moral characteristics determined by biology. But where Miller and others in the Senate saw in history evidence of essential cultural incompatibility determined by race or other biological characteristics, Hoar saw in the subtle and multiple varieties of races opportunities for assimilation and elevation. Obviously paternalistic, he assumed that race was irrelevant to the process of civilization. All races could be elevated to higher levels of culture, raised to heights of civilization—as he perceived it—and made worthy to live in a republic by the immortal truths of the Declaration of Independence, the Constitution, and the Golden Rule.[8]

Although on the losing side of the Exclusion debate, Hoar was not a dinosaur, a patronage party politician who had survived into an age of new history, but an amalgam of idealist, modern scholar, and pragmatist. In his response to Miller, Hoar reflected both the great romantic amateurs of the nineteenth century such as George Bancroft and Francis Parkman and the great Progressive historians such as Beard and Frederick Jackson Turner. Like the romantics, Hoar believed in the moral functions of history. A contemporary of Bancroft, Hoar shared his belief that facts led to historical truth and historical truth provided moral lessons for the human condition. Becoming a good friend of Bancroft after arriving in Washington in 1877, Hoar saw in him a mentor and colleague in his own studies. Bancroft, Hoar wrote in his *Autobiography*, was a great historian because he spared no effort in searching out the truth and he believed the history of the United States revealed the nation's dependence upon a free people moved by noble motives. Like the Progressives, Hoar saw historical scholarship as a means for deciding matters of public policy. An avid student of the past, he had wide-ranging interests that began with his family and extended through a belief in a functional, socializing approach for the discipline. In his presidential address to the American Historical Association, Hoar expanded upon this theme and urged writers of history "to develop among young people a love of country."[9]

George Frisbie Hoar (1826-1904). Photographer and date unknown.
Collection of the Massachusetts Historical Society.

In addition to writing a number of historical articles, his interests made
him an active participant in the professionalization of the craft through
organizations such as the American Historical Association and the American Antiquarian and Massachusetts Historical Societies. Like many of the
practitioners of the new scientific history, Hoar placed great value on primary documents. As early as 1850, he became concerned about the possible loss of archival materials held in state and local offices. While chairing

a Massachusetts Historical Society committee, he proposed legislation that ultimately led to a statewide program of documentary preservation. He also enthusiastically supported Smithsonian ethnological studies, helping to spread their influence by donating reports to Massachusetts libraries.[10]

Like Henry Adams, Hoar in his understanding of the methods and uses of history illustrated the transition from gifted amateur to professional that marked the closing decades of the nineteenth century. Despite the scorn that he heaped upon Hoar in 1899 for his anti-imperialism, Adams, whose American Historical Association presidency preceded Hoar's, shared a functionalist approach to the study of history. For both men history had utilitarian, prescriptive attributes that helped guide public policy. Ever the pessimist, Adams transformed the use of primary documents in the construction of historical narratives to see the essence of the human and national condition, even if the lessons learned were discouraging. More blatantly than Adams, Hoar, foreshadowing the rise of the Progressive historians, shared the assumption that history was an obvious and compelling guide to solving the problems of the late nineteenth century with his senatorial colleagues.[11] In his opposition to Chinese Exclusion, though, Hoar reversed the process much in the manner of Bancroft and Parkman, drawing on fact to make his conclusions more effective.

Characterized as a Half-Breed Republican, Hoar also brought to Exclusion the multiple divisions and tensions that marked the party's transition from Charles Sumner through Ulysses Grant to Theodore Roosevelt.[12] Hoar's speeches on the floor of the Senate represented a strain of egalitarianism on the issue of race that had been a family trait before the Civil War and was now out of place in the last quarter of the nineteenth century.[13] The son and younger brother of Samuel and Ebenezer Rockwood Hoar respectively, men who had helped to found the Free-Soil and early Republican Parties in Massachusetts, he had followed their abolitionist lead. Called to speak during a tumultuous public meeting convened to protest Daniel Webster's March 7 speech in defense of the Fugitive Slave Law, Hoar began his life in elected office shortly thereafter. An ardent Free Soiler, Hoar became the chairman of the Republican county committee in Worcester and a member of the Massachusetts senate by 1857.[14]

Like his father and brother, Frisbie, as his family called him, possessed an understanding of race that was at once paternalistic and hierarchical while radically egalitarian and assimilationist. Conflating race and culture, Hoar presumed a hierarchical construct partly determined by biology but that remained fluid in terms of culture. While, for him, lesser-civilized groups tended to be peoples of color such as Africans and Native Americans, there were no biological predeterminants preventing their ascension to higher levels of civilized behavior. Throughout his life, Hoar supported the elevation of African and Native Americans to what he considered higher levels of civilized society. Like his colleague Henry Dawes, he advocated funding for Native Americans that reflected a belief in race progress as defined in the acquisition of characteristics such as small-scale farming, literacy, and Protestant Christianity that marked their progress from savagery to civilization. Upon learning that Hoar had sponsored an appropriation that would provide two hundred dollars a year to pay the educational expenses of individual Indian students, R. H. Pratt, superintendent of the Carlisle Barracks School, expressed his gratitude in a letter on December 1881. With the legislation, Pratt wrote, Hoar would help to "inaugurate a paean for Indian civilization." Praising Hoar's support for Native American education, A. J. Standing in Yankton, Dakota Territory, wrote, "I do not know of any Indians who are not capable of being civilized by the school and results show that he can be taught to work and become a civilized person . . . [and] have every faith in the practicality of so moulding the rising generation of Indian youth by Education that the Indian Savage will be extinct in a generation."[15]

Repeating this Progressive assimilationist theme in his opposition to Chinese Exclusion, Hoar pointed out the irony revealed in the Senate's deliberations. "There are men in this body," he pointed out in rejoinder to Miller on March 1, "whose heads are not yet gray who can remember how the arguments now used against the Chinese filled the American mind with alarm when used against the Irishman." In his speech, Hoar cited the previous conceptualizations of African Americans as a savages and the supposed incompatibility of Irish and Jews with American institutions. The nation's treatment of Native Americans, Jews, Irish, and Africans was a moral stain on the history of the republic and provided Hoar with empirical proof that challenged the racial, economic, and cultural arguments Miller advanced. "Nothing is more in conflict," he declared,

> with the genius of American institutions than legal distinctions between individuals based upon race. . . . [The Founders] meant that

their laws should make no distinction between men except such as were required by personal conduct and character. The prejudice of race, the last of human delusions to be overcome until lately in our Constitutions and statutes, and has left its hideous stains on our history in crimes committed by every generation.[16]

Each of these groups, Hoar told the Senate, historically had been subjected to the same arguments now used in favor of Chinese Exclusion. "What argument can be urged against the Chinese which was not heard against the Negro within living memory?" Africans "were savages, heathens and wild beasts." Christians for ten centuries had charged that the Jew "did not affiliate or assimilate into the nations where he dwelt. He was an unclean thing, a dog, to whom [responsibility was given for] the crime of the crucifixion of his Savior." Members of the Senate should remember that it had been said of the Irish that "He will drive the American to starvation by the competition of his labor; he lives in squalor and filth; he wants only a few potatoes for food; . . . he owes obedience to a foreign potentate; he is incapable of intelligent citizenship."[17]

Hoar's recitation of these examples underscored his belief that racial distinctions were separate from culture and that the cultural attributes of seemingly different races could be changed for the better. "In forty years the Irish have become a source of wealth and strength to the nation." They raised "themselves from the bog or the hovel to the comfort of the New England home and placed his children in New England schools." The fear that cheap Irish labor would impoverish native American labor had come to naught as "Yankees became skilled laborers, merchants and landowner." In twenty years, "the children of the African savage were emancipated from slavery. In that brief space of time, they have vindicated their fitness for the highest duties of citizenship. These despised savages have sat in the House and Senate."[18]

Similarly, Hoar asserted, the Chinese were capable of living up to standards of civilized behavior. Their history of cultural achievement refuted Miller's lament that fifty centuries of development represented a hereditary or racial condition incapable of change. All races, Hoar argued, have capacities for degradation and elevation, and the Chinese were no different. Abundant testimony of positive developments in intellect, art, and character augured well for their abilities to assume the responsibilities of citizenship in a republic and to convert to Christianity. Centuries ago when Chinese philosophers had formulated a variant of the Golden Rule, Druids in Britain still offered human sacrifices. There was, Hoar announced, ample evidence that "this race can furnish able merchants, skillful diplomats, profound philosophers, faithful servants, industrious and docile laborers."[19]

When the details of his speech reached the press the following day, March 2, a number of correspondents wrote to Hoar confirming the ways in which one's position on Exclusion shaped one's use of historical evidence. Thomas Drew wrote to Hoar declaring that the proponents of Exclusion have abandoned the "doctrines of the declaration of independence, the faith of the fathers in the rights of man and all the traditions of our past history upon the subject of immigration."[20] Other correspondents weighed in with testimony of Chinese capacity for assuming civilized behavior. Included in a subsequent speech on March 8 by Hoar was a letter from Sarah Carrington of Colebrook, Connecticut. Speaking from a social background comparable to Hoar's, Carrington lamented that the blood of her brother, who had died in the Civil War, "cries out against those who are trying to make us believe that God and our Fathers meant only black and white" should live in America. As examples of the Chinese capacity for improvement, Carrington recounted the story of two students who had lived with her family and become virtually her brothers. "Taken from heathen surroundings," she wrote, the students "were not only as intelligent, courteous, and refined as any youths in this Christian land, but they were exceptionally noble and high-minded." Hoar, she thought, would understand how angry she was when she heard that others "who are not worthy to stand in their presence speak of one's beloved brethren as belonging to an essentially and irreclaimably inferior race."[21]

Responses to Hoar pointed to how the centrality of race in the debates led to a subtle shift in the understanding of whiteness. Hoar's assumption of the assimilationist capacities of disparate racial groups such as Jews, Irish, Native Americans, and Chinese required a distinction between race and culture, between fixed inalienable qualities and malleable characteristics, that were revealed in the historical record. To Hoar the physical attribute—race—was inconsequential. Culture mattered, and an individual's ability to assume characteristics of what Hoar considered civilized behavior provided ample evidence of this ability.

During the next eight days, from March 2 to 10, a bipartisan group, though one comprised mostly of Democrats and westerners, responded to Hoar with historical analyses that connected specific culture and nationhood to fixed, unmalleable physical characteristics—to race. Sen. Thomas Bayard (D-Del.) claimed to see the obvious lesson history taught. The Chinese represented a totally different civilization conditioned by centuries of development that precluded the blending of Chinese and American cultures in a positive fashion. No intelligent man, he argued, "studying the history and character of the Chinese people, their habits and tradition, the results consequences, and accompaniments of their peculiar and wonderful civilization, can believe that a republic is possible under such conditions." Bayard's Democratic colleague from Delaware, Eli Saulsbury, agreed: the history of the Chinese was that of a race incapable of civilization. "While they are industrious and may be intelligent in the matters with which they are familiar . . . they are a degraded people, and I know nothing of their civilization that has an elevating tendency." Furthermore, this cultural evidence indicated "they are a new, and different race, and they can not assimilate with Americans or adopt American principles of government or religion."[22]

On March 3 and 4, Samuel Maxey (D-Texas) and James Slater (D-Ore.) used history to blur distinctions between culture and race. They shifted the argument onto the latter, onto attributes that were incapable of change and thus of accommodation and assimilation. Slater noted that the Chinese had developed into a separate race of people that thrived under conditions in which whites would perish. The Chinese, according to Slater, had "developed into a race of such character and physical qualities" that were alien to American customs, religion, and civilization. Asserting the physical inability of the Chinese to assimilate American culture required Slater and Maxey to explain why Africans, whom they also construed as inferior, posed no threat to American institutions. Arguing that the historical experience of Africans in America had been different, Slater contested that they were thoroughly assimilated in ways that the Chinese could not be because whites had nurtured their limited capacities for civilized accomplishment. Also responding to Hoar's assertions of black political achievement, Maxey agreed with Slater's claims of African inferiority. While it was true, he acknowledged, that "we have had the colored race made citizens and voters, they were here; they had to be provided for; and they have been provided for by our civilization."[23]

According to the *Boston Globe*, the most devastating rejoinder to "Ah

Sin Hoar" came from an "unusually brilliant speech" on March 9 by John P. Jones, a fellow Republican from Nevada and an English immigrant. The *Globe*'s assessment of the unusual brilliance of Jones's performance may have rested on the fact, noted by the *Worcester Aegis*, that this was only his second speech after nine years in the Senate; the other had been on Free Silver. Disagreeing with Hoar, Jones claimed there was compelling scientific reason and logic that demonstrated that "the Senator's support for his ethnology [was] as faulty as his logic," that the Chinese as a race could not develop the characteristics of civilized or republican society. Challenging Hoar's evidence that the Chinese invented gunpowder and the compass as evidence of their capacity for achievement, Jones cited John William Draper's *History of the Intellectual Development of Europe* and an essay by W. F. Mayers in *The Journal of the North China Branch of the Royal Asiatic Society*. "History, written and monumental," Jones assured the Senate, establishes that "the Chinese people have lived in the conditions which conduces to crime for almost unnumbered centuries." The Chinese were a "race whose historical existence of fifty centuries shows that they have outlived all contemporaneous nations, and during that immense period never risen from the ranks of semi-barbarism."[24]

In the racial theory constructed by his opposition, Hoar's reliance upon the intent of the Founders shifted the discussions from restrictions on Chinese immigration to prohibitions against their naturalization. Although the Exclusion Act was ostensibly drafted in response to labor's demands to restrict immigration, the complex layers of discrimination and prejudice coupled with political opportunism quickly extended its reach.[25] On the evening of March 8, James Farley (R-Calif.) offered an amendment that, among other things, prohibited naturalization of Chinese immigrants. The amendment, at first glance, seems puzzling. If the intent of Exclusion was to regulate the flow of immigration, the prohibitions against naturalization should have been irrelevant. Prohibition of Chinese laborers alone would have diminished their competitiveness as workers and the pool of potential citizens even if they had been legally eligible for citizenship. To refute, however, Hoar's invocation of the Founders, the supporters of Exclusion could respond with historically authoritative documents that had a clear expression of original intent that was precisely on point: the Naturalization Acts of 1790 and 1795. In raising the problem of naturalization, Farley, Maxey, and the other senators could connect the Naturalization Acts, the authority of the Founders, and the necessity to solve a potentially dangerous and unregulated problem of un-American Americans.

Central to this discussion was the clear language in the Naturalization Acts of 1790 and 1795 and the presumption that the subsequent changes in the Act of 1870 extended its purview to blacks only.[26] Although language in the 1870 legislation restricted naturalization to whites, Africans, and those of African descent, the possible legal naturalization of Chinese had been considered in 1870. Indeed, when the 1870 bill had been reported out of committee, it included an amendment from Charles Sumner striking out "white" and thereby allowing for the naturalization of all free persons regardless of race. There was, however, a twofold concern: first, that somehow the language was insufficiently expansive to allow the naturalization of Africans (as opposed to African Americans) and, second, that there existed the potential for fraud by the Chinese. A subsequent reconsideration of the Naturalization Act in 1873 prompted a similar amendment in the House by George Villard of Vermont again to strike "white." It was again voted down in deference to the California delegation.[27]

Still, expansive and sympathetic courts had allowed the naturalization of Chinese. Prior to 1882, the legal jurisdiction for regulating immigration and naturalization had come under state courts. Before the Civil War, the nation had presumed that immigration and naturalization were a single integrated procedure. To enter the United States was to begin the process of becoming a citizen. Since American citizenship depended upon state criteria, relying upon states to document and regulate both processes was consistent with past practice and seemed eminently reasonable as long as the number of immigrants remained limited and they did not enter states with significantly different criteria for citizenship.[28] Until the post–Civil War waves of immigration took place, no one had considered the ramifications of the entry of large numbers of laborers recruited to come to the United States to fill specific niches in the labor force. Not only did these groups come from parts of Europe and elsewhere not represented in the established populations, but the patterns of recruitment, particularly with respect to the Chinese, reflected assumptions regarding the kinds of jobs they would fill.[29] The strains became especially visible when state and local jurisdictions allowed a number of Chinese to be naturalized. According to the *Boston Daily Advertiser*, a Chinese had been naturalized as early as 1845. The *San Francisco Chronicle* in 1880 reported that Democratic judges in New York had naturalized 12 to 15 Chinese. Indeed, the

New York Times noted that even after Congress had overridden the president's veto and passed the Exclusion Act, Pennsylvania courts naturalized 2 Chinese.[30] While the numbers could not have been large—Zhang Qingson reports 1,268 in 1900[31]—the very hint of any naturalization strengthened the case of those in favor of Exclusion.

On March 8, 1882, after debate had gone on for a week, George Edmunds (R-Vt.) shifted the debate to another focus, reaffirming the case for incompatibility, and rebutting Hoar's version of history while invoking his own ultimate authority, the Founders' intentions. Doing so required a reconsideration of the nature of race and whiteness.[32] Edmunds, possessed of long-standing Radical Republican credentials, surprised the Senate with a long speech that decried Hoar's opposition. Common sense, he argued, spoke to the futility of integration and assimilation, and that should be sufficient ground to enact what was a democratic decision. While following the argument of the irreconcilable differences between the Chinese and Americans, Edmunds shifted the crux of the argument to undermine Hoar's reliance upon the historic authority of the Declaration of Independence. In place of either purely historical or moral arguments, Edmunds invoked the government's unquestioned authority to promote the public welfare—its police powers—in its regulation of immigration and naturalization, "the right of every government, if it be a government to determine what persons shall come into it."[33]

In his rejoinder Hoar posed two questions, one historical, the other legal. First he asked how Edmunds could explain the success of the Swiss republic with its variety of "different races, of different habits of different religious faiths." How was it possible that the speaker of its Assembly might speak in French one day and in German the next? Second, he asked Edmunds to consider the fact that children born of Chinese parents in the United States became natural-born citizens. There was, Hoar pronounced, a "citizenship by birthright without regards to race, color or nationality: then the fifteenth amendment supplements it by the provision that this citizenship which is by birthright shall carry votes." Did Edmunds mean to infer that because government had the right to exclude a class of foreigners or to limit the period of naturalization, it was permissible to exclude and expel a class of citizens on the grounds of race?[34]

Hoar's questions forced Edmunds to respond by joining the historical, cultural, and, ultimately, racial arguments with a practical legal one. First, presaging the discussions over the Farley amendment, Edmunds denied the existence of Swiss racial heterogeneity. "The difference is in language, the difference is not in race (for there is no difference in race in the Swiss Republic) but the differences in the varieties of the same race that are analogous, that are consistent with each other." He then waffled with regard to Hoar's pointed question regarding the citizenship of natural-born children of the Chinese who, in all likelihood, were infinitesimal in number, and shifted the argument to one that could invoke clear and un-questioned authority. Constitutional precedents for exclusion by race were clear, and Congress, if it chose, could exclude even the English. "It was left to their judgment to determine and at the onset they determined that no Chinaman or other man, although they then confined it to white man, . . . could become one of the people of the United States until he complied with certain conditions and was subjected to certain tests."[35]

Within the context of this debate, the Farley amendment and the language of the Naturalization Acts of 1790 and 1795 took on added significance as it enabled a broadening of the terms of Exclusion. Speaking in the Senate in behalf of the Farley amendment, Jones reflected a substantial majority that the *Worcester Aegis* estimated would have been much larger had the original act not called for a twenty-year suspension of immigration of laborers.[36] Clearly justified under the police powers and the intent of the Founders, early statutes empowered the government to limit by race who might become a naturalized citizen of the United States. "A careful examination of that instrument [the first nationality act]," Maxey continued, "establishes the fact that the only people even dreamed to be naturalized citizens of the United States by the framers of the Constitution or by the people of the States which ratified it were people of the Caucasian race. . . . Does any man believe that the men who framed the Constitution ever for a moment thought of mingling the blood of the Caucasian race with any other?"[37] Bypassed in the process was Hoar's caveat that racial restrictions might limit the citizenship rights of American-born Chinese.[38] All that remained was to use the historical and ethnological evidence to reconstruct the multiplicity of white races into one, federally approved category.

Maxey's explanation for the different treatment that should be accorded blacks as opposed to the Chinese depended on his belief that Anglo-Saxons possessed an inherent racial strength that could be supplemented by other white races. The strength of Anglo-Saxon institutions had been sufficient to nurture the African, to educate him in ways that ultimately proved beneficial to whites. More whites were to be welcomed in this task; "the Englishman, the Scotchman, the Irishman, the Frenchman, the German and men of my own race and color . . . make valuable additions to the body politic." But the nation must reject "the refuse and dregs of the countless hordes of China" who were incapable of assimilation.[39]

As the debate continued into the second week in March, others picked up on Maxey's earlier merging of disparate concepts of whiteness. On March 8, Henry Teller (R-Colo.) gave a speech that illustrated the way in which Maxey's invocation of Anglo-Saxon identity was broadened to include other, non-Anglo-Saxon senators. Teller proffered somewhat apologetically that he did not mean "to claim that the Anglo-Saxon was in all respects superior for the blood that flows in my veins is not mainly from that source." He wished to assert, rather, that races were hierarchical—that in comparison to Europeans "there were other branches of the human family that stood lower in intellectual strength and essential vigor in moral worth." Moors, Egyptians, and Chinese were among these, and Teller believed this to be "an historical and ethnological fact."[40]

Jones affirmed Maxey and Teller's ideas of racial comprehensiveness by pointing to Europeans' common cultural heritage. That legacy, he argued, became apparent in light of the threat posed by Chinese labor. The Chinese were, he announced, like the miner's canary. Their competition with others for jobs was only one attribute of their overall disruptive impact upon American society. The real threat lay in their inability to assimilate the manners of democratic society as had European immigrants, whom Jones saw in increasingly singular racial terms: "the main objections to the incoming of the Chinamen cannot be brought against the Europeans of our own race and nearly related to us. . . . They [Europeans] readily adopt our manners, customs and language and soon become an indistinguishable part of our body politic."[41]

The debate that had begun on March 8 continued until March 16, when the Senate passed the bill and forwarded it to the House of Representatives for its consideration. As early as March 4, the *Boston Daily Traveler* reported that there was little doubt that it would pass, that the Democrats would support the bill to gain votes on the Pacific Coast, and that the Republicans would divide, thus providing sufficient votes for victory.[42] With the exception of Hoar, his Massachusetts colleague Henry Dawes, and Joseph Hawley (R-Conn.), few congressmen defended the Chinese. Like

Hoar, Dawes and Hawley reminded the Senate of the fading impulses of Radical Republicanism.[43] Others pursued more technical quibbles over the impact Exclusion might have on the recent 1880 treaty with China. Did it exclude only coolies and unskilled laborers? Did it violate reciprocal agreements that allowed the exchange of merchants and scholars? One's answer determined whether Exclusion had to be cast as an act enabling the operation of the treaty and not as an amendment to it; the former only required a simple majority in the Senate while the latter needed two-thirds of the Senate with the president's approval.

The House and Senate cast aside the procedural ambiguity and construed the bill as a separate piece of legislation. Pres. Chester Arthur, furthermore, made the distinction immaterial when he vetoed it on April 4. In sending it back to Congress, Arthur expressed his concern that the act was overly broad in its prohibition of coolies while allowing the immigration of merchants, students, and diplomats. Willing to regulate emigration on their end, the Chinese also considered Exclusion a material change in the Burlingame Treaty. While American merchants had expressed their willingness to cooperate in curbing Chinese immigration, they were concerned that any amendment placed recently won trade concessions in jeopardy.[44]

When the Senate reconsidered the bill in April after Arthur's veto, it shortened the period of suspension from twenty to ten years, but in the process of that debate Farley insisted on including the prohibitions against the naturalization of Chinese. When told the amendment was superfluous, that the Nationality Act already prohibited the naturalization of Chinese, he declared that state courts had been granting them citizenship for years and he meant to stop it. A supporter of Exclusion and the president, John Sherman (R-Ohio), perhaps mindful of the treaty considerations raised by Arthur's veto, sought to delay passage of the bill by referring it to the Foreign Relations Committee. Despite Sherman's efforts, the weight of opinion in the Senate was too great and the veto was overridden.[45]

In the last major speech before the override vote, John Morgan (D-Ala.) articulated the way in which the science of history had helped reconstruct race in the course of the debates. He refuted the suggestion that supporters of Exclusion were bigots or prejudiced as to color and race, and he charged that Hoar had read history in a false light. The use of historical facts, he contested, not personal emotion, led inevitably to certain obvious conclusions: "We are driven by facts which we cannot resist or avoid to the conclusion that it has become a solemn necessity on our part to protect the Caucasian race on this continent from the intrusion of the Oriental people." Further, in a defense of Edmunds's argument of police powers, Morgan lumped individuals into a four-part racial system: black, white, red, or yellow. Placing Europeans under the single rubric of "white," he asserted the rights and privileges of "the great race to which we belong, to move this continent and this hemisphere as to add to the glorious renown which this people have already won in the history of mankind."[46]

Hoar's opposition to Exclusion had little impact upon his standing in Massachusetts. While his reelection in January 1883 was bitterly contested, the fight reflected not an adverse identification with Exclusion but rather the complicated course of Gilded Age politics. In Massachusetts, the Republican Party was split into four fluid factions: Stalwarts such as George Boutwell, who benefited from Grantism and patronage; Half-Breeds such as Hoar—part machine politician, part reformer; outright reformers, including congressman and former governor John D. Long; and future Mugwumps and younger men such as Henry Cabot Lodge who were ambitious newcomers anxious over the party's recent decline in fortunes.

A supporter of Garfield, Hoar never reconciled himself to Chester Arthur, who had been nominated for the vice presidency as a sop to the Stalwarts and Roscoe Conkling. Despite Arthur's surprising retreat from the Stalwarts after ascending to the presidency and Hoar's half-hearted acceptance of machine politics, the two men remained at loggerheads. During the Exclusion debates, Arthur had nominated Roland Worthington to be the collector of the Port of Boston upon the recommendation of Boutwell, Grant's secretary of the Treasury and the man Hoar had replaced in the Senate. Protesting, Hoar and Dawes feared that this represented the use of national patronage by old Grant supporters to displace them as leaders of the Republican Party in Massachusetts. At the state convention in June 1882, a group of younger Republicans—characterized by historian Richard Welch as "Middle-aged Turks"—including Lodge rejected Congressman William Crapo, the preferred candidate of Hoar and Dawes, and nominated Robert Bishop for governor. Ben Butler, who with the retirement of Grant had switched his affiliation to the Democratic Party, then soundly trounced Bishop.[47]

While the Republicans made Hoar their official nominee for the Senate in January 1883, the party had two additional candidates, Long and Crapo; the Democrats nominated Stephen Bowerman. A champion of civil service reform, Bowerman, the Democrats believed, would attract the anti-Hoar votes and give them the office or enable them to name the Republican senator. Of the three Republicans, the *Herald* expected that Crapo would receive large numbers of Democratic votes. The Democrats would even count the election of any Republican other than Hoar a victory because of his role on the Electoral Commission that had denied Tilden the presidency. Of Hoar's two rivals Long was the more difficult to accept because he could not be bought. Representing the young, reform wing of the party, his supporters were, in the words of an unnamed independent observer, "upright men who believe in good faith that Long would make a more progressive senator." Crapo came into the race as a result of Hoar's early weakness. Crapo, the *Globe* reported, could have won had he been willing to make a deal with Butler. While the Long votes remained relatively steadfast, a few of his supporters were concerned that sticking with their candidate might cause either the election of Bowerman or Crapo. Ultimately, Crapo's supporters shifted their votes to Hoar in exchange for an unacknowledged agreement that their candidate would receive the gubernatorial nomination in 1884.[48]

In their coverage of the election, neither the *Globe* nor the *Herald* mentioned Chinese Exclusion. Hoar's initial weakness had been caused by his unwillingness to campaign. So sure of his election, Hoar supporters had not invoked party discipline at the nominating convention and had thus allowed dissidents to coalesce around Long. Once the slight possibility of his defeat emerged, it energized Hoar's traditional bases of support: churches; banks and manufacturers, for his position on the tariff; military men, for his vote restoring Fitz John Porter's rank in the GAR; and the machine. Dawes, the Republican *Boston Journal*, and party regulars rallied to Hoar's cause, holding court at the Parker House and working furiously to get him reelected. Ultimately, Long proved to be a poor alternative to Hoar. Because his positions were too similar to Hoar's, Long was unable to find political allies. Like Hoar, he had an ambivalent attitude towards patronage, holding its use by Butler and others in contempt but recognizing its place in winning elections. At the same time, he exhibited Hoar's genteel reform impulses and idealism.[49]

Hoar may also have been indifferent to his fate because he felt that a defeat would send him back full-time to his law practice, leaving him free from associations he preferred to avoid. While he, like his fellow Half-Breeds—leftover antebellum and Radical Republican idealists—accepted the necessity of the spoils system in the last quarter of the nineteenth century, politicking always seemed beneath him. Edward Farquhar, hearing of Hoar's death, recounted a story to Caroline Dall about his first run for the Senate. When urged to run, according to Farquhar, Hoar replied, "Now and any time possible in the next ten years I would rather have my ticket to the penitentiary than the Senate; for in the one, I could at least be spared the company I must submit to in the other."[50] Hoar would serve in the Senate until his death in 1904.

The Chinese Exclusion Act at the national level confirmed the Fourteenth Amendment's creation of a national citizenship that superseded state jurisdiction. With its prohibitions against the naturalization of Chinese, Exclusion reaffirmed and clarified the racial prerequisites that defined citizenship. This had two significant consequences: it necessitated the creation of a bureaucracy to enforce these prerequisites consistently on a national basis, and it required definitions of the racial classes prohibited from citizenship. Created in 1913 as a part of the Bureau of Immigration, the Division of Naturalization soon took on the task of eliminating fraud at the local level and insuring uniformity in recordkeeping and enforcing legislation.[51] But even here, the preoccupation with the Chinese as a prohibited class initially obviated the immediate necessity to create a special institutional structure to regulate immigration. The collector of the customs in Quangzhou (Canton)—the primary port of debarkation for the United States—assumed regulation of Chinese immigration during the first decade of Exclusion, and effectively limited immigration by refusing to provide certificates of entry. Notwithstanding threats that 20,000 Chinese were poised to enter from British Columbia or 8,000 from Cuba, a federal district court judge noted that in the first sixteen months following Exclusion only 3,425 Chinese had been allowed to enter San Francisco while over 17,000 had departed, a fact confirmed by the precipitous decline in the numbers of Chinese in the United States (excluding Hawai'i) between 1890 and 1900.[52]

Exclusion represented the culmination of trends that had made the Chinese scapegoats for the dislocations of post-Civil War industrialization. The Chinese provided a handy target for dramatizing the corrosive effects of immigration and industrialization without seriously impairing the supply of workers for the new factories or restricting the rights of

Europeans to enter. Whereas ethnic or racial characteristics associated with Europeans could be used for the purposes of recruitment, it was possible to see the Chinese as inherently or, perhaps more appropriately, genetically incapable of assimilation. Restrictions on immigration prior to Exclusion had rested upon moral or economic grounds: the Page Act barred the entry of Chinese women because they were potential prostitutes; the Fifteen Passenger Bill prohibited the entry of more than fifteen Chinese on any given passenger ship in order to limit the importation of coolie labor. The former represented a moral threat to Americans; the latter, to American workers. Restricting both classes of Chinese, Horace Page (R-Calif.) argued, would actually encourage more and better immigrant workers from Europe.[53]

Despite Page's argument, however, Exclusion provided a conceptual paradigm for justifying restrictions on European immigration when that became problematic at the beginning of the twentieth century. Exclusion provided an explanatory model for limiting new immigrants on objective, utilitarian, and historical criteria associated with supposedly cultural characteristics. A dual-edged argument, it could permit immigrants when they met a standard of social utility and stop them when they seemed dysfunctional. Initially used both in favor of and against the Chinese, the model also applied to European immigrants. For example, labor contractors advocated the recruitment of Italian women because they conformed to cultural, ethnic, and ultimately racial filters. Seen as specially attuned to domestic and unskilled labor, they could free native women for higher skilled work while moderating the behavior of supposedly volatile Italian men. As demand for labor dropped after World War I, American nativism found the ground for restricting Italians and other nontraditional European groups, and it is in the racial quotas of the National Origins Act (1924) that the conflation of racial and cultural categories initiated in Chinese Exclusion came to final fruition.[54]

After 1882, as Congress developed other classes of prohibited persons, it also necessitated the creation of the federal agencies for immigration control. Ironically, as these developments were translated into bureaucratic regulations, they served simultaneously to create more broad-based categories of white, black, and yellow while requiring mechanisms for differentiation within racial groups. Between 1882 and 1891, immigration operated under concurrent federal and state jurisdiction. In theory, states retained the right to determine who might enter from abroad, but with the passage of national moral and racial restrictions, that right was circumscribed by federal law. In practice, this meant that the secretary of state appointed agents, drawn from a pool of candidates nominated by state officials, to review new immigrants. The agents were responsible for examining immigrants and enforcing statutory exclusions for race and unfit persons while collecting a head tax to offset costs. In 1891, Congress authorized the creation of an immigration service; the agency's period of explosive growth occurred between 1896 and 1906, when it received powers to grant naturalization and its staff grew from 5 to over 1,200.[55] Until 1906, there was no central repository to administer naturalization, and frequently states and territories did not cooperate with federal requirements, a situation that led the Bureau of Immigration to initiate litigation to revoke certificates of naturalization. After 1906, in an effort to relieve courts of the burdens of suits, to provide more uniform grants of naturalization, to centralize recordkeeping, and to create adequate administrative and investigative structures, Congress enlarged the Bureau of Immigration to include a Naturalization Division.[56]

As long as the United States persisted in using racial categories for limiting immigration and naturalization, however, it condemned the INS to a half-century of confusion. In the course of defining the Chinese as the "other" during the Exclusion debates, the nation had begun the process of amalgamating whiteness as criteria for American identity. Left unsettled were the ambiguous borders between white and non-white. Anthropological evidence of difference seemed to offer a solution: if used as a guide to define groups whose racial complexions were not so apparent, it could distinguish whites from non-whites—Asians, Malays, and Americans (the last category for peoples indigenous to the Western Hemisphere in one theory). Still, this approach only encouraged legal parsing that sought bright-letter legal boundaries in ephemeral, indistinct racial composites produced by the ebb and flow of history. Were, for example, the descendants of Muslim Silk merchants living along the Silk Road Arab or Asian? Were the Japanese intended to be construed as Chinese?[57]

The confusion over race resulted from the inability of INS to recognize the way in which a historical moment had created contingent categories. In focusing the debate upon the historical justifications for discrimination, Hoar unwittingly opened the door to a specific, authoritative document from which a contrary historical conclusion could be drawn. In Chinese Exclusion the target had been, obviously, the Chinese, judged by the debates to be historically and racially incompatible with American life. It simply did not occur to the proponents of Exclusion that there might be other groups who would pose an equally dangerous threat to the republic but still pass whiteness tests. Exclusion created the need to prove legally one was not Chinese if one was to enter the United States or become a citizen. Given the specific context of turn-of-the-century circumstances, American law drove immigrants to assert they were not Chinese by proving they were white—to fit into a federally approved, if not privileged, racial category.[58] These demands to prove whiteness, however, placed legal judgments in the hands of a mixture of lawyers, judges, and physical anthropologists who, while confident that races existed, could not agree with any precision on what constituted authoritative physical or biological determinants. Using culture or common sense as a guide, as Hoar argued, might serve only if distinguishing traits created no "noticeable degree of repugnance." But America's racial distinctions were already full of inconsistencies when the law created general, definitive legal principles of separation that did not recognize the historicity of its constructions. Exclusion provided one set of contingent moments; Jim Crow, another. Even limiting the definition of whiteness to "Caucasian" could not permanently immunize the nation from European groups that under other circumstances would be deemed unacceptable.[59]

Unquestionably, Exclusion occurred because race so quickly inflamed the fears of many Americans. Whites thought that the Chinese threatened native workers' livelihoods, that they were racially and culturally alien and unassimilable, that they undermined the moral underpinnings of society. But the debates on the floor of the Senate also revealed the ways in which both friends and enemies of the Chinese used history to carry their arguments and in so doing lost sight of the way in which context—the confluence of historical moment, assumption, and debate—shaped their selection of facts and the development of conclusions. When John Miller claimed that his argument was supported by incontrovertible fact and when George Frisbie Hoar appealed to the authority of the Founders' principles, neither believed himself to be racist or a bad historian. They did reveal, nonetheless, the fragile, contingent nature of our historical narratives and racial constructions and how easily tragic consequences might flow from them. For those who would use history in the service of public policy or would construct federally approved races, the debates over Chinese Exclusion ought to pose a cautionary, humbling story.

NOTES

1. Dave Barry, "Counting the House," *Boston Globe Magazine*, Apr. 9, 2000.
2. *Congressional Record*, 47th Cong., 1st sess., pt. 1:1483. Because all subsequent references will be from the same record and part, it will be cited as *CR* with date and page number only.
3. *New York Times*, Mar. 2, 1882.
4. A summary of the literature on this issue may be found in Andrew Gyory, *Closing the Gate: Race, Politics, and the Chinese Exclusion Act* (Chapel Hill, 1998), 6-16. See also Stuart C. Miller, *The Unwelcome Immigrant: The American Image of the Chinese, 1785-1882* (Berkeley and Los Angeles, 1969), esp. 191, 204; and Alexander Saxton, *The Indispensable Enemy: Labor and the Anti-Chinese Movement in California* (Los Angeles and Berkeley, 1971), esp. 133-134, 230.
5. Matthew Jacobson, *Whiteness of a Different Color: European Immigrants and the Alchemy of Race* (Cambridge, Mass., 1998), 1-12.
6. *CR*, Feb. 28, 1882, 1482-1486.
7. *CR*, Feb. 28, 1882, 1483.
8. *CR*, Mar. 1, 1882, 1523.
9. George F. Hoar, *An Autobiography of Seventy Years* (New York, 1903), 2:202. For a charming description of Hoar's last meeting with the dying Bancroft, see 205-206. See also Robert L. Beisner, *Twelve against Empire: The Anti-Imperialists, 1898-1900* (New York, 1968).
10. Hoar was also instrumental in obtaining the return of William Bradford's manuscript History of Plymouth. Louis Leonard Tucker, *The Massachusetts Historical Society: A Bicentennial History, 1791-1991* (Boston, 1996), 65-67, 211-215. On Hoar's ethnological contributions, see *Salem Gazette*, May 12, 1882, and his "Report to the Council," *Proceedings of the American Antiquarian Society* 2(1883):108-135, which contains a discussion of the Smithsonian's North American Ethnological collections.
11. Richard Hofstadter, *The Progressive Historians: Turner, Beard, and Parrington* (New York, 1970 [1968]), 32-33, 40-43; Richard C. Vitzthum, *The American Compromise: Theme and Method in the Histories of Bancroft, Parkman, and Adams* (Norman, 1974), 206-210. See also John Garraty's comment that Lodge, who studied with Adams, tended to interpret the past in terms of his vision on current issues. *Henry Cabot Lodge: A Biography* (New York, 1965), 60. In 1899, Adams became extremely angry with Hoar over his anti-imperialism. "Hoar," he wrote Elizabeth Cameron, "is senile [and] I should be extremely relieved if some Hanna would intrigue him out of the Senate." Henry Adams to Elizabeth Cameron, Dec. 11, 1899, in *Letters of Henry Adams*, ed. J. C. Levenson et al. (Cambridge, Mass., 1988), 4:632-670. On historians and policy, see Peter

Novick, *That Noble Dream: The "Objectivity Question" and the American Historical Profession* (Cambridge, 1988), 69-70.

12. Richard E. Welch, Jr., *George Frisbie Hoar and the Half-Breed Republicans* (Cambridge, Mass., 1971), 2-4.

13. Fredrick Douglass to George Frisbie Hoar, Mar. 20, 1882, George Frisbie Hoar Papers, Massachusetts Historical Society (hereafter, Hoar Papers); *Worcester Aegis and Gazette,* Apr. 8, 1882.

14. Hoar, *Autobiography,* 148-150, 162, 176; Welch, *George Frisbie Hoar,* 11-12.

15. Pratt to Hoar, Dec. 29, 1881, and Standing to Hoar, Mar. 29, 1882, Hoar Papers. See also a letter from Edward Stewart, who had been born in slavery in 1859 in Prince Edward City, Virginia, to Hoar, Jan. 12, 1881, thanking Hoar for paying his tuition. Hoar Papers.

16. *CR,* Mar. 1, 1882, 1516.

17. *CR,* Mar. 1, 1882, 1517, 1519.

18. *CR,* Mar. 1, 1882, 1519, 1522.

19. *CR,* Mar. 1, 1882, 1520, 1523.

20. Drew to Hoar, Mar. 5, 1882, Hoar Papers. About two weeks later, Fredrick Douglass weighed in with two letters decrying the abandonment of traditional Republican principles. See Douglass to Hoar, Mar. 20 and Mar. 22, 1882, Hoar Papers.

21. Sarah Carrington to Hoar, Mar. 6, 1882, Hoar Papers. One of the young men was Lee Fun Tan, who wrote Hoar about seeing Carrington's letter reprinted in the newspaper. Tan to Hoar, Apr. 14, 1882.

22. *CR,* Mar. 3, 1882, 1584.

23. *CR,* Mar. 3, 1882, 1584.

24. *CR,* Mar. 3, 1882, 1741, 1745; *Worcester Aegis,* Mar. 18, 1882. A fifth edition of Draper published in London appeared in 1862; a New York edition, in 1863. Jones's citation is to volume 6 of *The Journal of North China.*

25. Gyory, *Closing the Gate,* 6-16.

26. *Statutes at Large of the United States,* 7 vols. (Washington, D.C., 1850-1873), 16:414.

27. Zhang Qingson, "Dragon in the Land of the Eagle: The Exclusion of Chinese from U.S. Citizenship, 1848-1943" (Ph.D. diss., Univ. of Virginia, 1994), 98-100, 148-147.

28. The most obvious authority for state-defined citizenship is, of course, *Scott v. Sanford,* 60 U.S. 393 (1857). On the singularity of immigration and naturalization, see Bina Kolola, "Immigration Laws and the Immigrant Woman, 1885-1924," *Georgetown Immigration Law Journal* 11(1997):555-556. On state jurisdiction for naturalization, see Darrell Hevenor Smith, *The Bureau of Naturalization: Its History, Activities and Organization,* Institution for Government Research Service Monographs of the United States Government, no. 43 (Baltimore, 1926), 18-24; and Congressional Research Bureau (hereafter CRB), *History of the Immigration and Naturalization Service* (Washington, D.C., 1980), 12.

29. Kolola, "Immigration Laws and the Immigrant Woman," 570-573; Gyory, *Closing the Gate,* 31-35; Saxton, *The Indispensable Enemy,* 53-65.

30. Zhang, "Dragon in the Land of the Eagle," 171-175; *New York Times,* June 27, 1882.

31. Zhang derives the figure from the 1900 census, which he believed was probably erro-

neous. "Dragon in the Land of the Eagle," 257. It was possible for Chinese legally to be naturalized citizens if they had formerly been citizens of the Republic of Hawai'i, and this may support the accuracy of the figure. The terms of the Organic Act provided for the mass naturalization of all citizens of the Republic upon its annexation to the United States. 31 Stat. 161.

32. Jacobson maintains that the amalgamation of whiteness in *Caucasian* occurred in the 1950s. Jacobson's analysis uses popular culture to make the case for amalgamation. *Whiteness of a Different Color,* 91-135.

33. *CR,* Mar. 8, 1882, 1711. On Edmunds's Radical Republican credentials and his pivotal role in raising the issue of popular votes, see Gyory, *Closing the Gate,* 231-232.

34. *CR,* Mar. 8, 1882, 1709, 1710.

35. *CR,* Mar. 8, 1882, 1709-1710; *Worcester Aegis,* Mar. 18, 1882.

36. *Worcester Aegis,* Mar. 18, 1882.

37. *CR,* Mar. 3, 1882, 1583.

38. See the example of the Bureau of Immigration justification for internal passports: "Certificate of Citizenship—Hawai'ian Islands—for citizens of Oriental descent in Hawai'i." Bureau of Immigration, Department of Labor, *Immigration Rules of July 1, 1925* (Washington, D.C., 1925), 116, and *Immigration Laws and Rules of March 1, 1927* (Washington, D.C., 1927), 127.

39. *CR,* Mar. 3, 1882, 1583-1584.

40. *CR,* Mar. 8, 1882, 1712-1713.

41. *CR,* Mar. 9, 1882, 1741.

42. *Boston Daily Traveler,* Mar. 4, 1882.

43. *CR,* Mar. 9, 1882.

44. Thomas C. Reeves, *Gentleman Boss: The Life of Chester Alan Arthur* (New York, 1975), 278-279; Hudson N. Janisch, "The Chinese, the Courts and the Constitution: A Study of the Legal Issues Raised by Chinese Immigration to the United States, 1850-1902" (J.S.D. thesis, Univ. of Chicago Law School, 1971), 2:468-470; Shirley Hune, "The Politics of Chinese Exclusion: Legislative-Executive Conflict, 1876-1882," *Amerasia* 9(1982):19-21.

45. *CR,* Apr. 25, 1882, 2609-2612. While the president's veto was overridden by a seemingly overwhelming margin, 32-15, the 29 abstentions raise an interesting question: many of the senators were "paired"—because their votes nullified each other, they abstained. This would appear to be an extraordinary number of abstentions, particularly since if all the votes were cast according to the pairing, the override would have failed.

46. *CR,* Apr. 25, 1882, 3267

47. Henry Cabot Lodge, *Memorial Addresses Delivered in the Senate and the House of Representatives, 58th Congress, 3rd Session* (Washington, D.C., 1905), 31; Geoffrey Blodgett, *The Gentle Reformers: Massachusetts Democrats in the Cleveland Era* (Cambridge, Mass., 1966), 13-14. According to Welch, Long declined to enter into negotiations with Butler's emissary. *George Frisbie Hoar,* 104-107. On Hoar's evaluation of Butler, see his *Autobiography,* ii, 335, 341-342.

48. *Boston Globe,* Jan. 16-19, 1883; *Boston Herald,* Jan. 16-19, 1883.

49. *Boston Herald,* Jan. 19, 1883; *New York Times,* Jan. 19, 1883; Welch, *George Frisbie Hoar,* 106-107.

50. Caroline Dall, diary, Sept. 30, 1904, Caroline Dall Papers, Massachusetts Historical Society; Welch, *George Frisbie Hoar*, 194-195.

51. Smith, *Bureau of Naturalization*, 5-7; CRB, *History of the INS*, 14-15.

52. Janisch, "The Chinese, the Courts and the Constitution," 2:514-517. Excluding Hawai'i, the Chinese population of the United States would have declined by about 16,500 (15 percent). United States Census Office, *Abstract of the Twelfth Census of the United States, 1900* (Washington, D.C., 1902), 41.

53. Gyory, *Closing the Gate*, 137-138.

54. Kolola, "Immigrant Laws and the Immigrant Woman," 553-554; John Hayakawa Torok, "Reconstruction and Racial Nativism: Chinese Immigrants and the Debates on the Thirteenth, Fourteenth, and Fifteenth Amendments and Civil Rights Law," *Asian Law Journal* 3(1996):97.

55. CRB, *History of the INS*, 12-15.

56. Smith, *Bureau of Naturalization*, 5-7.

57. See, for example, George W. Gold, "The Racial Prerequisite in the Naturalization Law," *Boston University Law Review* 15(1935):463-465. One of the most carefully crafted arguments critical of racial categories and the reasoning upon which they stood can be found in Dudley O. McGoveney, "Race Discrimination in Naturalization," *Iowa Law Bulletin* 8(1923):147-159. "So 'white persons' means the 'white race,' and thus we arrive at a position in which ignorance would be bliss." See for example the series of cases involving John Ali. In 1921, a Michigan district court had ruled that Ali should be granted a certificate of naturalization over the objections of the Bureau of Immigration on the grounds that he was Aryan—a high caste Hindu and therefore Indo-Aryan. Four years later, the certificate was revoked because of *U.S. v. Bhaghat Singh Thind*, 261 U.S. 204 (1923), which held that white persons were to be interpreted in the light of common speech, and Ali clearly was not white. *Ali v. United States*, 7 F (2nd) 732 (1925). For a slightly different perspective that supports this perspective, see Jacobson, *Whiteness of a Different Color*, 228-240.

58. Ian Haney-Lopez, *White by Law: The Legal Construction of Race* (New York, 1996), 123-125.

59. McGoveney, "Race Discrimination in Naturalization," 149; G. T. Stephenson, "Race Distinctions in American Law," *American Law Review* 43(1909):41-43. The obvious formulations of this problem can be seen in Madison Grant and the passage of the Johnson-Reed Act. See also Jacobson's analysis of Laura Hobson's *Gentlemen's Agreement* in *Whiteness of a Different Color*, 79, 88, 125-133.

"Have we no language of our own?"

Boston's Catholic Churches, Architects, and Communal Identity

PAULA M. KANE

OR THE PAST CENTURY in American Catholic urban life, to ask someone to name their neighborhood was the same as asking them to name their parish. Cities were cognitively mapped by the location of parishes.[1] The construction, decoration, maintenance, and survival of those parishes is what helped define many Catholic ethnic communities.

In 1994 I published *Separatism and Subculture*, a study of Boston's Catholic community in its intellectual, religious, and social forms in the early twentieth century.[2] As the title suggests, the book analyzed and highlighted what I described as a separatist subculture of mostly Irish Roman Catholics that coalesced at the close of the nineteenth century. Within it, Catholics built institutions and developed practices to parallel the Protestant-dominated culture of New England that had excluded them. A Catholic subculture gathered momentum through the 1920s and 1930s due to the combined and interactive forces of Irish dominance, numerical and institutional growth, the emergence of a Catholic middle class, and overall archdiocesan expansion.

The Archdiocese of Boston was not unique in this regard, although the local divide between Yankee Protestant and Irish Catholic was more pronounced there than in most cities. Throughout America wherever Catholics were concentrated in urban areas, an ethnoreligious subculture emerged in the early twentieth century and peaked in the 1940s and 1950s. As such, it gradually began to replace the particular ethnic loyalties of immigrants and their children with a broader concept of Catholic Americanism. Catholic identification with the nation became visible to an American public in activities that increasingly took place beyond the church walls, as Catholics took to city streets and athletic stadiums. There

Catholics staged massive eucharistic rallies, Holy Name Society parades, and Knights of Columbus pageants. Even in more intimate neighborhood settings, Block Rosaries and other practices that merged devotion and patriotism brought Catholics together in the streets of their communities and flourished in the interwar era and throughout the Cold War. New non-ethnic devotions, such as that to Our Lady of Fatima (dedicated to overthrowing godless communism in the Soviet Union), and the generic optimism of Fulton Sheen's television show, *Life Is Worth Living* (which avoided such potentially divisive topics as the Virgin Mary and the papacy), addressed the spiritual anxieties of the Cold War and signaled American Catholic mainstreaming. It has been argued that this devotional subculture eventually provided a way to unite Catholics across ethnic lines and thereby contributed to the creation of a generic American Catholic identity in the postwar era.[3] If so, then midcentury Catholic cultural isolation was being transcended "precisely as the Catholic community made larger claims to speak to (and even for) the culture itself."[4]

How Churches Mean

Between 1890 and 1950, roughly the era of transition from ethnic separatism to Catholic Americanism, sacred architecture played a role in the growth of Catholic power and prestige in Boston. The parish church provided Catholics' strongest point of contact with the Church, and both the building and the community that it contained were important markers of ethnic identity and neighborhood. In *Houses of God: Region, Religion, and Architecture in the United States*, Peter Williams has suggested that American religious architecture can be studied as an expression of liturgy, style, ethnicity, social history, and, his emphasis in that book, regionalism.[5] In New England, one can detect evidence of all of these in the attempts by Catholic priests and people to use sacred architecture to define the faithful. Here, I single out two elements of church architecture: its apologetic role and its reflection of the social history of Catholics in Boston. This essay will explore how the community of Boston Catholics used their churches to express something about themselves, their relation to Yankee Boston, and their vision of an ideal American society.

Catholic churches are polyvalent symbols, expressing local identities (ethnic, regional, national), as well as the universalism that Roman Catholicism claims for itself. At its best, a Catholic church embodies the spiritual dreams of humanity and provides a communal place to express those hopes. Theologically, the church symbolizes the house of God, the body of Christ, and the living congregation that is Christ's body on earth. Although the Church has never mandated an official architectural style, as houses of God, defined by tradition and decree, prior to Vatican II Catholic churches needed to meet certain distinctive canonical requirements: the centerpiece of the church must be the altar, which must be made of a single natural stone and permanently fixed to the floor. The church had to be consecrated by the local bishop when the church was dedicated, with holy relics installed inside the altar.

The design of a house of worship, therefore, involves more than meeting the practical demands of shelter. A Roman Catholic church tries to interpret the spiritual values of its congregation and convey something of that faith's ancient history as well as its relationship to contemporary society. As such, churches are repositories of personal and collective memory, but like any part of a cityscape, they are not eternal.[6] Churches house the sacramental rites of baptisms, marriages, and funerals where Catholics are "hatched, matched and dispatched," but they also are subject to natural disasters such as fires and floods and to economic forces and constraints that can lead to church closure, destruction, or adaptation into non-sacred use.

Within these parameters, parish churches functioned simultaneously to generate and represent Catholics' self-image in Boston. The architects, their design choices, the ideological uses of churches, and the social conditions and material relations that produce them provide the historical evidence. What did a parish church symbolize for Catholic religious identity at a particular moment? What did churches express about Irish Catholics' identity to some anticipated audience? This essay examines Boston in light of recent scholarship in urban religion and cultural change to explore the contribution of sacred architecture to the formation of community.[7]

Everybody's Gothic

Of the stylistic repertoire of Christian churches created since Greco-Roman antiquity, medieval Gothic enjoyed an enormous revival in the nineteenth century. Its return was largely inspired by English Catholic architect Augustus Welby Northmore Pugin (1812-1852), who declared in

1841, with equal measures of poetry and morality, that Gothic was the true Christian architecture.[8] Among his strongest advocates were John Ruskin (1819–1900), the English universities, and the High Church movements within the Anglican Church at Oxford and Cambridge. Ruskin held a direct connection to Massachusetts Gothicizers and Arts and Crafts practitioners through his longtime correspondence with Charles Eliot Norton (1827–1908), professor of Fine Arts at Harvard University and dévoté of the moral power of art. The combined efforts of these individuals and groups enabled the Gothic Revival to touch virtually every European nation, Canada, and the United States. The fact that by the early 1870s Gothic had been embraced by Low Church anti-ritualist Protestants (such as Ruskin), High Church Anglicans, and Roman Catholics suggests that the style had expanded its ideological content enough to represent generic Christian architecture to the churchgoing public.[9]

In its nineteenth-century revival, neo-Gothic combined aesthetic and social dimensions. Aesthetically, the Gothic Revival admired the "pageantry of worship," linking art to the service of God through the use of Christian symbols and designs and the manipulation of light inside churches. Socially, it represented the antithesis of industrialism by rejecting profit motives, machine production, and the loss of communalism that accompanied the expansion of industrial capitalism. Pugin himself set the tone in his first pamphlet of 1836, an attack on nineteenth-century poorhouse conditions.[10] Together with William Morris, a disciple of Ruskin, and the Arts and Crafts movement, Catholic Gothicists shared the view that industrialism was the source of modern rootlessness and loss of tradition.[11] Hesitant to endorse the social radicalism that stemmed from Morris and his circle, however, and more interested in the iconography underlying Gothic art than in labor radicalism, the Catholic Church maintained an ambiguous relationship to socialism as it tried to position itself as the unwavering third way between the excesses of capitalism and socialism.

Since Pugin, the Christian churches have undergone at least three phases of Gothic revivals, the final one put to rest by World War I. The current reappearance of the term *Goth*—to describe a youth subculture based upon a particular style of makeup, costume, and dance music called Gothic-Industrial—is highly paradoxical and, in postmodern fashion, shorn from coherent historical referents.[12]

Because the dramatic increase in the Irish population of Boston and the subsequent social assimilation of its Irish Catholics happened to coincide with several phases of the Gothic Revival, and because the Revival (both in its *fin de siècle* and post-World War I incarnations) shared affinities with Catholic antimodernist sentiments, many neo-Gothic churches were built between 1870 and 1940. Yet despite its seeming ubiquity, Gothic never became the "house" style of the Catholic Church. The Archdiocese of Boston, for example, while choosing Gothic for many churches built in Archbishop O'Connell's era, also produced an eclectic variety, which suggests that even churches were not immune to the impact of industrial capitalism on the arts.[13] After all, the vogue for historical revivals was the creation of the middle class that had emerged in the wake of the French Revolution. This new bourgeoisie tried to consolidate its position in European culture (and in America a century later) by ensconcing itself in "the picturesque and romantic associations of historical revivals."[14] The taste for the ancient affected church builders as well, who took pride in their choice of nonmanufactured materials and their reliance upon artisanal craftsmanship instead of industrial products and new building technologies.

The use of the past to embody premodern ideals against industrialism led to the resurrection of classical, Romanesque, Gothic, and Spanish mission style churches, all of which had their copies in Boston. The presence of these competing styles contributed to the failure of Gothic to become a universal preference.[15] Until at least the mid twentieth century, however, the idiom of Gothic aided the Church's belief in its unchanging moral principles, together with its anti-industrial and anti-utilitarian sentiments. The vertical appearance of its churches dominated the streetscape, a worthy competitor even to skyscrapers. But the unchallenged appeal of Gothic would come to an end with the arrival of artistic modernism.

Everybody's America

While rootedness and social stability were ideals associated with Gothic, rootlessness was the shared history of Hibernian immigrants. Indeed, it was the central motif of the Irish diaspora, according to Kerby Miller's massive 1985 synthesis, *Emigrants and Exiles: Ireland and the Irish Exodus to North America.*[16] In Ireland, since English Protestant oppression dating from the sixteenth century, Catholics had had to observe their religion in secret. The cultural memory of clandestine Masses offered in barns or hidden chapels without music or fanfare endures as a part of Irish American identity.[17]

Perhaps the enforced dampened liturgical style fostered the subsequent interest in exuberant church architecture in America's cities once Irish immigrants began to be successful. Even the most melancholy Irish immigrants from the Famine years became strongly attached to the idea of the United States and sang of the opportunities to be found "on the shores of Amerikay." A typical lyric celebrates

> America dear Eden land
> We fondly turn to thee
> Where still the homes and altars stand
> Of sacred liberty.[18]

Even as it perpetually mourned the Erin left behind, Boston's Irish Catholic population grew substantially amid the altars of "sacred liberty," despite the sickliness of the Famine arrivals of the 1850s. Although met with fierce social and religious discrimination that belied the image of America as a classless utopia, by the 1910s, and sometimes with cooperation from Protestant allies, Boston's Catholics began to demonstrate their desire to establish roots in Boston. They gradually abandoned their parochialism and insinuated themselves as agents of American patriotism, Christian civilization, and good government. Boston's Irish Catholic community achieved this civic-mindedness in part because it had gained an enviable degree of actual control of the city's political machines, police force, and public schools.

By 1920, first- and second-generation Irish Catholics had become integral to the city's administration, police department, public works, and public schools. Several Irish Catholic Democratic mayors had been elected, including Patrick Collins, Hugh O'Brien, John Fitzgerald, and James Michael Curley, who usually ran against the Brahmin establishment's Republican candidates. Massachusetts voters had even elected one Catholic governor in 1914.

In this environment of burgeoning Irish American power, Catholics began to build parish churches, convents, and schools at an unparalleled pace. In fact, architectural metaphors are commonly applied to the powerful pastors ("brick-and-mortar priests") and prelates ("builder bishops") who presided over this era throughout the United States. William

O'Connell, archbishop of Boston from 1907 to 1944, epitomized the kind of prince of the Church who micro-managed the expansion of the Catholic infrastructure, and at an amazing rate.[19] O'Connell could proudly boast to the Vatican in the 1920s (while under investigation for a juicy financial scandal involving embezzlement by his nephew, the chancellor of the Archdiocese) that he had created eighty-one new parishes, twenty-five missions, two colleges, and two retreat houses, all debt-free. The hegemony of Irish Americans over the American church was attested to in the *Official Catholic Directory*, the national annual listing of all Catholic parishes, religious orders, and related institutions. There, parishes were designated "German," "Slovak" or "Italian," but never "Irish."[20]

As Irish Catholics consolidated a network of institutions and anticipated a bright future in the land of the Cabots, Lodges, and Lowells, Boston's Brahmin leadership was experiencing a crisis. There was much talk about the creeping effeminacy of the Anglo-Saxon race, its falling fertility rates, and its waning control of New England. This feeling was even shared by some Protestants such as Ralph Adams Cram (1863–1942), who was eager to write obituaries for Puritanism.[21] Cram, an Anglo-Catholic, became America's leading Gothic architect and an enthusiastic supporter of medieval culture, which, as he understood it, culminated in England prior to the reign of Henry VIII. Known outside church circles for his buildings at West Point Military Academy and Rice University, Cram also served as the official architect of Princeton University where he designed its Graduate College and chapel. Although he lost the design competition for the Cathedral of St. John the Divine in New York City in 1889, Cram later became the project's overseeing architect from 1911 to 1942, during which time he shifted the design of the mammoth cathedral away from Romanesque-Byzantine to Gothic. As early as 1894, in an article on Catholic architecture for *Catholic World*, Cram had proclaimed with his usual boldness: "New England . . . is weary of Puritanism." Whereas Cram had his own mostly aesthetic reasons for trying to dislodge public taste in Boston away from Puritanism, he also encouraged Catholics to continue their allegiance to Gothic church architecture.

New England Catholic leaders, emboldened by their economic and political success, began to voice similar anti-Puritan sentiments in the public sphere shortly thereafter. As Mayor James Michael Curley said witheringly of the Brahmins, "The day of the Puritan has passed; the Anglo-Saxon is a joke; a new and better America is here."[22] Archbishop

O'Connell sounded the same theme in his sermon "In the Beginning," during the celebration of the centennial of the Archdiocese in 1908: "The Puritan has passed; the Catholic remains."[23] In this way, at least, Catholics made common cause with leading critics of Anglo-Saxonism, and embraced enthusiasm for the Gothic Revival to underpin what they hoped would be a Catholic Revival in the United States.

Maginnis the Magnificent

In the field of sacred architecture, Bostonians were led by Charles Donagh Maginnis (1867–1955). An immigrant from Ireland who became America's most prominent Catholic practitioner, Maginnis believed that "until we become racially homogeneous, it is clear that Catholic architecture in America must be largely and variously reminiscent of Europe.... Catholic art must have its roots deep in the past, though there need be much trimming of its dead branches."[24] Maginnis led a generation of traditional Catholic architects who skillfully borrowed from Europe's heritage and learned their profession through apprenticeship, yet whose careers overlapped with a rising generation of modernists who were breaking radically from the historicizing tradition and who were being trained in university degree programs that were shedding the constraints of Beaux Arts influence. As a conservative designer, Maginnis's career ended on the cusp of the major liturgical changes that would affect Catholic church design after Vatican II.

Born in Londonderry, educated in Dublin, and an emigrant to Boston via Canada in 1885, Maginnis moved up through the ranks of draftsmen in the prominent office of Edmund Wheelright before opening his own partnership with Matthew Sullivan (1868–1948) and Timothy Walsh from 1898 to 1907. Later, upon Sullivan's departure to start his own firm, the team of Maginnis and Walsh created a partnership that endured until 1954, although Walsh died in 1934.[25] Maginnis went on to become the nation's best-known Catholic architect, an American Institute of Architects (AIA) Gold Medal winner, and a two-term president of the AIA, despite never having received any formal architectural degrees. He married a poet and member of an established Boston Episcopal family, but Amy Brooks Maginnis, a Radcliffe alumna, kept herself modestly in the background. Timothy Walsh married one of Maginnis's daughters.

The firm of Maginnis and Walsh produced some twenty-four

A vista of the neo-Gothic buildings devised by Maginnis and Walsh for Boston College. Courtesy, Boston College Archives.

churches for the Boston area between 1900 and 1920, a sum exceeded only by the firm of Cram and Ferguson, whose total of forty-one commissions for mostly Protestant churches included restorations and interior remodelings. Maginnis and Walsh also specialized in projects that attested to the expanding presence of the Catholic Church in Boston: chapels, convents, hospitals, parish rectories, parochial schools, and collegiate buildings. The best-known of these include the Notre Dame Academy and Convent (later Emmanuel College) in the Back Bay; Immaculate Conception Church and School in Cambridge; the Cenacle Convent and chapel; the St. John's Seminary, Brighton; and the chapel and many campus buildings at Boston College. Maginnis and Walsh also produced noteworthy designs for high altars, including one for Trinity Episcopal Church in Boston, and the altar and baldachino for St. Patrick's Cathedral, New York City. Maginnis took part in contemporary discussion about architectural principles and church design as a frequent contributor to architectural and Catholic journals, including *Architectural Record, Brickbuilder* (and its successor *Architectural Forum*), *Christian Art, Columbiad, Donahoe's,* and *Liturgical Arts.*

A list of Maginnis, Walsh, and Sullivan's earliest churches for the Archdiocese of Boston includes Our Lady of Lourdes, Revere (1902); St. Margaret, Brockton (1903); and St. John the Evangelist, Cambridge (1904).
Maginnis and Walsh's ecclesiastical projects in the Boston area include St.
Aidan, Brookline (1911); St. Catherine, Norwood (1908); and St. George,
Norwood (1915).[26] Critics agree that Maginnis's finest church is St. Catherine of Genoa, Somerville, built between 1907 and 1916 in Italian Romanesque style, which predated the Gothic and tended to have a squat
heavy appearance. St. Catherine's Church was even chosen by Cram to
illustrate his "Architecture" entry for the *Encyclopedia Britannica*. Fortu-
nately for Maginnis, expense had posed no object for that project, since he
could rely upon the ample resources available to the pastor of St. Catherine, who was the grandson of Boston's first Catholic mayor.

A founder of the Liturgical Arts Society in 1928, and representing a relatively elite segment of the Catholic laity, Charles Maginnis shared Ralph
Adams Cram's love of the Middle Ages and especially for English perpen-
dicular Gothic. Whereas Cram had bluntly called the progress of Catholic
architecture in America "a carnival of horror," however, Maginnis acknowledged more generously that "until Catholics were homogenized
into American life, Catholic architecture must largely recall its European
roots," and that "the Church should be more intelligently eclectic in the
development of a vital architecture."

Maginnis, consequently, never restricted himself to Gothic designs.[27]
He admired the rounded arch style of Lombardy, and he frequently utilized Byzantine precedents, as in his prize-winning Shrine of the Immaculate Conception (1955) in Washington, D.C. In fact, Maginnis
contended that for the Catholic parish church in America, Gothic and
Italian Byzantine (Romanesque) styles were the most adaptable.[28] Cram
and Maginnis were acquaintances and members of the same professional
and social clubs, but they were apparently not close friends, although no
public record of their personal feelings toward each other exists. One sus-
pects from the exhaustive treatment of Cram's early career by biographer
Douglass Shand-Tucci that Cram's towering ego and personality quirks
did not earn him many close friends, and that in his private life his deep-
est affections were reserved for his partner, Bertram Goodhue.[29] Maginnis, by contrast, described himself as innately modest and shy, "based on
a democratic Christian regard of ideas and his fellowman."[30]

Maginnis, for all of his dedication to aesthetic standards, was a prag-

Charles Maginnis's masterpiece, St. Catherine of Genoa (1907–1916).
Courtesy of the author.

matist who was sensitive to the financial limitations of his Catholic clients, for whom he designed elegant yet cost-conscious churches.[31] In this sense he exemplified the immigrant who does not become alienated from his own community once he attains wealth and fame. Not every Catholic architect was willing to supply churches for congregations of modest financial means, and few architects could be as verbally extravagant and as insistent upon craftsmanship as Cram. Maginnis was so convinced of his fiscal principles that he sold designs to liturgical magazines in an attempt to prove that economy and beauty did not have to be enemies. He claimed that $10,000 was enough to construct an adequate church in 1917, whereas "every cent that is expended beyond $10,000, then, is expended for art, and for nothing else."[32]

Steeple Envy?

Apart from their liturgical function, the Catholic churches of Boston addressed a larger audience. As forms of cultural capital, they intended to impress all Bostonians by claiming an apologetic role for architecture and by contributing to an outlook that we might refer to as Catholic triumphalism. Archbishop O'Connell spoke fervently and frequently of his desire to cover Boston with Catholic buildings "from pinnacle to pavement," and he looked upon his residency at the seminary on the heights of Chestnut Hill as both strategic and symbolic.[33] Across Commonwealth Avenue from the seminary and archbishop's house was Boston College, a Jesuit institution that was likewise a source of great pride to local Catholics. O'Connell envisioned its campus as the Catholic "Oxford of America." Between 1909 and 1913 Maginnis and Walsh executed the Gothic plan and buildings that had won them the contract for the expansion of the institution.[34]

It is not surprising that once Irish Catholics began to achieve a bit of municipal prestige and power, their leaders used aesthetics and history to accuse Protestants of falsely appropriating the Gothic. How could a denomination in the Calvinist tradition, for example, claim any organic affinity with Gothic architecture?[35] In fact, Catholics could be rather dismissive of Protestantism in general by challenging the rationale for its houses of worship: "At the Reformation the Protestants rejected the Real Presence and thus converted the temple of God into a mere auditorium."[36] Such comments served to remind the Catholic faithful of the then-important theological boundaries that set them apart from other Christians. This defensive posture also became a way for Catholics to assert cultural and social superiority. Hence, Catholics were taught to take pride in the unique elements of their sacramental theology that defined a sacralized space: the presence of Christ in the tabernacle, the burial of relics inside the immovable stone or marble altar, and the dedication of each new church by the local bishop.[37]

To some degree Protestants *had* turned their sacred spaces into auditoriums. A structure known as an auditorium church had first emerged in the 1830s in cities affected by the Second Great Awakening, notably the Chatham Chapel (1832) and the Broadway Tabernacle (1836) in New York City. Auditorium churches had become quite common by the last quarter of the nineteenth century, but not for the reasons the Catholic priest above had suggested. Instead, this trend arose from quite different liturgical norms. The theater-cum-chapel was introduced to enhance the teaching authority of the preacher, who became an actor on a stage and who could be seen and heard equally well by anyone in the comfortable seats ar-

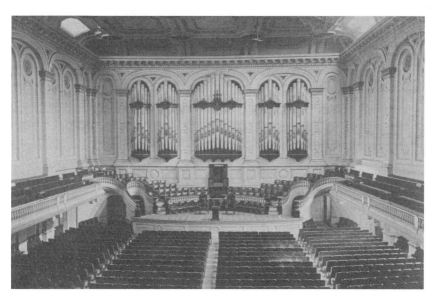

The Boston Tremont Temple of the Baptists, an auditorium-style church.
Photograph, 1874, courtesy of the Boston Public Library.

ranged in a circular fashion on a sloping floor. Large spaces, good sight-lines and acoustics, elevated and thrust stages, and proscenium arches all contributed to a corporate identity of Protestants centered upon the preached word of God.[38] Eventually, as one phase of the Gothic Revival took hold in the 1850s, Protestants returned to traditional aisle seating in a rectangular space and abandoned the square auditorium interior. It returned in the Gilded Age and lasted through about 1910, epitomized by the remodeled Tremont Temple in Boston.[39] With the next Gothic Revival, Protestants shunned the auditorium style, and even liberal Protestants and Unitarians turned to updated medieval forms for their remodeling plans.[40] President Charles Eliot of Harvard, for example, was horrified when Unitarians of Boston chose Ralph Adams Cram's design for an elaborate renovated altar.

Charles Maginnis was no fan of the principles guiding the "chunky" auditorium church, finding it commendable optically and acoustically, but in the end, unacceptable to Catholics because of its un-Catholic emphasis on the sermon rather than on the eucharistic sacrifice. "Worship of God at the altar had been forgotten," he lamented. "This principle is the fundamental one in its demand on the architecture."[41] Catholics would not abandon their emphasis upon the altar and the Eucharist, yet the

church architecture of Maginnis's generation itself would become out-
moded by the recommendations of Vatican II, which called for a simpli-
fied church interior centered visually around the key symbols of the faith
(including the altar). In effect, Vatican II did "Protestantize" Catholic
church interiors.

The Professionalization of Architecture

Architects of the *fin de siècle* derived their artistic principles and prejudices
from the training they had received, but not all Catholics came to the profession through the same channels. Many of the early Catholic architects
of Boston were immigrants who had received training as draftsmen. Their
prototype was Irishman Patrick Keeley (1816–1896), the designer (it is
said) of more than 600 Catholic churches in America during the nineteenth century, mostly in the French Gothic mode. The twin-towered
Cathedral of the Holy Cross (1867–1875) in Boston's South End is one of
his schemes. It is apparent from the career limitations facing Catholics
entering the field of architecture after 1900, or facing those who aspired
to the profession through experience in the construction industry, that
no one could build as many churches as Keeley, that only a handful would
achieve the success of Maginnis and Walsh, and that ever fewer would devote themselves to penning reflections on the spiritual impulses guiding
Christian architecture.

Charles Maginnis arrived in Boston in 1885 as the vocation of architect
was becoming professionalized and specialized, departing from its divided existence as either a patrician pursuit or a vocation learned via apprenticeship and at the drafting board. In Boston these divergent paths
were represented on one hand by the elite enclave of Harvard's School of
Architecture and the venerable Massachusetts Institute of Technology
School of Architecture and on the other by the more progressive approach
of the Boston Architectural Club (BAC), founded in 1889 with an atelier-
style evening program for drafters who held daytime jobs. In both of these
settings, a student was gradually transforming into a professional who
learned the canonical principles and discursive field of architecture at a
school.[42] Graduates would then supply distinguished firms with the
"best" designers for low wages. Because American schools usually followed the French curriculum and formalism of the Ecole des Beaux-Arts,

the lack of a distinctive, American architecture was something that Maginnis and his generation acknowledged. Of that deficiency, he wrote: "What, then, is meant here in America by the jumble and conflict of styles which are not of us? Have we no language of our own? We seldom ask ourselves the question."[43] This would appear to be an especially important question for Catholic church architecture.

Certain aspects of professionalized architecture were already entrenched by the late nineteenth century: large firms, specialized publications, and professional organizations that conferred awards and honors. For Catholic practitioners and their clients, use of artistic traditions to promote their worldview depended on the formation of a professional class of Catholic architects, contractors, and craftsmen. It was not an easy task, given the elite nature of the field, the exclusion of Catholics from Boston's WASP institutions of higher learning, and the lack of family heritage and incomes to undertake such essential pilgrimages as the Grand Tour of Europe, where young men aspiring to artistic or architectural careers could see first-hand the stones of Florence; the churches of Lombardy, Tuscany, and Ravenna; and the cathedrals at Chartres, Reims, Florence, and Siena. Perhaps it is no accident that the overwhelming majority of Catholic architects practicing in Boston contemporaneously with Maginnis were of Irish backgrounds, and some were already experienced continental travelers.

In addition to the professional credentials increasingly required to train an architect to design a church, by 1900 a battery of artisans were employed to construct and furnish the buildings. These skilled craftsmen included carpenters, engineers, glaziers, interior designers, landscape architects, marble carvers, plasterers, stained glass designers, and wrought-iron workers. Judging from the surnames in advertisements appearing in church and city directories, many of the craftsmen initially active in New England came from Irish or Irish American backgrounds.[44] Maginnis encouraged these allied arts and crafts and made regular visits to the studios and shops of his subcontractors and craftsmen. The interest in craft production, moreover, was a major emphasis of the Gothic Revival, which regarded the Middle Ages as a time when the tasks of designers and craftsmen were not separated.

Through their involvement in the liturgical arts, architects and craftsmen developed a symbiotic relationship with the Catholic hierarchy, which provided them with steady commissions for a seemingly infinite demand for new churches. Although church commissions created jobs for skilled laborers, they nonetheless did not generate guaranteed profits for architects. Even the agreeable Maginnis confided in his unpublished memoirs that "churches rarely yield any profit to an architect who is dependent for his income upon the more secular side of his practice."[45] In Maginnis's day, architects generally received a flat fee of 6 percent of the cost of the church, which, in his opinion, barely covered a "perfunctory performance" by the architect. In language that drew comparisons between the growing specialization of the arts and the emergence of celebrity athletes in America, Maginnis grumbled that architects were treated like surveyors rather than honored like "musicians, authors and baseball players."[46] It was not until several decades later that a minimum fee of 10 percent of the cost of a church plan was established by agreement of architects nationwide, with a bonus for customized items such as sanctuary and baptistery designs. In 1938 Maginnis contributed one such design for the altar and chancel of H. H. Richardson's Trinity Episcopal Church in Copley Square.

Some Catholic architects of the late nineteenth and early twentieth centuries learned their craft, as did Maginnis, by serving as apprentices to practicing architects. Others acquired experience through surveying or civil engineering jobs. But there were still other ways to secure employment in architecture despite the handicap of being Irish and Catholic. We usually imagine Irish Catholics choosing a career as one of the three "p"s—priest, policeman, or politician—but they also excelled as civil servants. Hence, some Catholic builders and contractors were able to secure contracts through personal connections with city managers and administrators. Other Catholics secured positions in city administration as building inspectors, supervisors of plans, and urban planners, while pursuing careers in architecture simultaneously. Charles Bateman provides one example. He became the city architect of Cambridge in 1883 and served that city for four administrations. He built St. Cecilia's Church, Back Bay, in one of the city's wealthiest parishes, especially after Archbishop O'Connell became its rector. Bateman also designed apartments, tenements, and schools. He followed Catholic families who were moving to the streetcar suburbs and secured commissions there, which proved to be a lucrative venue for both Catholic and non-Catholic builders. Like Bateman, most of Boston's Irish architects, such as immigrant Patrick Ford (1848-1900), were obliged to earn a living constructing wooden tenements, apartments, and other domestic buildings. Locally, "the penetration of Catholic architects of Maginnis's caliber into the elite realm of independent practice was far less typical than a broader diffusion of Catholic entrepreneurs into the building arts and trades in Massachusetts."[47]

Maginnis summarized the contemporary scene in the draft of his memoirs: "Architecture in the Boston of that day, and for generations after, was regarded as an aristocratic occupation whose practitioners were usually to be found in the proper clubs." As a gentleman's vocation it had always counted upon patronage from within the WASP elite. The social and class biases of New England had traditionally excluded Catholics from the few existing American schools with architectural programs, such as at Harvard and MIT. Since 1867 the latter (which relocated to Cambridge in 1916) had offered the first four-year architectural curriculum in the nation, while Harvard's architecture history curriculum (1874; B.A., 1893) added graduate programs in 1906 and remained the preserve of the Brahmins. The BAC, whose faculty included those from Harvard and MIT volunteering their services, probably attracted more Catholic students because of its populist orientation and evening classes.[48] Maginnis, who took pen drawing lessons there, recalled it being "made up of the ambitious younger element."[49] Relatively few Catholic students attended any of these institutions until social and economic conditions had changed enough to produce an Irish Catholic bourgeoisie.[50] Catholic architecture students arrived on the scene, therefore, just as the professionalization of architecture by degree-granting university programs was emerging in the United States.

Maginnis was one of the last draftsmen to achieve national prominence, both for his designs and as a moral spokesman for aesthetic uplift of America's Catholic population. He was a lifelong critic of mediocre church design and of the dispiriting effects of commercialization: "We must seek the sources of true art production instead of complacently accepting what the highly organized commerce of today offers at our doors," he preached. "For art is not to be had merely by paying for it. To select an architect as one would select a hardware dealer, assuming that one is as good as another, is being simply unintelligent at the critical moment."[51] On the other hand, Maginnis realized with his customary common sense that eclecticism must dominate stylistic choices in America for some time to come:

National and racial identities are growing more and more indefinite. There is constant mingling of peoples. . . . So it is that the art of the time is intensely self-conscious and, of necessity, eclectic. Our architecture for years to come must continue to be reminiscent. . . . No one architectural system, however, intellectually satisfying, may hope to reconcile such variances, nor will a national style of architecture develop in this country until we are one coherent race, probably not even then.[52]

Given his assumptions that national and racial boundaries would melt together in America, was there anything innovative in Maginnis's continued preference for European Gothic architecture? Probably not, but nor was there anything demeaning about his talent as an excellent copyist. It was the noble purpose of neo-Gothic, as he understood it, that inspired him. Architects of the medieval revival committed themselves to repudiate modernist shortcuts in construction techniques, to emphasize the solidity and structural honesty of stone (or even "unpretentious" brick, which Maginnis recommended for less affluent parishes), to avoid imitation in building materials, and to link their utopianism to the precapitalist past. In this respect, Maginnis seems to embody Pugin's four organic "true principles" of architecture: that even the smallest details have spiritual or functional meaning; that construction be adapted to accessible materials; that ornament be integral to the structure of the building, not simply picturesque additions; and that the exterior and interior of a building correspond to its spiritual or functional purpose.[53]

In the United States, where the Irish began as underdogs in an Anglo-Protestant environment, figures like Maginnis were understandably preoccupied with claiming a benign and symbiotic relationship between architecture and national identity, but they also imagined that nation as one dedicated to pluralist ideals. Therefore, Maginnis esteemed Europe's medieval past but did not intend to reproduce it slavishly in America: "I hold no brief for a modern Gothic architecture. We can all admit that under other conditions than ours, it interpreted, as no other system ever did, or perhaps ever can, the complex genius of religion. . . . What we do want is the *spirit* of Gothic if we are to give the Church in America responsible standards of art."[54]

Synagogues, Churches, and Neighborhoods

Foreign-born Catholics were not the only immigrants who wanted to infuse the United States with their own spirit of sacrality. The debates between Protestant and Catholic in New England take on greater depth when we compare Catholic investment in the styles of churches and the ideology of sacred architecture with similar conflicts facing Boston's Jews. Focused on Protestant-Catholic conflict in Boston, I had not explored this possible connection in *Separatism and Subculture*. Recent scholarship, however, has opened a new perspective on the history of Boston's ethnic communities by comparing the worship spaces and neighborhood loyalties of Jews and Catholics in light of their shared outsider status in Protestant America.[55] In *Urban Exodus: Why the Jews Left Boston and the Catholics Stayed* (Cambridge, Mass., 1999), Gerald Gamm set out to explain why Catholics maintained their residences in the suburbs of Dorchester and Roxbury while most of the Jewish population departed by 1970, joining the white flight that emptied many American cities in that decade.

Among the factors that encouraged Catholics to remain in their neighborhoods, he found, were the intense investment of Catholics in parish life and the territorial limitations of such attachments. Overall, according to Gamm, Catholics who decided to leave their parishes faced greater penalties, such as loss of access to the parochial school, which probably acted as a strong deterrent to departure and a strong impetus for laity to remain devoted to their parish center.[56] Clearly, the Catholic parish functioned as more than a scenic backdrop to Sunday, devotional, and civic forms of Catholic religious life.[57]

In *Urban Exodus* Gamm concludes that concepts of sacred space, whether embodied in a church or synagogue, had meaningful effects on the social construction and ultimate fate of neighborhoods. Gamm chronicles the fate of key parishes in Dorchester, including St. Paul's, designed by Charles Maginnis. Indeed, Ralph Adams Cram had praised this design as "undoubtedly one of the really fine Catholic Churches in the United States. So far as its exterior is concerned it is a notable model of what Catholic architecture should be."[58] For Cram, the aesthetic experience of a church was paramount; for Catholic parishioners, the parish church symbolized belonging and identified a neighborhood. Further, because of their rootedness in territorial parishes, Catholics shaped the pattern of future stability of their neighborhoods by effectively limiting where Jews and later, blacks, could find housing. As Gamm suggests, "Catholic churches successfully coordinate residential behavior because they restrict membership to local residents and because the church itself can make a long-term commitment to its neighborhood."[59] Jewish congregations, by contrast, are not territorially bound. Because they have had to compete for members and often coexisted with dozens of nearby congregations, synagogues also faced competition for membership and lacked a permanent neighborhood base. Further, because synagogue financing depended heavily on the revenue raised by sales of seats for the High Holy Days, the American synagogue became "an essentially private institutional organization for dues-paying members."[60]

Gamm contends that Jews and Catholics diverged dramatically on the essential notion of how to constitute a sacred space. He suggests that the aesthetic concerns of Protestants and Catholic elites in Boston were unmatched among Jews, who regarded the synagogue as merely a shell.[61] What was stored inside the building—the Torah scrolls—were the most sacred objects of Judaism, but even these could belong to private individuals who kept them at home. Whereas this fact led Gamm to conclude that Jews entertained little concern for synagogue design, it seems probable that factors other than aesthetics better explain the uneven pace of synagogue building in Boston and the frequent migrations of Jewish congregations. The shifting locations of Jewish settlement could have had an impact, as could ethnic conflicts among German, Polish, and Russian Jews, or the congregational autonomy of Judaism in general. Only three Boston congregations had built synagogues by 1870, but many congregations formed in the following decades existed without a permanent structure of their own. Consequently, worship took place in storefronts, rented rooms, family homes, and recycled spaces, including former Congregational and Unitarian churches. Because frequent discord among Jews over issues of reforming ("Protestantizing") services led splinter congregations to form, the same neighborhood could contain dozens of Jewish groups, in contrast to the strict geographic boundaries separating each Catholic parish and delineating its territorial membership.

Against Gamm's claim, however, there is ample evidence that Boston's Jews did use architecture, in a fashion similar to Catholics, as an expression of ethnoreligious identity that over time adapted to an American context as greater financial resources became available.[62] Three examples from different generations of local Jews illustrate this passage. Temple Israel, the first architecturally important synagogue in Boston, dates from 1885. It adopted the Romanesque Revival style of Bavaria, the homeland of many of its members. David Kauffman compares this "ethnic church" for Jews to the many unpretentious parishes built by Patrick Keeley for immigrant Catholics of the same era.[63] By 1906, Boston's Reform Jews were able to hire a leading local architect to design a grander second Temple Israel on Commonwealth Avenue, replete with Egyptian and Byzantine motifs chosen for their meaningful historical connections for Jews. The temple also incorporated an organ, an innovation that stemmed from Reform Judaism as well as from Jewish exposure to Protestant church interiors in the United States.[64] Twenty years later, Temple Israel bought prime land on the Riverway and planned construction of a massive classical temple and affiliated buildings, although the project was halted by the stock market crash and the Great Depression. In the wake of the Holocaust, some Boston congregations retreated from grandiose building programs and chose smaller, enclosed synagogue designs, for which brick Georgian Revival was unobtrusive and popular.

By the late 1940s, new synagogues built in Brookline and Newton, where the Jewish population then clustered, selected modernist designs. An excellent example is Mishkan Tefila, a Conservative congregation that moved to Chestnut Hill from Roxbury, where it had occupied a Gothic Revival Congregational church from 1907 to 1924, followed by its creation of an innovative synagogue-center on Sever Street from 1925 to 1957. In Chestnut Hill, the congregation opted for a sleek structure by modernist architect Percival Goodman on a wooded site with the typical large suburban parking lot.[65] These transitions in style and locale of Jewish synagogues suggest that, like Catholic churches, temples and synagogues have reflected contemporary social debates about their members' status within a religious tradition as well as their position in Boston and in American society.

The Future of Catholic Community

Neo-Gothic churches proved to be an important but not final stage in
Catholic sacred architecture in America. Their impact may have lingered
with greater force in the Archdiocese of Boston because few new parishes
and churches were created after Vatican II, by which time the Catholic
population of many areas of the Archdiocese had already begun its exodus
to the suburbs. Yet even in places such as Roxbury where black residents
were moving into neighborhoods vacated by fleeing Jews, Catholic enclaves survived. As Gerald Gamm found, "The parish was a fortress for
old-time residents, stoutly maintaining familiar rituals, social events, and
the neighborhood's disappearing ethnic character. Its pastor and curates
continued to provide vigorous leadership, reinforcing for white Catholics
the permanence of the parish's commitment to the neighborhood. In a
time of change, the parish offered stability."[66] Thus, Catholic parishes endured through a contradictory set of behaviors: the Church remained
committed to their neighborhoods, but also adopted "conscious policies
of racial discrimination."[67] Departing Catholics left behind an infrastructure of churches in Boston that was solidly traditional, among which the
Gothic style was the epitome of solidity and permanence. Of the nineteen
new parishes formed and built in the archdiocese after 1960, at least eleven
featured "modern" architectural designs or features—more than half of
the new construction—yet they still comprise only a small percentage of
the total churches in the Boston area.

Between 1940 and 1960 the ideological force of Gothic had faded and
modernist tendencies had made inroads into sacred architecture. As the
descendants of Catholic immigrants became Americanized through the
cultural effects of World War II—access to higher education and subur-
banization—postwar architecture likewise took on new meanings associated with new opportunities to succeed in America, and after 1945 with
the globalization of American culture. References to medieval Europe no
longer wielded the same kind of power that they could once command,
even for Cold War Catholics. The waning of neo-Gothic style seems related also to the upsurge in pro-American feeling after World War II, for
which the stasis of medieval forms and its teams of art producers seemed
to be an unconvincing idiom for American individualism, democratic institutions, and the dynamic nature of capitalist development. If American

St. Gerard Majella parish, 1960, Canton, Massachusetts, one of the archdiocese's few modern-style churches. Courtesy of the *Boston Globe.*

Catholics wished to be a part of that prosperous America, they would need to follow suit.

Another historical factor affected Catholic thinking about sacred architecture: the adoption of new liturgical norms generated by Vatican II (1962–1965) revised many of the ideals that guided the architects discussed above.[68] The historical context had changed as well: designing a copy of a Gothic church no longer seemed appropriate for the 1960s because, as a premier Catholic modernist architect reasoned, "practically all the living elements which then went into the creation of those older churches are now lacking—the honesty of construction and directness of expression, counterbalanced by the simplicity of their lives, the feelings for the materials at hand; the long training of the building crafts who [*sic*] had wonderful traditions of craftsmanship."[69] Groups such as the Liturgical

Arts Society, which had resisted the spread of medieval revivalism among
Catholics, believed that contemporary churches could reflect the intent of
medieval builders to be contemporary without simply copying their
style.[70] Between 1965 and the present, Catholic churches became less dec-
orated, less filled with statues, and less "medieval." They have come to resemble modernism's "unadorned box," without necessarily sharing the
tenets of modernist architecture. Catholics in the pews, however, have not
abandoned their traditionalism as rapidly.

Because of the decline of a Catholic subculture since Vatican II, the diversity of opinion that prevails today on every religious question, and the
non-European origins of the most recent immigrant arrivals, it is no
longer possible to speak of a shared Catholic America. As forecast by Will
Herberg in the 1950s, Catholics seem to have opted for becoming a "culture religion"—one of three major denominations in American society
that pose no challenge to the status quo.[71] New patterns of immigration
have meant that some of Boston's Catholic churches are now home to
congregations of recent arrivals from Italy, Brazil, and Haiti.[72] New economic pressures and changing demographics have induced Boston's
archbishop to respond by merging and closing some congregations.[73] Still
other churches have been de-sacralized ("relegated to profane use," in
Chancery parlance) to become non-Catholic worship sites.[74] In the present situation of ever-expanding pluralism, however, it is unclear whether
Catholicism (and organized religions in general) will survive in forms
that have any recognizable connection to the subcultural strategies of the
first half of the twentieth century.

Catholicism may endure in the future as fragmentary traces of that
past, or as a tradition that successfully rebuilds itself as a global religion,
based upon new identifications with the marginalized peoples of the
world. Just as the Gothic Revival attempted to address the spiritual crisis
of the industrial age by recalling a time of moral absolutes and guild communalism, new artistic forms have already emerged to comment on the
accelerated pace of change and new social realities of a post-industrial,
postmodern milieu. Nevertheless, there is some evidence that instead of a
progressive agenda directing sacred architecture, neotraditionalism is
making headway, proof perhaps of Fredric Jameson's claim that "the nostalgia mode" itself is one of the traits of postmodernity.[75] A recent example of reactionary resistance occurred in the summer of 2001, when a
group of Milwaukee Catholics persuaded the Vatican to order their arch-

bishop to halt approved renovations to St. John the Evangelist Cathedral. Although Archbishop Rembert Weakland was able to demonstrate that his opponents misstated his position on liturgical norms as well as the actual nature of the renovations, the episode was a reminder that dissenting conservative factions often exert disproportionate influence and devote immense energies to policing perceived threats to tradition.[76] Conservatives have continued their agitation against contemporary church design, directed now against the American bishops' recently approved directive on sacred art and architecture, "Built of Living Stones."[77]

Despite the laments of Catholic traditionalists, the phase of revolutionary change known as "the modern" never had time to be nurtured properly in Catholicism, and now, a mere forty years after Vatican II, postmodern conservatives (many of whom never experienced the preconciliar church) are demanding a return to "tradition": in liturgy they would revive the Latin Mass; in church design they want to bring back side altars, fixed pews, and rectilinear naves. Critics of a modernist aesthetic for Catholic churches argue that it has contributed to a loss of sensual experience and mystery during Mass and has amplified the rejection of Catholicism's rich artistic heritage.[78] Since Vatican II, Catholic conservatives have advanced what amounts to conspiracy theories in their bashing of modernism's "totalizing" control of contemporary sacred architecture.[79] It seems that the real target of their frustration, however, is "modernistic" art of often poor or mediocre quality that has been produced for parishes in the last forty years.[80] This says more about the lack of a vital support for the arts among postconciliar Catholics than it does about Vatican II.

Proponents of Vatican II's liturgical norms maintain that the relatively uncluttered appearance of contemporary church interiors highlights essential liturgical elements that the Council had agreed upon: the non-hierarchical space unifying priest and people rather than segregating them into choir and nave, bread and wine, altar and pulpit. Because the longitudinal aisle plan of former centuries no longer worked well with the participatory post-Vatican II liturgy, circles, semicircles, and fan shapes became popular as alternatives. Perhaps the simplest way to denote the change that occurred in thinking about Catholic church design before and after Vatican II was that the former conceived of churches as *forms*, whereas the latter imagines sacred architecture as *space*. The most difficult aspect of the shift, though, has been to produce a change in lay Catholic opinion about the meaning of tradition.

Compounded with that, a different set of forces is needed today to build religious community, which can no longer be taken for granted as synonymous with one's parish and neighborhood. Ethnographic scholarship continues to reveal how city life has changed and continues to change in the United States since the nineteenth-century era of immigration, within which Catholic citizens comprise just one among many religious groups striving to maintain what they have while making room for newcomers. The fading of white ethnicity, the naming of "postethnic" identity, the arrival of non-European immigrants, and the shrinking presence of churches as part of urban fabric all suggest that Boston will have to contend with this new set of social factors. Equally significant has been the recognition (among historians at least) that, in American historiography, ethnic conflict has often displaced discussion of class conflict, thereby constantly deferring analysis of the real sources of inequality and discontent in the United States while focusing instead on friction between immigrant factions. While the parish still remains the cherished focal point of American Catholic experience, urban congregations now possess demographic and economic profiles as diverse as the cities themselves. In this context, the symbolic premium of Irish American identity may decline, Gothic architecture is unlikely to experience yet another revival, fewer new churches are likely to be built, and the reform of aesthetic values loses out as a favored cause of patrician intellectuals. Perhaps the greatest dilemma now facing church architects and Catholic parishes concerns the fluid and indefinite nature of contemporary "community." If, as sociologists speculate, community is no longer a product of geography but of experience, then the very buildings within which people strive to make religious community a reality may begin to make changes to reflect that situation.

Seventy years ago in the heyday of Mayor Curley, Archbishop O'Connell, and Charles Maginnis, one sees an earlier stage in the history of Catholic notions of community. Then, community was dominated by white Irish Catholics and tied securely to the neighborhood and parish boundaries of Boston. Social opportunities for Irish Americans seemed boundless, Catholics made convincing gains toward social and economic parity with Protestants in New England, and the demand for more churches grew. In some cases, the conservatism and organicism of Gothic worked hand-in-hand with the forces of industrial and corporate capitalism that had helped assimilate Irish Catholics. At other times, the values of the Middle Ages seemed impossibly at odds with the traits attributed to the modern metropolis: "improbability, multifunctionality, multiplicity, and lack of organic structure."[81] Across the decades one can imagine the shared appeal among Catholics for Maginnis's imagining of the medieval age as a time when "The glories of the past have been magically visualized to us, revealing the glamour of the days when Art was the handmaid of Religion, when the hands and imaginations of genius were busy in God's service."[82] But one also hopes that Catholic nostalgia for that era of ethnoreligious vigor does not stifle necessary change in the present.

NOTES

1. Kevin Lynch, an urban planner and writer, used the term "cognitive mapping" in his seminal book, *The Image of the City* (Cambridge, Mass., 1960). He defined cognitive maps as essential and necessary tools that people use to orient themselves in cities, as constituted by five elements: paths, edges, landmarks, nodes, and districts. Lynch used Boston as his initial example. For my more limited purposes, Catholic Bostonians certainly relied upon their notions of paths, nodes, and districts in thinking about the urban environment and the function of churches within it.

2. Paula M. Kane, *Separatism and Subculture: Boston Catholicism, 1900-1920* (Chapel Hill, 1994).

3. See Robert S. Ellwood, *The Fifties Spiritual Marketplace* (New Brunswick, 1997); and Christopher Owen Lynch, *Selling Catholicism: Bishop Sheen and the Power of Television* (Lexington, 1998).

4. Mark S. Massa, *Catholics and American Culture: Fulton Sheen, Dorothy Day, and the Notre Dame Football Team* (New York, 1999), 8-9.

5. Peter W. Williams, *Houses of God: Region, Religion, and Architecture in the United States* (Urbana, 1997), 180. See also Williams, "The Medieval Heritage in American Religious Architecture," in *Medievalism in American Culture*, ed. Bernard Rosenthal and Paul E. Szarmach (Binghampton, 1989), 171-191.

6. Even "finished" buildings are subject to constant remaking: "Moreover, all buildings are, to an important degree, perpetually under construction; never are they 'done' in the sense of fixing and fully stabilizing their meanings.... The idea of the fully finished building is a fiction that cannot be sustained." Linsday Jones, *The Hermeneutics of Sacred Architecture* (Cambridge, 2000), 263.

7. I am revisiting *Separatism and Subculture* particularly in light of three recent studies of urban religion: Robert Orsi, ed., *Gods of the City* (Bloomington, 1999); Gerald Gamm, *Urban Exodus: Why the Jews Left Boston and the Catholics Stayed* (Cambridge, Mass., 1999); and R. Stephen Warner and Judith G. Wittner, eds., *Gathering in Diaspora: Religious Communities and the New Immigration* (Philadelphia, 1998).

8. See Augustus Pugin, *The True Principles of Pointed or Christian Architecture* (1841; London, 1853), and *An Apology for the Revival of Christian Architecture in England* (London, 1843).

9. In part this blending of low-church Protestantism and Romanism came about because of Ruskin's personal spiritual struggles. As a young man he denied any influence of Pugin as he tried to rescue Gothic for the low-church tradition. He then went through an agnostic and atheist phase, before returning to Christian belief (though not Roman Catholic), after an experience at a spiritualist séance in 1875.

10. Pugin's account of the horrendous conditions of contemporary workhouses undoubtedly resonated strongly with the Irish during the Famine decades, when they were frequently forced into English workhouses that often caused death from malnutrition and disease.

11. See the helpful essay by Richard Guy Wilson, "American Arts and Crafts Architecture: Radical though Dedicated to the Cause Conservative," in "*The Art that is Life*": *The Arts and Crafts Movement in America, 1875-1920*, ed. Wendy Kaplan (Boston, 1987), 101-131.

12. See Dick Hebdige, *Subculture, the Meaning of Style* (London, 1979); and Sarah Thornton, *Club Cultures: Music, Media, and Subcultural Capital* (Hanover, N.H., 1996).

13. See Michele H. Bogart, *Public Sculpture and the Civic Ideal in New York City, 1890-1930* (Washington, D.C., 1997).

14. Magali Sarfatti Larson, *Behind the Postmodern Façade: Architectural Change in Late-Twentieth-Century America* (Berkeley, 1993), 21.

15. George Germann, *Gothic Revival in Europe and Britain: Sources, Influences and Ideas* (Cambridge, Mass., 1972), 188.

16. Kerby Miller, *Emigrants and Exiles: Ireland and the Irish Exodus to North America* (New York and Oxford, 1985).

17. As reported in Thomas Day, *Why Catholics Can't Sing* (New York, 1990), 20. The inability to express Catholicism publicly in Ireland led to a subdued liturgy without processions, hymns, instruments, or church bells.

18. Quoted in Leon B. Litvack, "Songs and Hymns of Irish migration," in *Religion and Identity*, ed. Patrick O'Sullivan (London and New York, 1996), 72-73.

19. See, for instance, the superb biography by James O'Toole, *Militant and Triumphant: William Henry O'Connell and the Catholic Church in Boston, 1859-1944* (Notre Dame, Ind., 1992).

20. Day, *Why Catholics Can't Sing*, 23.

21. Cram's impact is summarized by Richard Guy Wilson, "Ralph Adams Cram: Dreamer of the Medieval," in *Medievalism in American Culture*, 193-214.

22. Thomas O'Connor, *Bibles, Brahmins and Bosses*, 2d ed. rev. (Boston, 1984), 145.

23. William O'Connell, *Sermons and Addresses*, 11 vols. (Boston, 1911-1938), 3:121-139.

24. Charles Maginnis, "Movement for a Vital Christian Architecture and the Obstacles— the Roman Catholic View," *Christian Art* 1(1907):25.

25. Timothy Walsh, from a leading Catholic family of Cambridge, had already studied drawing in the Paris ateliers and had worked in the Boston offices of Peabody and Stearns by the time he joined Maginnis.

26. As of 1999, St. Aidan in Brookline was closed because of its dwindling congregation, but activists are mobilizing to preserve the church for its architectural and historical merit (John F. Kennedy was baptized there in 1917). Douglass Shand-Tucci, "Beyond Bricks: Is There a Spiritual Value to Inspired Architecture?" *Boston Phoenix*, June 3-10, 1999.

27. Shand-Tucci calls Maginnis "perhaps the most gifted follower" of Cram. "Beyond Bricks."

28. Charles D. Maginnis, "Catholic Church Architecture," *Architectural Forum* 27(1917):37. Architects debated the perfect style for the American parish church. Some upheld the English "village" church as the model for America, although these charming rural stone structures did not always conform to the limitations of urban sites.

29. Douglass Shand-Tucci, *Boston Bohemia, 1881-1900: Ralph Adams Cram: Life and Architecture* (Amherst, 1995). For a discussion of Cram's anticapitalist sentiments, see Robert Muccigrosso, *American Gothic: The Mind and Art of Ralph Adams Cram* (Washington, D.C., 1980).

30. Charles Maginnis, memoirs, 10, Charles Donagh Maginnis papers [microfilm], Archives of American Art/ Smithsonian Institution, Washington D.C. [hereafter AAA/SI].

31. Kane, *Separatism and Subculture*, 143.

32. Maginnis, "Catholic Church Architecture," 33.

33. The phrase comes from a sermon by O'Connell in *Sermons and Addresses*, 3:397.

34. Interestingly enough, the rectory at Boston College was by Louis Weissbein, a German Jew who designed the first Temple Israel.

35. David Morgan helps explain this anomaly by noting that in the age of mass mechanical reproduction, Protestants began to reconsider their distaste for and fear of the highly visual world, long associated with popery and antidemocratic values. Following this radical shift in their visual piety, Protestants filled their churches with Gothic iconography, stained glass, ornate altars, screens, and baptismal fonts. Morgan, *Protestants and Pictures: Religion, Visual Culture, and the Age of American Mass Production* (New York, 1999).

36. John B. Pastorak, *Sermons for Forty Hours Devotion* (St. Louis, 1949), 204. The heyday of Forty Hours devotion was the 1940s and 1950s, in conjunction with movements to get Catholics to receive Communion more frequently than the once per year that had been required since the year 1215. In 1905, Pius X urged more frequent reception and lowered the age of first communion from about 12 to 6 or 7, but it was slow to take effect. Not until Vatican II did frequent communion become a prized property of the laity.

37. As Catholic apologists of the early to mid twentieth century saw it, no matter how grand your architecture, how educated your builders, without the Real Presence of Christ housed in your tabernacle, Protestants and others had nothing more than a hall or a meetinghouse. The tabernacle was the focal point of much Catholic ritual behavior that characterized lived religion of the devotional subculture. It was the heyday of perpetual adoration societies, of Holy Name Societies dedicated to prevent swearing and blasphemy against the Lord's name, of Forty Hours eucharistic devotions and novenas.

38. Jean Halgren Kilde, "Architecture and Urban Revivalism in Nineteenth-Century America," in *Perspectives on American Religion and Culture*, ed. Peter W. Williams (Oxford, 1999), 174-186.

39. Kilde, "Architecture and Urban Revivalism," 183.

40. Kilde, "Architecture and Urban Revivalism," 184.

41. Maginnis, "Catholic Church Architecture," 35.

42. An excellent discussion of the professionalization of architecture appears in Larson, *Behind the Postmodern Façade*, chap. 1.

43. Maginnis, "Catholic Church Architecture," 36.

44. Italian surnames do not begin to appear in significant numbers as church architects until after 1950. From the list maintained at the Boston Public Library, some examples include Bossi, Caputo, Caruso, Cascieri, Cuneo, D'Orsi, and Pasqualucci and Sons.

45. Maginnis, memoirs, 69-70, Maginnis papers, AAA/SI.

46. Maginnis, memoirs, 70, Maginnis papers, AAA/SI.

47. Kane, *Separatism and Subculture*, 134.

48. See Margaret Floyd Henderson, ed., *Architectural Education and Boston: Centennial Publication of the Boston Architectural Center, 1889-1989* (Boston, 1989).

49. Maginnis, memoirs, 27, Maginnis papers, AAA/SI.

50. "The emergence of Catholic consciousness about architectural styles emerged only with its middle class and with the firmer financial footing of the second and third generation removed from immigration." Maginnis, memoirs, 126, Maginnis papers, AAA/SI.

51. Maginnis, "Catholic Church Architecture," 34. The situation of Catholics had improved again by 1950, when MIT invited an Italian Catholic, Pietro Belluschi, to be dean of architecture and urban planning, a position he held between 1951 and 1965. Internationally known as a designer of religious buildings, especially in the Pacific northwest, Belluschi became a popular lecturer on the question of style and liturgical reform in churches. Ultimately, although Belluschi was a committed modernist, the more orthodox modernists of eastern establishment regarded his defense of traditional symbols and associations in church design as "soft" and not intellectual enough. Meredith L. Clausen, *Spiritual Space: The Religious Architecture of Pietro Belluschi* (Seattle, 1992), 23.

52. Maginnis, "Catholic Church Architecture," 37.

53. Wojciech G. Lesnikowski, *Rationalism and Romanticism in Architecture* (New York, 1982), 158-159.

54. Charles Maginnis, "Recent Roman Catholic Architecture," *Proceedings of the Boston Society of Architects* (Boston, 1909), 9.

55. Such as Gamm, *Urban Exodus*, and *The Jews of Boston*, ed. Jonathan D. Sarna and Ellen Smith (Boston, 1995).

56. An excellent treatment of the nature of the parochial school and its relationship with the public school system appears in James W. Sanders, "Catholics and the School Question in Boston: The Cardinal O'Connell Years," in *Catholic Boston: Studies in Religion and Community, 1870-1970*, ed. Robert E. Sullivan and James M. O'Toole (Boston, 1985).

57. On the features of Catholic piety, see Thomas E. Wangler, "Catholic Religious Life in Boston in the Era of Cardinal O'Connell," in *Catholic Boston*, 239-272.

58. Kane, *Separatism and Subculture*, 122.

59. Gamm, *Urban Exodus*, 93.

60. Gamm, *Urban Exodus*, 126.

61. Gamm's perspective is shared by Lindsay Jones: "both the synagogue's visual appearance and mode of construction (or expropriation of previous structures) were largely inconsequential so long as the congregation was, in the end, afforded a safe interior space in which to study the Torah, pray, and foster a sense of community in diaspora." *Hermeneutics of Sacred Architecture*, 269. A different perspective is offered by David Kauffman, "Temples in the American Athens: A History of the Synagogues of Boston," in *The Jews of Boston*, 167-207.

62. Kauffman, "Temples," 202. Gamm's claim may be more aptly directed at the practice of some Orthodox congregations of converting existing houses into synagogues (known as *shtibls*) without much concern for architectural style. Kauffman, "Temples," 200.

63. Kauffman, "Temples," 176.

64. Today the building is the Morse Auditorium at Boston University. Kauffman, "Temples," 177.

65. Kauffman, "Temples," 197-198.

66. Gamm, *Urban Exodus*, 239.

67. Gamm, *Urban Exodus*, 239.

68. I have written about the dilemma of church architecture and sacred space for modernity and postmodernity in "Is that a Beer Vat under the Baldochino?: From Antimodernism to Postmodernism in Catholic Sacred Architecture," *U.S. Catholic Historian* 15(1997):1-32.

69. Pietro Belluschi, "Report on Project for Catholic Church Submitted by the Catholic Diocese of Portland," 1936, Belluschi Collection, George Arents Research Library, Syracuse University. Like Maginnis, Belluschi published thoughtful articles throughout his career, reflecting upon the challenge of contemporary architecture to churches. A sampling includes "An Architect's Challenge," *Architectural Forum* 91(1949):72; "Architecture To-Day: A Symposium," *Liturgical Arts* 19(1950):21; "The Modern Church—or Traditional?" *New York Times Magazine*, Mar. 14, 1954.

70. Susan J. White, *Art, Architecture, and Liturgical Reform* (New York, 1990), 154.

71. This is the well-known thesis of Will Herberg in *Protestant, Catholic, Jew* (Garden City, N.Y., 1955), in which membership in one of those religious traditions constitutes a valid form of Americanism as well as a compromise of former ethnic identifications.

72. On new demographics of Boston see Thomas H. O'Connor, *Boston Catholics: A History of the Church and Its People* (Boston, 1999). For national examples of urban religious diversity, see the essays in Orsi, *Gods of the City*.

73. According to the *Boston Catholic Directory* (2000), in the city of Boston proper 15 parishes have been suppressed and/or merged. I thank Boston's Archdiocesan Archivist Robert Johnson-Lally for his assistance with statistics.

74. One example is St. Leo, Dorchester (1902), which was suppressed in June 1999 and "relegated to profane use" in July 1999.

75. Fredric Jameson, "Postmodernism, or the Cultural Logic of Late Capitalism," *New Left Review* 146(July-Aug. 1984):53-92.

76. "Weakland Asked to Stop Cathedral Renovations," *America*, June 18-25, 2001.

77. The directive, approved in 2000, is available online from the National Council of Catholic Bishops at www.nccbuscc.org/liturgy/livingstonesind.htm. The document is

significant as the first set of guidelines presented in over 20 years, since the publication of "Environment and Art in Catholic Worship" in 1978, which it replaces but does not override.

78. From a gendered perspective, feminists have targeted the masculinist preoccupation of post-Vatican II design insofar as it privileged abstraction and rationality in an attempt to eliminate the "feminine" clusters of statues and pastel-painted interiors of the previous century.

79. This position is represented by the journal *Sacred Architecture* (Notre Dame, Ind.), which includes traditionalist commentators who attack the major documents guiding the understanding of Catholic liturgy, "Environment and Art in Catholic Worship" (1978) and the latest document, "Built of Living Stones" (2000).

80. See Kane, "Is that a Beer Vat under the Baldochino?"

81. Manfredo Tafuri, *Architecture and Utopia* (Cambridge, Mass., 1976), 124.

82. Maginnis, "Movement for a Vital Christian Architecture," 24.

No More the Faith of Our Fathers

Immigrant Converts and Boston-Area Churches, 1890–1940

KRISTEN A. PETERSEN

> *My parents were Lutheran to start with. When my father [Joseph Sundin] was a young man he played organ for the [Swedish] Lutheran Church in Waltham, but to go to that church he had to walk a long way and cross the Charles River. He became interested in Beth Eden Baptist, because he liked the minister and it was in our neighborhood. He wanted me to be able to walk to church and to Sunday school. If you're Lutheran in the old country and you go through what I just described, it makes sense to change churches—we're all Protestants, after all. It's not like that great leap to Catholicism.[1]*
>
> —LILLIAN SUNDIN SHIRLEY

HEN JOSEPH SUNDIN arrived in Waltham, a small industrial center located ten miles west of Boston, he found several hundred Swedish families settled there. Despite the relatively small number of Swedes in a city dominated by Irish, Italians, and French-speaking Canadians from the Maritime provinces, there was no single, cohesive Swedish community. There were two Swedish churches, one Lutheran and the other a Free Church (later Covenant Congregational). The former was the state church, the latter a dissenting sect that was rapidly gaining momentum both at home and in the U.S. The members of these congregations worked in different factories and appear to have maintained social distance.[2] Waltham's case was by no means atypical for U.S. cities. Scholars have reported similar patterns among Swedes in Worcester, Italians in Boston's North End, and Germans in Boston.[3]

The phenomenon of an ethnic community religiously bifurcated into distinct subcommunities contradicts generations of scholarship that embraces a very different model of the immigrant ethnic community. The prevailing model posits a cohesive community either centered around or anchored by one church traditional to the group. To historian Marcus Hansen, the trauma of uprooting compelled immigrants to use religion to "provide group stability in the face of the bewildering new array of choices and the absence of traditional institutions of control."[4] Thus they recreated homeland churches and residential enclaves in order to shape a space in America that was familiar and safe. Hansen and other historians argue that immigrants turned to the faith of their fathers and mothers to achieve this stability and security. Since the majority of this scholarship examines Catholics, the model has encountered little contradiction, even from scholars researching Protestants or homelands with a tradition of multiple religions.

The case of Joseph Sundin suggests the possibility of an alternative model of immigrant communities and religion in the U.S. Immigrants from some nations carried divergent religious affiliations; some, such as Sundin, transferred their religious affiliations once in the U.S. These religious changes were defined by the need to adjust the role of religion to accommodate new social and cultural circumstances. In the immigrant context, conversion is inextricably linked to the process of becoming American.

Changes in an immigrant's religious affiliation did not necessarily qualify as "conversion" as described by William James at the turn of the last century.[5] While his model of conversion as a spiritual awakening dominated discourse throughout much of the twentieth century, recent scholarship identifies more complex patterns.[6] Some sociologists now "defin[e] conversion as a change in religious community."[7] The transformations described in this article reflect choices motivated by the need to resolve practical issues of cultural environment, geography, language, love, community, and poverty. Because Lillian Sundin Shirley's description of her family's change in affiliation encompasses many of the major factors that intersected to compel a conversion, her father's story provides the framework of the following narrative.

My parents were Lutheran to start with.

Lillian Sundin Shirley's parents came to Massachusetts from Sweden in the 1890s. They joined other Swedes in Waltham following a typical chain migration pattern. As members of the Lutheran State Church, they initially sought membership in Waltham's Swedish Lutheran Church. As at home, First Lutheran served as the organizing center of the Swedish community. Everyone was welcomed into—indeed, expected to join— the First Lutheran Church. But those who came to Waltham, Boston, Worcester, Quincy, and other New England immigrant centers had other choices of where they went to worship in their native language. Many who were disenchanted with the Church of Sweden for political or theological reasons or who had joined Free Churches or Mission Covenant churches prior to emigrating changed their affiliations once in the U.S.[8] Here, Episcopal, Baptist, Congregationalist, and Methodist missionaries organized churches in every significant Swedish settlement. Nonetheless, immigrants who left the faith of heritage, such as the Sundins, have been overlooked by historians; their stories are not a part of the typical ethnic-group biography found in either immigration or urban historiography.

Historians have long agreed that most immigrants maintained traditional church affiliations after arrival in the U.S. In the archetypal experience of pre-1965, immigrants came to the U.S., settled in congested neighborhoods, and created ethnic enclaves, the social and religious center of which was a church. But churches—infused with the spirit of a people who were becoming something new in the U.S.—were more than spiritual sites or community centers. As immigrants' ethnic identities developed, the churches—with their dual mission as a place of worship and as a place to preserve and celebrate community and old-world culture— became natural homes for the characteristics and sensibilities that comprised the group's ethnic identity. The church reinforced the cultural and linguistic barriers of the enclave, protecting immigrants from the American mainstream, allowing for cultural retention, and slowing the assimilation and Americanization processes.

For Italian immigrants the religiocultural home was a Catholic church. For Swedes it was a Lutheran church. Because this model does not allow for deviation, however, it inadequately addresses the relationship of ethnic sensibility and religion when an immigrant people are divided *at home* by religion and carry that distinction to the U.S., as with Boston's Germans, who arrived in the mid nineteenth century and established both a Catholic church and a Lutheran church. The model also excludes immigrants who left their old world churches and joined American Protestant missions, through which they created unique ethnoreligious communities. Still, the model endures.[9]

Historians also give considerable significance to the fact that a sizable percentage of immigrants of all national origins joined no churches in the U.S. This simple point makes it all the more apparent that the model fails to represent the totality and complexity of the immigrant experience. Because not everyone affiliated with traditional churches upon arrival, despite the efforts of transnational religious institutions to retain them, those new arrivals encountered two novel religious options: proselytism by American Protestant organizations and the nation's commitment to freedom to worship (or not). Immigrants found that in American cities and towns they could choose where and how to worship.

In the Boston area, as in most other immigrant centers in the United States, newcomers exhibited several patterns of religious affiliation. Some came as members of dissenting sects formed in the old country; they were seeking the freedom to worship as they chose. Italian Waldensians and Swedish Covenant Congregationalists exemplified this trend as it occurred from the 1870s through the early decades of the twentieth century. Immigrants also had at least three other religious experiences. For example, some attended the nearby church with a liturgy and style that best matched those of the church of heritage or with religious services available in their language. Other immigrants were befriended by missionaries or pastors of unfamiliar neighborhood churches and chose for a variety of reasons to affiliate with a new faith—to convert. Finally, of the immigrants in these latter two categories, some failed to commit to any new faith and changed affiliations several times during their lifetimes, maybe even deciding to return to their original communion.

Many of Boston's newcomers exemplified the traditional model of immigrant religion since they maintained a connection with their home cultures by joining the local church of the same denomination that they had left behind in Europe. For example, when Italians and other Catholic immigrants arrived in the U.S., they were automatically absorbed into the local Roman Catholic church. Similarly, Lutheran immigrants who arrived in the late nineteenth and early twentieth centuries found Lutheran synods well established and positioned to aid in the construction of new churches. Religious transnationalism characterized by the international Roman Catholic church and by the Lutheran Church of Sweden, both of which retained members regardless of their place of residence, took on other forms late in the nineteenth century. For example, Baptist, Methodist, and Congregational foreign mission work in immigrant-sending countries in Europe and Asia introduced potential migrants to American forms of Protestantism. In addition, return migrations of converts contributed to the spread of American Protestantism abroad.

In Boston, the Roman Catholic Church and the Church of Sweden (Lutheran) demonstrated the burgeoning transnationalism of European-origin religious institutions in different ways. Because both the Vatican and the Swedish government regarded the United States as a mission field, emigrants theoretically remained under their respective authority. Rome resolved the problem of growing communities of non-English-speaking Catholics in the U.S. by creating the national parish, which existed conceptually, uniting people by culture across geographic boundaries. Catholic parish territories and memberships had long been determined by geography; national parishes differed from typical urban parishes because membership was based on ethnicity (really defined by language) rather than address. The national parish also kept all Catholics, regardless of ethnic origin, under the umbrella of the American church hierarchy, precluding the splintering of American Catholicism into many synod-like groupings. There would be one Church in the U.S.; there would not be a German Catholic Church structure and an Italian Catholic Church with independent relationships to one another and to Rome. By 1925 national or ethnic parishes accounted for fully one-fourth of all the Catholic churches in the Archdiocese of Boston. In the absence of a convenient national parish, Catholics could attend the appropriate neighborhood Catholic church, although the language barrier often impeded full participation.

The Church of Sweden counted all Swedes as members, including emigrants. Maintenance of missions to Swedish immigrants and sailors at Boston's docks was only one way in which the Church retained contact with and supervision over citizens who traveled and lived abroad. Nonetheless, in the event that a Swede found him- or herself somewhere lacking a Lutheran presence, the Church approved an alternative. As early as the 1850s, the Church of Sweden instructed emigrants to "join

Episcopal churches where there were no Lutherans around."[10] In the early twentieth century, American Episcopalians took advantage of this long-standing arrangement and incorporated it into their mission outreach. For example, Boston Episcopalians urged Swedes to join St. Ansagarius' Episcopal Church in Boston because, as they claimed, it was the closest thing to the Church of Sweden (Lutheran).[11]

Despite the options available to immigrants, many of Boston's church pews remained empty on Sunday mornings. Studies of Swedish and Italian immigrants in the United States support the claim that large numbers of each group remained unaffiliated. In his investigation of American Swedes, George Stephenson found that "in proportion to the total Swedish population, church members were greatly in the minority. . . . [T]he mass of the immigrants were nominal Lutherans with a leaven of pietists."[12] The Episcopal Diocese of Boston offered two reasons why "a very large percent" of the 10,000 Swedes in the city at the turn of the century did not join any church. First, their experience as members of a state church made them take it for granted. The church existed whether they supported it or not; they did not have to work to create or maintain a place of worship. Second, an uneasy tradition preceded them. Previous immigrants who arrived and found no familiar place to worship or no place to worship in their own language simply remained unaffiliated. This was especially true of young immigrants who had not yet made the commitment to remain in the U.S. permanently.

Proselytizing institutions used such data to justify their mission work. As early as 1917, Protestants who surveyed East Coast Italians determined that most were marginal Catholics if they considered themselves members of the Church at all. Antonio Mangano, himself a convert to the American Methodist Episcopal Church, reported that "Ninety-nine per cent. of the Italians landing on our shores would give the Roman Church as their religious belief, but if questioned a large number would add that they were not faithful to its celebrations nor its services, except perhaps at times of births, deaths, and marriages."[13] Mangano's account of Italian immigrants' departures from the Catholic Church found corroboration later in the century. In a 1939 study of Italian Americans, John V. Tolino found that of six million Italian Americans residing in the United States just two million were "good Catholics," while one million lived "entirely outside" the Catholic Church and claimed to have had no religious instruction. The remaining three million identified themselves as marginal

Catholics. He concluded from his data that "the large majority of Italo-Americans have little or no connection with the church."[14]

Failure to affiliate was especially true of unmarried male immigrants.[15] Single men were less likely to join a traditional church community than were men with families. Unmarried men, however, or men who were in this country without their families, were susceptible to conversion because of their isolation from the social mores, familial expectations, and civic and religious pressures (and laws) that tied them to their churches at home. Indeed, some of the most consistent mission work emerged in Chinatown, which was for all intents and purposes a bachelor community throughout the decades of this study. Female missionaries in Boston logged long hours teaching Chinese men English and offering Sunday School classes. Not only were missionaries welcomed into Chinese workplaces, but the missionaries found that many of the converts became active proselytizers among their own people both in Boston and at home. Italian men in Boston who converted to Protestantism tended to be active and regular church members. The Italian Congregational Church in the North End was the denomination's only church in Boston and the only church of any confession in the North End in which male members outnumbered females.[16]

Boston's South End exemplifies the general state of immigrant affiliations during the first quarter of the twentieth century. Morgan Memorial, a Methodist Episcopal church located in that ethnically and religiously diverse neighborhood, conducted surveys in 1915 and 1923 to determine the

TABLE 1. Boston's South End: Ethnic Composition and Church Affiliation, 1915[17]

Nationalities	Percent with Protestant Connection	Percent Unaffiliated with any Religious Body
Jewish	.9	39.5
Italian	2.0	13.2
Irish	5.3	5.8
Syrian	3.5	4.2
American	32.7	14.4
"Colored"	26.9	4.9
Greek	1.2	2.4

Source: Community Survey of Morgan Memorial Parish Boston

religious status of the parish's residents. As Table 1 shows, both Jews and Italians, the predominant immigrant groups in the South End during this period, preferred to remain unaffiliated rather than join Morgan Memorial's Church of All Nations or any other Protestant church. The question, then, may not have been about finding the right religious affiliation. Some people apparently preferred not to attend religious services or join a church community at all.

In Boston, and throughout New England's other immigrant centers, newcomers experienced the freedom to choose whether and where to affiliate. Boston offered an especially complex ethnoreligious landscape. Italians, for example, had plenty of national parish options within the Archdiocese of Boston, but many chose not to join a Catholic church at all. Others found something appealing, comforting, or relevant in one of the city's many Protestant missions. As newcomers settled down, their processes of identity and community formation were peculiar to the immigrant experience. Here, they became Italians rather than Genoese or Calabrese. Here, the archdiocese helped them to organize socially and culturally through national parishes, creating new ethnoreligious communities based on linguistic and cultural similarities that segregated them from mainstream American Catholics. The process of settling down also brought with it negotiations of identity, needs, and desires that shaped the cohesiveness of the group. And each individual had to decide whether traditional ethnoreligious communities offered solutions to the many issues life in America presented. Immigrants learned to strategize in very individual ways the best path to survival and success in this new environment. For many, the role of religion and the selection of an organization to affiliate with played a part in the development of a strategy. Immigrants had choices, and one of the factors that compelled them to exercise their options was access.

When my father was a young man he played organ for the [Swedish] Lutheran Church in Waltham, but to go to that church he had to walk a long way and cross the Charles River.

Joseph Sundin was attracted to the Boston suburb of Waltham by employment opportunities at the Waltham Watch Company. Other Swedes worked at the company as well as at the Boston Manufacturing Company (BMC), a textile mill downriver. When he arrived in Waltham in 1898, the city's Swedish population was divided into two churches: First Lutheran (established in 1889) and the Swedish Covenant Congregational Church (established in 1888 as the Swedish Free Mission Church).[18] The latter congregation was organized by employees of the BMC and located in that neighborhood. Joseph Sundin lived in the vicinity of the Watch Company, and he met his wife in a boardinghouse that catered to the factory's Swedish employees. After they married, they built a house near the Watch Company. That South Side neighborhood had many churches but none that was ethnic or immigrant. The Sundins' new home was a stone's throw from Beth Eden Baptist Church, whose pastor and congregation were committed to mission outreach among the neighborhood's burgeoning immigrant population.

For many immigrant converts, convenience provided a compelling reason to change religious affiliation. For those ethnic communities in the Boston area that remained relatively small—such as those of Scandinavians, Germans, Poles, and Lithuanians—it was often difficult to find a church of heritage within walking distance of their place of residence. This problem plagued the first waves of immigrants to arrive in the Boston area; it was up to them to lay the groundwork for the ethnoreligious communities that they and subsequent immigrants would build. The organizational boom among Boston's Germans occurred by the 1840s, while Scandinavians took root in the 1880s. For Poles and Lithuanians, who arrived after 1890, the struggle to build churches endured through the 1920s. The influx of Irish after 1850 accounted for the growth of the Archdiocese of Boston in the nineteenth century.

Once established in specific neighborhoods, churches could appeal powerfully to a new community's need for social connectedness and cultural presence. They organized people into communities, they nurtured ethnic languages and cultures, they gave their members a cultural and spiritual center, and they provided an institutional structure through which immigrants networked with others of their faith and ethnicity. Churches also made statements by their locations and architectural styles. The church was "the religious center of the neighborhood," as Jay Dolan described, even as it was the conceptual organizing site of the community. As such, the edifice announced an ethnoreligious community's existence and made a statement of permanence to both insiders and outsiders. In Boston, with the construction of each new Catholic church, the archdiocese asserted to Catholics and to Protestants alike that the Church was strong and growing, claiming more territory for the faith. Kathleen Conzen recalled her epiphany that a Milwaukee Catholic church was "not just a building but a declaration of war. Here in stone was documented a clash of spiritual mentalities, of alternative conceptions of cultural integration, of competing visions of the place of religion in the secular order of this frontier city."[19]

Catholic churches remained fixtures of both the physical and social landscape long after congregants left. Indeed, as Gerald Gamm found in his study of Catholics and Jews in Boston, national parishes stabilized immigrant groups geographically and encouraged long-term maintenance of ethnic communities in those neighborhoods. However, as the children and grandchildren of the first generation moved out, the churches built by and for the immigrants faced the dilemma of filling the emptying pews and retaining contact with former members. Catholic churches did not move with the people.[20] Some of the faithful attended nearby mainstream Catholic churches in their new neighborhoods even though there was no priest to hear confession or preach in their native languages. For example, Lithuanians in Waltham attended a local Catholic church except for special occasions or holidays, when they took the train to South Boston to attend the Lithuanian Catholic church.[21]

The city's Protestant missions and immigrant-convert churches had a different relationship to the people and to the landscape. Some were neighborhood mission-campaign anchors, such as the Boston Baptist Bethel in the North End and Morgan Memorial in the South End. Pastors affiliated with these institutions reported year after year that transience constituted a major problem for their development and financial strength.[22] More often than not, immigrants who converted in one of these churches moved on within a few years and settled in a new community and a new church. Other convert churches, such as the First Swedish Baptist Church (now Calvary Baptist Church of Dorchester), changed homes from four to six times before merging, closing, or settling permanently near their respective members in the suburbs.

In other cases, Protestants identified potential mission fields when they discovered new immigrant communities, such as among Italians in Hyde Park and West Quincy. They then sent either a missionary or a pastor who spoke the appropriate language to establish a mission church. For example, when the Malvesta family moved into West Quincy there was no Italian-speaking priest nearby and no national parish to serve the area's growing Italian population.²³ A neighbor told them about a nearby Baptist church that had an Italian pastor, who, with the help of a Swedish missionary, had organized neighborhood Italians into a community. The Malvestas, and many other immigrants who settled in areas in which they were isolated from their traditional ethnoreligious communities, accepted foreign language-speaking pastors of Protestant mission churches as an alternative to having no religious affiliation at all. Through these convert churches, immigrants were able to retain ethnic traditions and languages as they constructed new ethnoreligious identities and continued on the path to Americanization.

While the immigrant experience loosened traditional religious ties for some newcomers, religious institutions remained an important part of their communities. As immigrants reconstructed families and communities in peculiar American urban environments, they used churches and religious affiliation as just one of many strategies for negotiating both the new sociopolitical, occupational, and religious terrain and the process of assimilation. In so doing, the first generation made choices about how and with whom to affiliate, or they chose not to affiliate at all. Among the many factors contributing to such choices, changing family needs and geographic issues had great influence. The challenge for ethnic churches was to remain culturally relevant for subsequent generations. Members of the second generation made linguistic and cultural demands that compelled ethnic churches to accommodate them along with their parents—constituents from two different worldviews.

When children of immigrants demanded services in English and American-style programs and organizations, they challenged the extent to which traditional ethnic churches served as the embodiment of old-world identity and heritage. For many of their parents, the ethnic church was the one place that would always connect them to the old world, that would, in essence, bring them home each Sunday. The church's ability to survive with its ethnic culture intact reassured parents that they could belong in both worlds. The fact that so many immigrant churches survived into the late twentieth century and continue to celebrate old-world cultural heritage attests to the ability of community leaders to keep an ethnoreligious identity attractive, meaningful, and relevant.

Ultimately, however, the capacity to change churches depended upon access. Convenience, one of the most critical factors in immigrants' decisions to change religious affiliations, took many forms. The Sundins chose

Beth Eden Baptist Church because the pastor opened the church to immigrants, but it was also important that the children had easy access to Sunday School. Likewise, the availability of foreign language-speaking clergy and missionaries introduced immigrants to alternative religious and social affiliations. In addition, clergy and missionaries drew connections between Protestantism and Americanness that appealed to some immigrants' desire for socioeconomic advancement and citizenship. As some immigrant converts have written, these "friendly visitors" embodied America's guarantee of religious liberty. Indeed, many Protestants told immigrants that the proper church affiliation would help them become better Americans and thus grant them access to greater opportunities for socioeconomic advancement.

He became interested in Beth Eden Baptist, because he liked the minister . . .

No family lore exists to elaborate on Joseph Sundin's relationship with the pastor of Beth Eden Baptist Church, but existing church histories and denominational reports suggest that the congregation's pastor and lay leaders gave priority to outreach among immigrants in the community.[24] In Boston, as at Beth Eden, clergy and the women missionaries who worked in immigrant neighborhoods played an important role in both leakage and conversion. Together, clergy and missionaries formed a team of gatherers; home visitors, who were employed by churches and stationed by missionary societies, served as reconnaissance troops. They canvassed neighborhoods, going from tenement to tenement and visiting women in their homes. They shepherded immigrant children into Sunday Schools and mission programs and organized mothers' meetings. From these contacts, immigrants then made their way into the churches, where it was the clergy's job to bring them into membership. Factors influencing a clergyman's success in attracting converts included his longevity in a parish and his sensitivity to the changing needs of the congregation (such as American-born congregants' need for English-language sermons).

Throughout Boston, the churches that boasted the greatest number of converts and the most stable ethnic mission churches were those that had clergy of long tenure. Across Boston, certain priests' tenures were marked by sharp increases in numbers of conversions performed, with sharp declines in conversions evident upon their replacement.[25] Statistical analysis of priests' assignments taken from parish census cards indicates that just 13 percent of priests in the archdiocese served as pastor of more than one parish in their career. Forty percent of priests spent more than ten years in one parish, with the majority of them serving between ten and twenty years. However, the connection between longevity of tenure and conversion rates is not as clear-cut as some of the evidence would suggest. For example, four priests whose terms in Roman Catholic parishes were marked by high rates of conversion also served other parishes in which no such escalation occurred (other than an increase in converts in the mid 1930s that took place throughout the archdiocese).[26] Any hypothesis must of course take into account other factors, including the priest's relationship with the congregation and the peculiarities of the new parishes, such as the character of the neighborhood, socioeconomic and ethnic makeup of the congregation, generational mix, and language needs.

Longevity posed a constant problem for Boston's Protestant mission churches, especially during the missions' first decade. Baptists and Methodists staffed such churches with students from area theological schools. Boston University, for example, provided divinity school students to Morgan Memorial in the South End and to other foreign-language Methodist Episcopal churches in Boston. Typically, student preachers remained for only one to three years. The first two pastors of the Italian Mission of the Methodist Episcopal Church of Our Saviour, South Boston, were Boston University seminary students. The first, John Buono, worked with Miss Laura Walker to organize Italians into the church between 1925 and 1927.[27] Stephen Genoitis, a Lithuanian-born student in Boston University's School of Religious Education, preached "an earnest evangelistic message" to South Boston's Lithuanians. He became their pastor when the group organized as a Methodist church in 1922, and he served them for four years, until he graduated from Boston University.[28]

Poor funding plagued of all Boston's immigrant churches. It considerably undermined a church's capacity to retain staffing and clergy. Both native-born Protestants and Catholics expected that eventually the immigrant congregations would become self-supporting; in the interim they assisted with the initial organization. Congregations were expected to raise money in order to rent, purchase, or erect their own buildings. As the new religious communities stabilized and their members achieved stronger socioeconomic footing in the new world, they took on more financial responsibility, including that of funding clergy salaries. Still, ministers could only stay when they were paid. After the organization of Boston's Swedish Congregational Church in 1881, the members called Axel Mellander to be their first pastor. He "remained in Boston only a short time, however, because the congregation was so poor that it was unable to pay the minister's salary and rent a place for worship too."[29] Few of the immigrant churches were self-supporting during their first decades, while many never achieved that status. Protestant missions and churches received steady aid from local churches and city and state home mission societies. The Swedish Congregational Church, for example, obtained a monthly stipend of $25 from the Massachusetts Congregational Home Missionary Society to help pay its pastor's salary.[30] Leakage and conversions were thus affected by a denomination's ability to staff churches with foreign language-speaking clergy and by the churches' ability to pay their pastors and to maintain church buildings on the meager offerings of working-class congregants.

Ethnic origin and language abilities often outweighed denominational particulars in the contest for immigrant souls. Both Protestants and Roman Catholics faced a shortage of clergy who spoke foreign languages. The preferred preacher was a member of the ethnic group's heritage. But Italian, Polish, German, French, or Swedish clergy of any denomination were hard to come by, and Lithuanian, Armenian, Portuguese, Chinese, Norwegian, Finnish, and Danish clergy were even rarer. In some cases church communities with healthy bank accounts were able to send to the old country or to divinity schools in the Midwest for pastors. However, many Protestant denominations accepted clergy ordained by other denominations to serve foreign-speaking congregations rather than give up the mission field. The Reverend Henry Sartorio was a Presbyterian minister in Delaware when he was called to organize North End Italians into an Episcopal mission. This fact necessitated a change in affiliation (for both Sartorio and his wife, Lydia, whose conversion is recorded in the St. Francis of Assisi record books). Sartorio "was admitted as a candidate for Holy Orders and in due time made a priest," reported *The Church Militant*, the Episcopal Diocese's organ.[31] And, interestingly, the next two men to serve that mission began their careers as Baptists. Sartorio's successor in 1921 was his brother-in-law, Baptist minister Henry J. Chiera.[32] East Boston Unitarians stretched even further, hiring a social worker who worked in the neighborhood to lead their Italian mission.[33]

Individual clergy who worked with immigrant converts had magnified roles both as spiritual and community leaders and as negotiators between the immigrant world and the mainstream. This role was in great part due to the fact that convert churches were small and their members were isolated from both their prior ethnoreligious communities (because they converted) and the mainstream culture (because of their lack of familiarity with English and American customs). Some clergy wore more than one hat, such as the Unitarian pastor who was also a social worker or the Methodist minister to Italians in the South End who was also a physician. Not only did clergy organize the parishes, but they also acted as interpreters, housing agents, and employment contacts for immigrant members. The intimacy of the clergy-parishioner relationship thus extended well beyond the spiritual to the secular.

In addition to his function as institutional representative, each clergyman's personal style and interests influenced his reception among immigrants. Any individual's success in this regard may be measured in church growth patterns as printed in denominational annual reports. For example, under the pastorate of Ludwig Petersen, membership in Boston's Norwegian Congregational Church increased dramatically. In his first decade of service, the number of full members increased from 75 to 156. Petersen's significance in attracting new numbers is borne out by his return to the congregation after a twenty-year absence, during which membership was stagnant if not in decline. In his first year back membership began to climb, and during the first three years he welcomed 31 new members on confession of faith, alone.[34] Likewise, Swedish Congregational Church pastor August Eriksen brought in 50 to 60 members a year on confession of faith during his decade of service. Membership rates plummeted upon his departure in 1910 and throughout the tenure of his successor, Charles V. Bowman, but rebounded with the arrival of a new pastor in 1918, Carl O. Swanson.[35]

If a pastor were well liked and respected, he nurtured a devoted following. Francis Debilio, who grew up in the North End's Methodist mission, credited the Reverend Giuseppe Merlino of the Congregational Italian Church of the Evangel for the church's longevity. It was, Debilio declared, "because of the excellent character and sincerity of the minister [that] this work drew its constituency."[36] In another case, Father Carlo Celotto was so popular among Sacred Heart parishioners in the North End that he was even able to attract non-English-speaking Italians from the North End and neighboring towns who had left the Catholic Church. Parishioners praised "his sweet words and nice ways," which "convert[ed] many people, some of whom had not received the Holy Sacraments for about 40 or 50 years."[37]

Conversely, while his primary motivation was to bring people into the church, a clergyman's politics, personal style, or even region of origin could work against him and cause people to withdraw. Catholic records illustrate such factors with the greatest clarity. The most frequently cited complaints against Catholic clergy included the pastor's financial ineptitude or misuse of funds, alleged improper behavior, alcoholism, inability to serve both immigrant and American-born generations, territorial machinations, and involvement in nationalistic or local politics. Many such complaints masked deep-rooted schisms in the parish such as regional prejudices (for example, when the pastor was from northern Italy and the parishioners hailed from the southern provinces).

Clergy in immigrant congregations dealt with increasingly schizophrenic communities. While the founding generation consisted of foreign language-speaking immigrants for whom the church was a linguistic and cultural necessity (if not lifeline), subsequent generations of members had different needs. The question of how to serve both immigrant and American-born congregants plagued—or at least challenged—all clergy in ethnic churches. The case of Father D'Alphonso of the Sacred Heart Italian Catholic Church in the North End illustrates the divisive effect of Americanization in ethnic parish communities. During the summer of 1920 several of his parishioners wrote letters in broken English and in Italian to Cardinal O'Connell complaining that Father D'Alphonso was secretly consorting with the church organist. At the same time that these parishioners decried his morals, D'Alphonso acknowledged to the cardinal his inability to make peace among his congregation. He was, however, making important inroads among the young Italian Americans in his church. D'Alphonso's attention to the needs of American-born congregants, through week-long missions as well as sermons and confessions in English, endeared him to many. But others saw these activities as a threat to the parish's traditional ethnic culture and old-world memory. They used malicious gossip to get the cardinal's attention.

Upon D'Alphonso's departure two years later, members warned the cardinal that without a priest who could (and would) preach in both Italian and English, Sacred Heart would soon lose its young people, and with them the future of the community. "The few old women who go to church will go anyway," wrote parishioner A. Caleri, "but the younger generation [*sic*] tendencies are to strive away from the Catholic Church and run into other religions especially in the North End. . . . [W]hat will become of them?"[38] Fellow parishioner Angelo Bonighi echoed this sentiment: "although we are Italians we are living in the good old USA and we want to bring up our children in the American ways and ideas."[39] Likewise, when asked by the cardinal what Boston's Poles needed in a priest, the pastor of St. Stephen's Church in the North End emphasized the significance of language in immigrant communities and national parishes. "The pastor needed," the Reverend Edward F. McLeod wrote, "is one who speaks Polish for the benefit of the older people—and English for the newer generation, who do not know the Polish language and wish to be known as Americans."[40]

As these examples illustrate, clergy in immigrant churches walked a fine line between the spiritual world and the complicated and evolving social and political cultures of the ethnic peoples they served. They faced another challenge in other religious institutions that sought to draw away their people.

. . . and it was in our neighborhood.

When Joseph Sundin and his wife decided to build a house in Waltham's South Side neighborhood far from the city's two Swedish churches, they made a critical decision regarding their relationship to the religious community of which they had been a part. Before the advent of automobiles, one's primary community institutions and jobs were within walking distance of home. Once ensconced on Robbins Street, the Sundin family found itself in an ethnically mixed working-class neighborhood. While there were no ethnic congregations on the South Side, there were a number of American Protestant churches, including a Salvation Army headquarters. Beth Eden Baptist Church had already committed itself to outreach work in its neighborhood. Although neither family memory nor documentation illustrates how the Sundins came to worship at Beth Eden, it is most likely that the pastor or a missionary assigned to the neighborhood knocked on the door one day and made an introduction.

In Waltham and Boston, as in other American cities, denominations and home mission societies viewed working-class and immigrant neighborhoods as mission fields. Indeed, the term "friendly neighbor," used by

TABLE 2. Churches and Missions to Ethnic Groups in Boston, 1890–1940

Ethnic Group	Baptist	Congregational	Episcopal	Lutheran	Methodist
Armenian	1	2	1		
Chinese	3	1	1		1
Danish				2	1
Finnish				2	
French	1	1			1
German	2			3	2
Greek		1			2
Italian	7	2	2	1	7
Lettish	1				
Lithuanian					1
Norwegian	3	1		2	1
Polish					1
Portuguese	1				1
Swedish	5	2	1	5	1
Syrian	3		1		1
Ukrainian					
Totals:	27	10	6	15	20

Sources: American Baptist Churches of Massachusetts, Yearbook of the American Baptist Churches of Massachusetts (Mass., 1969-present); American Unitarian Association, Unitarian Year Books (Boston, 1901-1940); Archdiocese of Boston, Official Catholic Directory (Boston, 1910-1940); Commission on Boston Methodism, Boston Methodism Survey (Boston, 1914); Francis DeBilio, "Protestant Mission Work among Italians in Boston," in The Episcopal Diocese of Massachusetts, 1784-1984: A Mission to Remember, Proclaim, and Fulfill, ed. Mark J. Duffy (Boston, 1984); Emmet E. Eklund, "Acculturation in the Swedish Lutheran Congregations of the Boston Area, 1867-1930" (Ph.D. diss., Boston Univ., 1964); The General Association of the Congregational Churches of Massachusetts, Minutes of the Annual Meeting with the Statistics (Boston, 1890-1940); Massachusetts Baptist Convention, Annual Reports of the Massachusetts Baptist Convention (Boston, 1890-1940); Massachusetts Baptist Convention, The Massachusetts Baptist Year-Book, containing the annual reports of the Massachusetts Baptist State Societies with Minutes of Proceedings at the

Pentecostal	Roman Catholic	Unitarian	Miscellaneous Protestant	Total
	1			5
	3		3	12
	1	.		4
				2
	1			4
	1		2	10
	1			4
1	6	1	3	30
				1
	1			2
				7
	5		1	7
	1			3
		1	2	17
	1			6
1	1			2
2	23	2	11	116

Anniversaries *(Boston, 1908-1951); Massachusetts Council of Churches, Department of Research and Strategy,* Protestant Ministry to Italian People in Massachusetts *(Boston, 1951); Methodist Episcopal Church—General Conference, Minutes (Boston, 1890-1942, incomplete); New England Conference, Boston Missionary and Church Extension Society of the Methodist Episcopal Church,* Annual Reports *(Boston, 1890-1940); Ulf Pettersson, "The Formation of Different Christian Congregations within the Swedish Community in Boston-Cambridge, Mass., USA," unpublished paper, University of Uppsala, 1987 (available at Boston University archives); Arthur W. Smith,* Baptist Situation of Boston Proper: A Survey of Historical and Present Conditions *(Boston, 1912); William J. Villaume, ed.,* Protestantism in East Boston, 1920-1946: An Underchurched Minority in an Overchurched Community *(Boston, 1947); Works Progress Administration, Church Records Survey, Massachusetts Archives, Boston, Mass.*

Protestants, emphasized a spatial orientation and sense of responsibility to new residents. None of Boston's neighborhoods lacked a constant mission presence between the 1890s and the 1930s. No matter where an immigrant lived in the city, he fell within someone's mission territory. These friendly neighbors developed a variety of strategies to reach immigrants and their children, including home visits, distribution of tracts and Bibles, practical aid, children's programs, and mothers' meetings. Not only were missions and Protestant-sponsored reform and welfare agencies made easily accessible to newcomers by virtue of their location in poor and immigrant neighborhoods such as the North and South Ends, but they provided a range of services and programs.

Boston's Protestant community targeted neighborhoods with large and complex concentrations of immigrants. In the North and South Ends and in South Cove, in particular, Baptists and Methodists planted mission churches in the middle of the action. Table 2 illustrates the total distribution of religious work among immigrant groups throughout the period of this study, 1890 to 1940; however, not all the missions and churches endured for the duration of the period, while some were still in existence after 1940. A closer look at several neighborhoods underscores the argument that immigrant communities were multichurched. Table 3, adapted from Arthur W. Smith's *Baptist Situation of Boston Proper: A Survey of Historical and Present Conditions,* illustrates the distribution of churches by neighborhood. In the North End, which had twelve churches in 1912, the residents were overwhelmingly Italian, some 20,000 strong by 1910. State census figures for 1905 show Italians at 65 percent of the neighborhood's population, with Jews at 16 percent and Irish at 10 percent. Since 1905 to 1914 saw the greatest influx of Italians into Boston, the percentage of Italians in the North End only escalated.[41] Of the twelve religious institutions in the neighborhood at the time of the Baptist survey, two were Italian national Roman Catholic churches (St. Leonard's of Port Maurice and Sacred Heart of Jesus). Between them, the two encompassed all the neighborhood's Italians. They were enormous parishes: on annual census cards pastors at St. Leonard's estimated the number of souls at approximately 19,000 between 1907 and the early 1920s, while Sacred Heart clergy claimed between 15,000 and 18,000 members. However, these numbers suggest inflated estimates.[42] The Protestant congregations were much smaller, counting members in the low hundreds rather than thousands. First Italian Methodist Church was the only organized ethnic convert

TABLE 3. The Distribution of Churches in Three of Boston's Immigrant Neighborhoods, 1912

	North End	West End	South End	Total
Baptist	1	1	6	8
Congregational	1	0	3	4
Episcopalian	1	2	4	7
Jewish	3	4	2	9
Lutheran	0	0	2	2
Methodist	1	2	4	7
Presbyterian	0	1	5	6
Unitarian	1	1	2	4
Roman Catholic	4	1	5	10
Total	12	12	33	57

Source: Smith, Baptist Situation of Boston Proper.

church at that time, although the Boston Baptist Bethel had been the cornerstone of Baptist mission work in the North End beginning in 1852. In the coming decade Congregationalists, Unitarians, Baptists, and the Salvation Army established missions there.

The South End was a much more heterogeneous ethnic and religious neighborhood than the North End. With a total population of 31,000 people, the South End was one of Boston's more congested places to live. It was also extremely poor. Ward 9, which comprises much of the South End between Eliot-Kneeland Streets and Dover-Berkeley Streets, was 73 percent foreign-born at the time of the Baptist study. Forty percent of these people were Irish, 12 percent were Italian, 6.5 percent were Jews, 8 percent were Syrian, and the rest were Canadian, English, French, Swedish, and Greek.[43] In addition to the thirty-three churches enumerated in Table 3, there were two other Protestant churches and one each for Armenians and Greeks (the latter was Orthodox).

In this neighborhood, even more so than in the North End, the churches illustrated Boston's ethnoreligious complexity. Of the thirty-seven churches noted here, twelve served ethnic communities. These churches included Swedish Baptist, Norwegian Congregational, First Swedish Methodist, Emmanuel Lutheran Swedish, Scotch Presbyterian, Greek Orthodox, and Armenian, as well as Roman Catholic national parishes for Italians, Syrians, French, and Germans. The neighborhood also had at least seven churches for African Americans.[44] Tables 2 and 3 give some indication of how extensively Protestant denominations were committed to immigrant work in Boston. There was no neighborhood in Boston, and no substantial immigrant group in the city, which did not have access to an alternative form of worship (in their language, no less) thanks to Protestant mission activity.

The Protestant mission churches used a variety of strategies to attract their neighbors to services, from location to free refreshments to clothing. In Boston's North End, despite the existence of two Italian national parishes, Episcopalians sought to draw in Italian immigrants. One of the tools they employed was altar décor. In at least two Italian Episcopal churches in the city, including at St. Francis of Assisi Episcopal Chapel in the North End, the priests hung red lanterns in the sanctuary, reminiscent of the Roman Catholic "high church sanctuary lamp."[45] Diocesan leaders argued that they sought to reach only unchurched Italians, and they used such gimmicks to make their sanctuaries familiar and nonthreatening to lapsed Catholics who may still have harbored deep fears and wild notions about Protestants. One minister went to great lengths to subvert deep-rooted prejudices against Protestantism among the Italians with whom he worked. Recognizing that Catholics are taught from a young age to distrust Protestants, he introduced himself as a "Christian Catholic man," rather than as a Protestant. To emphasize the familiarity of his particular faith when approaching potential converts, he "recites the Apostles' creed."[46]

In 1916, the Massachusetts Baptist Convention reviewed the most successful strategies for reaching immigrants. Popular programs included "lectures, church sociables, concerts, settlement work, industrial school, shop preaching, employment aid, vacation Bible school, Sunday afternoon forum, the observance of Recognition Day, and the purchase of books in foreign languages for the public library."[47] Sunday Schools remained the most utilized and most conventional tool.[48] Of all these instruments, the convention's survey showed that even though there was no one perfect method for attracting immigrants into Baptist churches, one-on-one contact had the greatest return. "After all," the secretary reported, "it seems to be the spirit of sympathy and friendship that is the essential element rather than any particular method."[49]

The offers of friendship made by missionaries and other "friendly visitors" were welcome in many immigrant homes in which mothers were isolated and alone. Husbands and children had social contacts and opportunities to learn English that most mothers did not have, and their isolation and loneliness must have been quite oppressive. City Missionary Society workers reported regularly their successes with women of all ethnicities and religions, who were pleased to have people come to talk with them. Missionaries made door to door visits and identified those women who they thought were in need of friendship and Christian affiliation.

The Congregationalists used mothers' meetings as one strategy for bringing women into their missions and churches. It usually took several visits by a missionary to convince a mother to attend a session, in some cases because of reluctance on her part and in others because of the language barrier. The gatherings had a semiformal structure divided among hymn-singing, Bible study, and attention to one woman's particular case. According to the City Missionary Society annual reports, "At each meeting the subject for the next is given, and those present read or repeat from memory appropriate passages from the Bible."[50] One missionary described her visit with a Swedish family that lived near her church. "Neither the mother nor children could speak a word of English," the missionary wrote. "They lived near the church, so by taking the mother to the door, pointing first to the church then to the figure twelve on my watch, I was able to make her understand with the aid of a few gestures that I wanted the children to go there with me the next Sunday at twelve o'clock." The mother agreed, and the children began to attend Sunday School regularly. They learned English there and at public school, and they taught their mother their new language at home. The missionary brought her to a mothers' meeting "and although she did not understand a word that was said, she seemed to enjoy the friendly greetings and the handshakes."[51]

Immigrants should not be perceived as unwitting accomplices to these strategies. Surveyors for the Massachusetts Council of Churches in the 1940s found that some immigrants "went over to the Protestant missions which in the early days required little from these 'poor people' and gave freely to meet their physical needs."[52] And since the missions held their services at different times, at least in the North End, visitors (who were quickly recorded as members) attended several meetings a week and reaped the benefits of each. Roman Catholic Bishop P. J. Muldoon of Rockford, Illinois, viewed immigrants who attended Protestant missions as more concerned with the "opportunity to better their material condition" than the "salvation of their souls."[53] Constantine Panunzio, who was pastor at the Methodist mission to Italians there, wrote that the North End's three different missions to Italians suffered from overlapping memberships that were encouraged by the respective clergy. He wrote that "One Sunday I attended them all and found the same constituency, meager as it was, swelling the ranks of all three. Later, by mere accident, I learned that 75 per cent of the membership of one was enrolled on the books of the second, and 35 per cent on the books of the third." And while the "members" attended one service after the other, Panunzio found that they "went on pretty much their own way, practising their Old World customs and habits as if nothing American were within a thousand miles of them."[54]

While some immigrants voluntarily took advantage of the missions' offerings, others had no choice but to avail themselves of goods and services. Poverty served as yet another means to changing religious affiliation. Thus some immigrant parents succumbed to mission offers in order that their children would have basic necessities. In her memoir of her childhood in New York's Lower East Side, Rose Cohen wrote that when her parents could not afford to feed their children, they instructed them to "bow your heads and pray" in school in order to receive bread and honey.[55] Rob McDonald grew up with the unquestioned assumption of his family's Irish Catholic heritage. But one day as an adult, he discovered an unexpected truth: his roots lay not in Ireland but in Scotland, and his family's Catholicism could only be traced back two generations, to a time of family crisis. After the premature death of his grandfather MacDonald in the 1920s, his grandmother was left with several small children and no income to support them. A Scottish Presbyterian by birth, she requested aid from the minister of her Presbyterian church. Rebuffed by him, she sought out the local Catholic priest, who offered assistance to her and her children. Gratitude to the priest and disappointment in her own church led her to bring her children to Catholicism, and for nearly two generations, surprisingly, no one was the wiser. Somewhere along the way the "a" disappeared from the "Mac" in "MacDonald," and the ethnic ambiguity of the name, combined with the family's Catholicism, led John and his relations to assume that they were of Irish Catholic descent. In this case, the family's survival and the willingness of another church to assist during a time of crisis acted as more than an introduction to a new faith and ethnoreligious community.[56]

In each of Boston's immigrant neighborhoods Protestant religious and social agencies established organizations and missions to aid newcomers in settlement and the negotiation of assimilation issues. As a result, the enclaves became saturated with Americans and their peculiar social reform, welfare, and religious creations; the promulgation of a message that linked Christianization and Americanization; and the social and religious complication of what would otherwise have been isolated immigrant communities. Protestants saw the conversion of immigrants as a way to save the newcomers from poverty and vice, as well as the city from foreign culture and papal control, and they used many outreach strategies to achieve those ends. Immigrants saw mission offerings as a solution to a variety of needs, from childcare to linguistic assistance to feeding, clothing, and sheltering their families. Some immigrants also accepted missionaries' claims that American Protestantism would put them on a fast track to Americanization, acceptance, and socioeconomic improvement.

While Protestant institutions and "friendly visitors" penetrated ethnic enclaves' boundaries, they had a tougher time breaking through the barriers erected by language and culture. One segment of the immigrant population, however, routinely crossed those barriers to participate in the American mainstream. The children of immigrants were the key to reaching the family and to perforating the shell of the ethnoreligious community.

He wanted me to be able to walk to church and to Sunday school.

Children played a critical role in familial changes in religious affiliation. Not only did immigrants make important choices to improve the lives of their sons and daughters, but both Protestants and Catholics recognized that bringing the young into the fold (or keeping them) enhanced their chances of making headway with their parents. Thus the most important strategies used by missionaries and immigrant parents focused on the needs of the children.

Immigrant parents had dual expectations and hopes for their children. They hoped that as Americans their sons and daughters would live better than they had, but they also expected that their children would retain ethnic memory, respecting their old-world culture and values. Because immigrant parents were also, in many cases, desperately poor, they broke some of their own rules so that their children would have basic necessities. Even so, Boston Methodists recognized a fine line that many parents would not cross. Although they would send their children to Sunday School, settlement houses, mission daycare, and recreational programs, and would accept practical aid from Protestants, most would not join the churches themselves. Methodists blamed parents' refusals to attend religious services on the "well-organized propaganda" that was preached regularly in neighborhood Roman Catholic churches. Indeed, clergy of all faiths admonished their members of dreadful fates should they even enter another house of worship. "Many of these folks are ready to accept the benefits of our institutions that minister to their bodies," complained one missionary, "but the same are warned to shun all ministry to the soul."[57] Baptists complained in 1899 that "the children in the North End are accessible; but they call forth constant effort as they are watched by jealous eyes and often hindered." Missionaries found they had to start from scratch with Catholic children, who were "utterly ignorant of the very name of Jesus and the fact of there even being a book of Life."[58]

Children were the key to Americanizing an ethnic community. All of Boston's Protestants recognized this fact and designed programming to use—as well as serve—children. In 1935 Baptists reported that "the large number of second and third generation of young Americans, often needing help in adjustment between foreign born parents groups and older American groups, many of them with no church home and little Christian training, offers a real challenge."[59] Sunday Schools and daycare centers were critical components of mission outreach in immigrant neighborhoods. For the Gulinello family in the North End, the "Club," a childcare center at the North End Italian Methodist Mission/Church, served as the family's entry into a new religious affiliation.[60] Attendance at Sunday School was a practical compromise for immigrant families who desired that their children learn English. Denominational annual reports are filled with stories of families who sent their children to Sunday School and later joined the church. Baptists offered yet another reason to work on the children of immigrants. "So many of them have drifted away and have no vital connections with the church of their fathers," reported Baptists in their yearbook of 1938. "So many of the fine young people will be the husbands and wives of our sons and daughters, that even a selfish interest should make us eager to win them."[61]

Programs aimed at attracting children included daycare, afterschool classes, and clubs sponsored by settlement houses and missionary societies, vacation camps, and Sunday Schools at neighborhood churches.

Baptist missionaries in the North End explained that the denomination's success with children of Italian Catholic immigrants was because "it is hard to make men and women believe that a person who cares lovingly for their children and provides for their happiness, is an agent of the devil."[62] Thus immigrant parents allowed their children access to American religious and social programs that were educational, many teaching language skills and vocational activities such as woodworking and sewing. Parents such as the Gulinellos entrusted the spiritual education of their children to neighborhood churches despite differences in denominational affiliations. Baptists hoped that the children could "be led into the way of salvation, and that through the children the parents can be interested and often won for Christ."[63] The Congregational City Missionary Society reported with pride and hope of its vacation school's concluding ceremony in 1913. The secretary wrote that in the final moments "the entire number salute the American flag and sing 'America' and return home. Are we not, even in our small way, making some little impression upon the hearts and minds of these little ones, teaching them to be better citizens and better 'soldiers of the cross'?"[64]

Children of immigrants straddled culturally and geographically disparate worlds. They experienced their parents' ethnic culture and their American identities differently than did either their parents or their own future children. They learned English faster than their parents did and often had the responsibility of interpreting and negotiating for their parents. And they felt more American than Italian, Swedish, Polish, or German even as they carried their parents' cultural baggage. They were the first American generation, but they would also be the keepers of the family's ethnic cultural traditions. They lived in two worlds; by day they attended public schools (for the most part, although parochial schools flourished among Catholics), but after school they mixed and mingled with immigrant children of many nationalities in the streets, in tenements, and in city- and Protestant-sponsored recreational facilities. On weekends, and sometimes after public school let out, they attended Sunday Schools and religious classes sponsored by their ethnic churches. As children came of age, they made choices about which identity served their changing needs. For many sons and daughters of immigrants, the call of higher wages, education, and suburban life led them out of immigrant or ethnic enclaves and into American neighborhoods. Giving up the benefits within the community of close contact to an extended family, an ethnic church, and cultural opportunities, children of immigrants sought instead mainstream associations. All of these changes increased the importance of the child—now adult—as an entity independent of the extended ethnic family. The Massachusetts Council of Churches researchers argued that in such an isolated state "the Protestant church may appeal to his sense of what is American. If the church can offer him . . . the warmth of fellowship and the sense of belonging which he sacrificed by turning from the solidarity of the Italian community, it may help prepare him for his journey to the suburbs and his integration into American life."[65]

If you're Lutheran in the old country and you go through what I just described, it makes sense to change churches—we're all Protestants, after all.

Although not as socially cataclysmic as the move to or from Catholicism, the change from Lutheran to Baptist or Anglican to Methodist still reflected complex social, political, and theological decisions. As Lillian Sundin Shirley's story suggests, many immigrants apparently neglected to differentiate among Protestant denominations. But there is also some indication that Protestants muddied the waters themselves. To many proselytizers, the main issue was to win converts to Christ to save their souls—and thus also to save Boston and the United States. How immigrants got to the point of conversion was not as important as the fact that they did so; for example, Congregationalists surveyed Protestant work among the state's immigrants and submitted a report outlining which denomination should work among which immigrant peoples. The written justification asserted that some denominations simply made better progress with certain immigrants in certain areas than did others. For example, Congregationalists recognized that the city's Syrian population was too small for the number of Protestant missions among them, so they closed their own on the grounds that a successful Protestant Christian outreach was already in place.[66]

Indeed, after completing a survey of Protestant work in the West End, the board of the Massachusetts Council of Churches concluded that ethnic identity might be a stronger factor in peoples' religious affiliation choices than denominational particulars. Thus, as Alexander von Hoffman found, "German-speaking residents of Jamaica Plain, free to select their own institutions, often chose to attend German-language churches, even if it meant going outside the neighborhood."[67] In its review of

Pentecostal work in the West End, the Council found that "the group is more dominantly a national than a sectarian denominational one," and its primary purpose was "a means of fellowship between fellow nationals, sharing the common values due to the common background from which the worshippers came, that is, Italian homes."[68]

These reasons, especially the significance of ethnicity and/or language, help to explain why many immigrant converts made more than one change in affiliation. Usually the first change was the most pronounced, whether from Catholicism or Scandinavian Lutheranism to an American Protestant denomination. Subsequent changes tended to be confined to the circle of American Protestantism, such as moves between Baptist, Congregational, Episcopal, Methodist/Methodist Episcopal, and Presbyterian churches. These shifts frequently resulted from geographic moves that brought a convert to a neighborhood too far from the church in which he had converted and without a church of that denomination and ethnicity. Instead, if the new neighborhood harbored a different Protestant church of his ethnicity, the immigrant joined that church. In one such case, Raffaele Mazzeo immigrated first to Pennsylvania coal mining country and joined a Presbyterian church there. Later, when he came to South Boston for a job at the Boston Elevated Railway, there happened to be a Methodist church with an Italian mission on his street, but there was no Italian or American Presbyterian church. He joined the Italian Methodist church.[69]

Protestant denominations' annual reports show that foreign-born convert clergy also moved freely among denominations. Antonio Mangano blamed the ease and frequency of "denomination switching" on religious leaders who either failed to inculcate institutional loyalty in convert clergy or who encouraged miscreants or less than suitable pastors to change affiliations.[70] Indeed, such switching underscored the significance and power of the foreign language-speaking clergy. For example, in one striking case the Baptist missionary to the city's Syrians abruptly "transferred his allegiance to the Congregationalists, and he very naturally carried the mission with him."[71] Pastors who worked with immigrants in the nineteenth century also described this pattern. In the 1850s, a Lutheran pastor in Wisconsin named Adolph Preus described a "constant flux in religious affiliation. If a person is a Presbyterian today, he will become a Methodist tomorrow and a Baptist the next day."[72]

On the other hand, many immigrant converts became devoted to their new faiths through lay leadership positions or through evangelism. Swedes, for example, were often described as exemplary converts. Baptists claimed that "the most successful work is among the Swedes. These men from the North become most active Christians once they have adopted the faith, and they propagate it with the most commendable zeal."[73] Likewise, Chinese men who were introduced to Christianity in Boston Sunday Schools were known for returning home to convert wives and family. In addition, many of Chinatown's Christian converts sent money home to support foreign missionary work sponsored by their denominations of choice. In its annual reports, the Congregationalist's City Missionary Society reported an extensive connection between Chinese converts in Boston and the work of a foreign missionary in China. The converts not only sent money back to support this man's church, but they also traveled back to live or to visit with the intention of bringing family members to Christ.[74]

It's not like that great leap to Catholicism.

The leap to or from Catholicism, on the other hand, set the convert on a path away from ethnic community and family. The repercussions of such conversions erupted in a variety of situations. Italian children whose families joined Protestant churches were isolated in their schools, singled out by teachers and students. Their parents found it difficult to obtain housing once Catholic landlords learned of their Protestantism. Extended families often ostracized converts to varying degrees, making them the black sheep of the family. In cases in which the new affiliation arose from an interfaith marriage, ostracism from family may have been particularly intense. Converts who remained in the neighborhood of their prior ethnoreligious community faced more immediate and daily reminders of their choices, whereas those who joined new churches far from their original communities appear to have fared better.

Conversion isolated family members from one another. Missionaries recognized that those people who were already exhibiting a rebellious spirit, particularly Italian men, were most susceptible to evangelistic suggestion. But they also remained aware of others attending their open mission meetings and mothers' meetings who risked alienating husbands and family. Sympathetic researchers wrote that "It is not hard to visualize the difficulties of Protestant missionaries in East Boston trying to sever a few

Italians from the religious values in their extended family and 'paesani' group at the risk not only of their excommunication from the Roman Church, but much worse, of excommunication from their communal identity."[75]

For some, participation in mission activities and conversion created an open break with family. Methodist minister Constantine Panunzio described his conflicted feelings when a young Italian man with whom he was working in a mission church was "cast out of his home by his parents because they did not approve of his attending the meetings held in our little chapel. He came very near going insane."[76] To Panunzio, it seemed clear that the missionaries should have been more sensitive to the man's household strife, and he blamed them rather than the potential converts for the "very serious breaks in the home life of some of the people."

Families that converted could not avoid alienation from the larger ethnic community. Hostility took the form of discrimination in employment and housing, and it occasionally manifested as violence. While in many circumstances conversion led to work opportunities, for other immigrants the change in affiliation was an obstacle. One missionary reported her work with a family recently arrived from northern Italy. The parents sent their children to a Congregational Sunday School in the neighborhood, and the father struggled to find work. He told the missionary that "the other Italians hate him because he is not a Roman Catholic, and make it hard for him to get work."[77] Young Frank Gulinello often wondered that his family, all converts to Methodism, moved so frequently. In his memoir he wrote, "Landlords would not have a Protestant as their tenant."[78] But even within the "strong, supportive fellowship" of the ethnic convert community, there was a sense of being an outsider from both the immigrant community at large and from the new religious community. Virgil Olson recalls that "non-Swedish Baptists felt that we were strange people, really not a part of the 'regular' American church culture. . . . Those of us who were growing up in this separatistic, ethnic church community felt within our social context a kind of churchy inferiority."[79] Baptists summarized the experiences of converts with their former communities. The Massachusetts Baptist Convention reported that even by 1897 some of the opposition had been surmounted. They wrote,

> We . . . little know of the great trials of these Canadians, Portuguese, and Italians who endure persecution of family and of friends, of the

ostracism and isolation, and even bodily injury, because of their renouncing the belief of their families and their countrymen for ours,
for the simple gospel; for until a little church is gathered . . . they are
without mutual sympathy and encouragement. . . . When the first
converts from Romanism began to be gathered there was considerable opposition, and they were compelled to suffer much from their
former friends and associates. As they have had since their conversion equal prosperity in matters temporal, . . . it has come to pass that
the feeling towards them has changed for the better. . . . It is also worthy of note that whether in the chapels or open-air meetings, all violent opposition seems to have ceased, and disorderly proceedings,
where services have been held, have become rare and exceptional.[80]

Children of convert families faced ostracism in public schools as well
as on the streets, where fights between Catholic and Protestant children
were not uncommon. Frank Gulinello recalled that Ash Wednesday was a
particularly dangerous day for Protestant children, since they stood out
for their lack of smudges on their foreheads. In order to avoid persecu-
tion by classmates and even by teachers, he wrote, Protestant children
would stay home on that day, and "thus some fights were avoided." He
recalled that "many a day 'Mr.' [Salvatore Giambaressi, pastor of the
North End's Italian Methodist Mission] would go to the several schools
and speak in behalf of his 'children.'"[81]

Conversion from Catholicism to American forms of Protestantism
initiated social changes beyond isolation from family and ethnic community. Integration into American neighborhoods and suburbs, especially
through the mainstream church memberships that replaced the ethnic
mission churches, not only facilitated Americanization but also enhanced
socioeconomic opportunities. In the missions, Protestants used the promise of socioeconomic improvement as a reward of conversion. Thus their
message to potential converts conflated spiritual and physical salvation, a
message that was particularly potent in intemperance cases. The editor of
The Converted Catholic, the vitriolic organ of ex-priest Father O'Sullivan
of New York City, wrote that "for most Roman Catholic girls marriage
with a Protestant means social advancement, as well as higher ethical standards on the part of the prospective husband."[82] In a less biased study,
Thomas Sowell found that when Italians intermarried with people of
other ethnic groups, "it was not so much a step toward the amalgamation

of groups as an isolated event in the lives of upwardly mobile individuals who had already drifted away from the ethnic community."[83]

The greatest measurements used in assessing socioeconomic improvement included advanced education of children, alcohol abstinence, gainful employment of family members, and home ownership. If, as Stephan Thernstrom suggested, residents of institutionally complete ethnic communities faced a variety of community-imposed barriers and mainstream prejudice that stifled socioeconomic improvement, then the inverse may be true. Members of ethnic groups who lived outside the enclave might have improved their circumstances faster than did members within the enclave.[84]

The extent to which converts retained their ethnic group identities and contacts is difficult to determine. One important aspect of lifestyle and community that changed for male Catholic converts was participation in voluntary (especially fraternal) associations. One historian found that "more than half of the Swedish immigrants to New England never joined any church. Instead many consciously formed Good Templar temperance lodges, Male Glee clubs, provincial societies, fraternal orders, gymnastic societies and political clubs as an alternative to church affiliation."[85] Consequently, it may be possible to draw conclusions about identity and ethnic community relationships from memberships in Odd Fellows or Masons as opposed to membership in ethnic or village-specific mutual aid societies. Ex-Catholics found associational options in fraternal lodges that had once been forbidden to them. Despite the fact that a search for records has proved futile, oral history and anecdotal information connects Italian American members of the Church of Our Saviour Methodist Episcopal Church in South Boston with an Odd Fellows lodge. Francis Mazzeo recalled that his father, Raffaele Mazzeo, and a number of other Italian men from that church joined the Bethesda Odd Fellows Lodge and were not members of the Sons of Italy.[86] Lodge membership was also an issue for Germans in the 1890s and for Poles, who informed the cardinal of the founding of a Polish Freemason lodge in Boston in the 1910s.[87]

In the previous section I argued that retention of converts was a constant issue for the clergy of immigrant churches. Most Protestant denominations recognized that ultimately the greatest loyalty among converts would be found in the children; parents who were socialized and religiously affiliated in the old country did not make the best of converts, for the most part. John Daniels, writing in 1920, reported that "only a small proportion of adults who have been Catholics even nominally become permanently attached to the Protestant church" after their exposure to Protestantism via settlements, mothers' meetings, and Sunday Schools. Rather, he wrote, "recruits come mainly from the children as they grow up. As a rule, Protestant missions and churches are not organic factors in neighborhoods of Catholic immigrants."[88] For his doctoral dissertation, written in the 1940s, Francis DeBilio conducted a survey to ascertain retention rates among Italians who converted to Protestant denominations. After reviewing the cases of 654 "former members of Italian missions in Boston," he was able to disprove the belief that "many of the converts returned to Roman Catholicism." DeBilio found that of the 654 "only 16 or less than 2.5 percent had returned to Roman Catholicism. The rest are generally not active in any church." Of the 16 who returned to the Catholic Church, half did so after marrying observant Roman Catholic women.[89] DeBilio interviewed 100 former members of mission churches and surveyed 171 Protestant churches in Boston's immediate suburbs. He concluded that "unlike the old line American Protestants these 'new Protestants' are not relating themselves with the American Protestant Churches in the communities to which they are moving."[90] By way of explanation, he surmised that, "because many of them did not have any new religious experience, they gradually abandoned the mission when their material needs were met."[91] By 1930, however, all the Protestant denominations reported in their annual publications that the missions struggled with membership retention because out-migrating children of converts joined American mainstream churches in their new neighborhoods. When the children of immigrant converts chose new churches, they identified religiously rather than ethnically.

Conclusion

The journey from old-world to new-world religious affiliation varied from person to person and from family to family. In each case, however, a constellation of common factors marked the conversions of immigrants. For some people, geography compelled a change in affiliation, while for others it was a need or desire for linguistic familiarity. Still others found friendly and persistent clergy and missionaries to be persuasive and comforting in what could often be a harsh and unfriendly urban environment. Ultimately, however, an individual's decision depended on faith in the new community and opportunities that a conversion could offer, and on faith in the suitability of a new religious home for one who sought to make sense of a new lifestyle and identity in America.

The relationship between religion and ethnic identity sits at the center of any discussion of immigrant conversions. For many Catholic peoples, Catholicism and ancient folk traditions were inextricably intertwined with one another and with ethnic or communal sensibilities. For Swedes, on the other hand, the role of Lutheranism as the state church set up a separate set of relationships and identities. Some things are clear: conversion did not erase national or linguistic attachments in the immigrant generation. Immigrants who converted and changed religious affiliations overwhelmingly sought, and to a greater extent were organized into, segregated mission churches. The capacity of many of these mission churches to become vital, permanent ethnoreligious centers proves the permeability of ethnic communities and the ability of immigrants to create alternative ethnic communities. The ethnic sensibility and old-world attachment of Swedes at Calvary Baptist Church in Dorchester rival those at Waltham's First Lutheran Church. Despite these certainties, some important questions remain unanswered. Did the construction of an ethnic identity by immigrants themselves and by the mainstream society for them make newcomers question the structural or associational features that comprised or supported their communities? What features did a community need to make it feel "ethnic"? How did these features or institutions operate as boundaries? Was religion on the inside, embedded in the individual immigrant's understanding of what it meant to be Italian or Swedish, or was religion on the outside, embedded in a church as an external symbol of ethnic belonging? Could it be both?

Immigrant converts belonged to multiple and often overlapping communities. They were members of the dominant ethnic group when perceived or approached by outsiders. Some maintained a strong sense of nationalist pride and involvement. They were also members of American denominations (despite the tendency for the mission churches to have secondary standing). They were residents of neighborhoods, employees of companies, and members of voluntary associations such as the Swedish Order of Vasa or the Italian Sons of Italy. The degree to which converts disassociated from the primary ethnoreligious community depended upon a variety of circumstances including the conversion experience, familial relationships, and occupation.

Joseph Sundin was attracted to Beth Eden Baptist Church in at least three ways. First, it was within walking distance of the watch factory in which he worked and the boardinghouse at which he met his wife. After they married, they built a house just two blocks from the church on a street that soon became a little enclave of Scandinavian Baptists. Second, the pastor was friendly and had made a good impression. Finally, Sundin found the church and what it represented appealing. Relatives in Sweden remember that Sundin wrote to express his fascination with this American innovation that placed bells in the tower of the church.[92] The Sundin family offers a useful glimpse into the complex religious sensibilities and ties of immigrant converts.

When Joseph Sundin died in 1919, he and his family had been active members of Beth Eden Baptist for many years. He and his wife had raised all their children in the church's neighborhood, and the church remained an important part of family culture. Still, Joseph Sundin's ties to his homeland and to the church of his birth transcended his death. His family, following his wishes, returned his remains to Sweden, where they were buried in a family plot in the cemetery of his family's ancestral Lutheran Church.

The family's ties to their ethnic heritage (and to Beth Eden Baptist) remained strong after his passing. Lillian assumed his devotion to the church bells, climbing the tower to ring the bells each day of the American hostages' period of captivity in Iran in the 1970s. Years later when Lillian was planning her wedding to John Shirley (whose family had long been members of Waltham's First Baptist Church), it was more important to the family that she be married by a Swedish pastor than in the Baptist church of which she was a member. So Episcopal priest George Ekwall, a son of Swedish immigrants, performed the ceremony. The Shirleys still raised their children in Beth Eden Baptist Church. Yet their eldest son left that church and is now an Episcopal priest. The three-generation religious journey of the Sundin-Shirley family illustrates the multiplicity of choices and the ethnoreligious complexity of an as yet little known constituency of American immigrants.

Notes

1. Lillian Sundin Shirley, interview by author, Oct. 10, 1994, Waltham, Mass.
2. Kristen A. Petersen, *Waltham Rediscovered: An Ethnic History of Waltham, Massachusetts* (Portsmouth, N.H., 1988).

3. Roy Rosenzweig, *Eight Hours for What We Will: Workers and Leisure in an Industrial City, 1870-1920* (New York, 1983); William M. DeMarco, *Ethnics and Enclaves: Boston's Italian North End* (Ann Arbor, 1981); Alexander von Hoffman, *Local Attachments: The Making of an American Urban Neighborhood, 1850 to 1920* (Baltimore, 1994). See also Stanley Nadel, *Little Germany: Ethnicity, Religion and Class in New York City, 1845-1880* (Urbana, 1990).

4. Laura Becker, "Ethnicity and Religion," in *Encyclopedia of the American Religious Experience: Studies of Traditions and Movements*, ed. Charles H. Lippy and Peter W. Williams (New York, 1988), 1479.

5. William James, *The Varieties of Religious Experience* (New York, 1982).

6. See Lewis Rambo, *Understanding Religious Conversion* (New Haven, 1993); and Christopher Lamb and M. Darrol Bryant, eds., *Religious Conversion: Contemporary Practices and Controversies* (New York, 1999).

7. Alan F. Segal, *Paul the Convert: The Apostolate and Apostasy of Saul the Pharisee* (New Haven, 1990), 300. Segal writes that new "sociological research stresses the social dimension of the conversion experience and a subject who actively develops a new world of meaning by conversion and entrance into a new community" (294).

8. The Covenant Congregational Church was the outgrowth of the Free Mission Church movement begun in Sweden in the last quarter of the 19th century. This was a pietistic faith that sought a pure form of worship that believers claimed Swedish Lutheranism had lost. See Ulf Pettersson, "The Formation of Different Christian Congregations within the Swedish Community in Boston-Cambridge, Mass., USA, 1987" TMs (photocopy), 27, New England Methodist Historical Society Collection, School of Theology Library, Boston University, Boston. See also Mark A. Granquist, "Smaller Religious Groups in the Swedish-American Community," *The Swedish-American Historical Quarterly* 44(1993):221.

9. Recent scholarly research examining the religions of late-20th- and early-21st-century immigrants offers validation that the Boston examples of the 19th and early 20th centuries represent a pattern in immigrant experience rather than an anomaly. See, for example, R. Stephen Warner and Judith G. Wittner, eds., *Gatherings in Diaspora: Religious Communities and the New Immigration* (Philadelphia, 1998).

10. Pettersson, "The Formation of Different Christian Congregations." Pettersson quotes George M. Stephenson, *The Religious Aspects of Swedish Immigration: A Study of Immigrant Churches* (Minneapolis, 1932), 221.

11. A. W. Sundelof, "The Opportunity among the Swedes," *The Church Militant*, Jan. 1903 and Feb. 1910.

12. Pettersson, "The Formation of Different Christian Congregations," 6.

13. Antonio Mangano, *Religious Work among Italians in America: A Survey for the Home Missions Council* (Philadelphia, 1917), 8. In 1918 this organization published a survey of Methodist Episcopal work among all immigrants to the U.S. Methodist Church, *The Centenary Survey of the Board of Home Missions and Church Extension of the Methodist Episcopal Church* (New York, 1918). See also Kate Holladay Claghorn, "The Italians in America," *The Home Mission Monthly* [Baptist] (May 1905):177-201.

14. John V. Tolino, "The Future of the Italian American Problem," *Ecclesiastical Review* 101(1939):221-232. The relationship between Southern Italian men and the Italian

church has been well documented by historians, including Robert Orsi, *The Madonna of 115th Street: Faith and Community in Italian Harlem, 1880-1950* (New Haven, 1985); Sylvano M. Tomasi, *Piety and Power: The Role of the Italian Parishes in the New York Metropolitan Area, 1880-1930* (New York, 1975); and Tomasi, "The Ethnic Church," in *The Italian Experience in the United States*, ed. Tomasi and Madeline H. Engel (New York, 1977). Contemporary studies suggest similar affiliational practices among Mexicans.

15. Sundelof, "Opportunity among the Swedes," 8.
16. The General Association of the Congregational Churches of Massachusetts, *Minutes of the Annual Meeting with the Statistics* (Boston, 1890-1940).
17. Helen Lacount and Pauline Helms, *Community Survey of Morgan Memorial Parish Boston* (Boston, 1923), 5, table 3.
18. Petersen, *Waltham Rediscovered*, 238-241.
19. Jay Dolan, *The Immigrant Church: New York's Irish and German Catholics, 1815-1865* (Baltimore, 1975), 4; Kathleen Conzen, "Forum," *Religion and American Culture: A Journal of Interpretation* 6(1996):108.
20. Gerald Gamm, *Urban Exodus: Why the Jews Left Boston and the Catholics Stayed* (Cambridge, Mass., 1999), 131. Gamm explains that the Catholic national church as neighborhood and cultural center gave way to the Catholic national church as a cultural center for a largely nonresidential membership.
21. Petersen, *Waltham Rediscovered*, 491. This raises an interesting issue for Catholics. People who spoke Lithuanian in Boston automatically became members of the Lithuanian national parish rather than the geographic parish in which they lived. Lithuanians who moved out of the city still perceived the South Boston or Cambridge Lithuanian churches as their cultural centers and true parishes, even generations after moving out.
22. Not only did immigrants return to their native lands and/or move into and out of Boston and her near suburbs, but movement within the city was also quite common. Mary Antin, whose family arrived in Boston in the 1890s, described the frequent moves from neighborhood to neighborhood in her memoir, *The Promised Land: The Autobiography of a Russian Immigrant*, 2d ed. (Princeton, N.J., 1985), as did Italian immigrant and convert Constantine Panunzio, in *The Soul of an Immigrant* (New York, 1921). On the mobility of urban residents, see Stephan Thernstrom, *The Other Bostonians: Poverty and Progress in the American Metropolis, 1880-1970* (Cambridge, Mass., 1973).
23. Daniel Malvestra, interview by author, Aug. 7, 1996, Boston, Mass.
24. The Rev. Michael Shirley, interview by author, July 28, 1998, Amesbury, Mass.
25. Priests in the Archdiocese of Boston with high conversion rates from 1907 to 1940, and their churches: Peter Abouzeid, Our Lady of the Annunciation; Francis Archdeacon, Church of the Immaculate Conception; William Casey, St. Patrick's (Roxbury); William Crawford, Church of the Immaculate Conception; Neil Cronin, Cathedral; A. J. Duartes, St. Mary's, North End; William B. Finigan, Cathedral; Edward F. Hurley, St. Phillips; C. E. Lane, Church of the Immaculate Conception; Ignatius Limont, Our Lady of Ostrabrama; John J. McGarry, St. Cecilia; George H. Quigley, St. Philip; F. Reilly, St. Mary's, North End; David Ryan, St. Cecilia; Flavin Zohar, Our Lady of the

Annunciation. Several churches reported high conversion rates under the leadership of several different pastors: the Cathedral of the Holy Cross, the Church of the Immaculate Conception, Our Lady of the Annunciation (Syrian), St. Cecilia, and St. Mary's in the North End. Parish Census Cards, 1907-1940, Archives, Archdiocese of Boston, Boston.

Although most converts to Catholicism were not immigrants, they provide an important comparison with immigrant converts. National parish pastors were more concerned with daily operations and with stemming the tide of leakage than with proselytizing, and they were confined to working among people who would belong to their parish based on ethnicity (or language).

26. The four priests were William Casey, St. Patrick's (Roxbury); Neil Cronin, Cathedral of the Holy Cross (South End); Edward F. Hurley, St. Phillip's (Roxbury); and John J. McGarry, St. Cecilia (Back Bay). Parish Census Cards, 1907-1940, Archives, Archdiocese of Boston, Boston.

27. Italian Methodist Church of Our Saviour, Boston, Massachusetts, Historical Record of Permanent Data, Book 1, page 5, New England Methodist Historical Society Collection, School of Theology, Boston University, Boston.

28. Methodist Episcopal Church, New England Conference, *Minutes, 1920* (Boston, 1921), 47; *Minutes, 1922,* 389; *Minutes, 1924,* 50.

29. Gustav Anderson, "Swedish Congregational Church (Scandinavian Free Church) Historical Sketch," TMs, Works Progress Administration, Church Records Survey, Box 113: Congregational Churches, "Boston Swedish Congregational Church," Massachusetts State Archives, Boston.

30. Anderson, "Swedish Congregational Church Historical Sketch."

31. George G. Chiera, "A Church Mission in the North End," *The Church Militant,* Apr. 1929.

32. Massachusetts Council of Churches, *Protestant Ministry to Italian People in Massachusetts* (Boston, 1951), 52.

33. The Rev. Samuel L. Elberfeld came to the East Boston Unitarian Italian Mission in 1930. Francis DeBilio, "Protestant Mission Work among Italians in Boston" (Ph.D. diss., Boston Univ., 1949), 118.

34. The General Association of the Congregational Churches of Massachusetts, *Minutes of the Annual Meeting.*

35. The General Association of the Congregational Churches of Massachusetts, *Minutes of the Annual Meeting.*

36. Massachusetts Council of Churches, *Protestant Ministry to Italian People,* 46.

37. Sacred Heart Church Parishioners to William Cardinal O'Connell, July 19, 1932, TLS, RG 5.3 Parish Correspondence Files, Boston (North End) Sacred Heart (Italian), 1915-1939, Archives, Archdiocese of Boston, Boston.

38. A. Caleri to William Cardinal O'Connell, Aug. 22, 1922, LS, RG 5.3 Parish Correspondence Files, Boston (North End) Sacred Heart (Italian), 1915-1939, Archives, Archdiocese of Boston, Boston.

39. Angelo Bonighi to William Cardinal O'Connell, Sept. 19, 1922, LS, RG 5.3 Parish Correspondence Files, Boston (North End) Sacred Heart (Italian), 1915-1939, Archives, Archdiocese of Boston, Boston.

40. Edward F. McLeod to William Cardinal O'Connell, June 19, 1917, LS, RG 5.3 Parish Correspondence Files, Boston Our Lady of Ostrobrama (Polish), 1916-1939, Archives, Archdiocese of Boston, Boston.
41. Arthur W. Smith, *Baptist Situation of Boston Proper: A Survey of Historical and Present Conditions* (Boston, 1912), 40.
42. Parish Census Card File, Archives, Archdiocese of Boston, Boston. The neighborhood's Catholic community was more complex than this survey indicates. At the time it was conducted, the Portuguese Catholic church had only recently moved, and St. Stephen's Church had not yet begun its mission to North End Poles.
43. Smith, *Baptist Situation of Boston Proper*, 52-53.
44. Smith, *Baptist Situation of Boston Proper*, 52, 55.
45. James O'Toole, *Militant and Triumphant: William Henry O'Connell and the Catholic Church in Boston, 1859-1944* (Notre Dame, 1992), 165. An Episcopal church in East Boston also used the lamp to attract Italian worshippers.
46. Massachusetts Council of Churches, *Protestant Ministry to Italian People*, 108.
47. Methodist Episcopal Church, New England Conference, *Minutes, 1909* (Boston), 91.
48. Methodist Episcopal Church, New England Conference, *Minutes, 1909*, 91.
49. Social Service Commission to the Baptist Churches of Massachusetts, *The Massachusetts Baptist Year Book, Minutes of the Proceedings of the Massachusetts Baptist State Societies* (Boston, 1916), 196.
50. [Congregational] City Missionary Society, "Influence of the Mothers' Meetings," *Annual Report of the City Missionary Society, Boston, for the Year 1893* (Boston, 1894), 17.
51. [Congregational] City Missionary Society, *Annual Report of the City Missionary Society, Boston, for the Year 1909* (Boston, 1910), 30.
52. Massachusetts Council of Churches, *Protestant Ministry to Italian People*.
53. P. J. Muldoon, "Immigration to and the Immigrants in the United States," address at the Second American Catholic Missionary Congress, in James Edward Quigley, *The Two Great American Catholic Missionary Congresses* (Chicago, n.d.), 138.
54. Panunzio, *Soul of an Immigrant*, 240-241.
55. Rose Cohen, *Out of the Shadow: A Russian Jewish Girlhood on the Lower East Side* (Ithaca, 1995), 162.
56. Robert McDonald, interview by author, fall 1994, North Attleborough, Mass.
57. Methodist Episcopal Church, New England Conference, "Report of the District Superintendent," *Minutes, 1939*, 831-832.
58. Boston East Baptist Association, *Annual Meeting of the Boston East Baptist Association, 1899-1900*, 21.
59. Massachusetts Baptist State Societies, *Massachusetts Baptist Year Book, Minutes of the Proceedings of the Massachusetts Baptist State Societies* (Boston, 1935), 50.
60. Frank Gulinello, Sr., "Biography," TMs, n.d. 8, Family Papers of Frank Gulinello, Jr. (private collection), Londonderry, N.H.
61. Massachusetts Baptist State Societies, *Massachusetts Baptist Year Book, Minutes of the Proceedings of the Massachusetts Baptist State Societies* (Boston, 1938), 38.
62. Massachusetts Baptist State Societies, *Massachusetts Baptist Year Book, Minutes* (1935), 41-42.

63. Massachusetts Baptist State Societies, *Massachusetts Baptist Year Book, Minutes* (1935), 31.

64. [Congregational] City Missionary Society, *Annual Report of the City Missionary Society, Boston, for the Year 1913* (Boston, 1914), 35.

65. Massachusetts Council of Churches, Department of Research and Planning, *Protestantism in East Boston, 1920-1946: An Underchurched Minority in an Overchurched Community* (Boston, 1947), 22-23.

66. The General Association of the Congregational Churches of Massachusetts, *Minutes of the Annual Meeting with the Statistics* (Boston, 1890–1940).

67. Von Hoffman, *Local Attachments*, 132.

68. Massachusetts Council of Churches, Department of Research and Strategy, *Boston's West End: A Study of Church and Community* (Boston, 1949), 107.

69. Francis Mazzeo, interview by author, Mar. 15, 1996, Concord, Mass. In her recent study of contemporary Brazilian immigrants from the city of Governador Valadares in the Boston area, Peggy Levitt found similar behavioral patterns. Immigrants change churches when they "fail to meet the spiritual needs of their members," and "the hardships of migrant life also prompt many non-believers to seek religion." Peggy Levitt, "Transnationalism or Assimilation: Paradox or Possibility?" (unpublished paper, 2000), 28-29.

70. Mangano, *Religious Work among Italians in America*, 26-27.

71. Massachusetts Baptist Convention, *The 102nd Annual Report of the Massachusetts Baptist Convention* (Boston, 1904), 25. See also Frederick Hale, "Baptists and the Norwegian-American Immigrant Milieu," *Foundations: A Baptist Journal of History, Theology and Ministry* 24(April-June 1981):126.

72. Hale, "Baptists and the Norwegian-American Milieu," 126.

73. Massachusetts Baptist State Societies, "Report on the New Americans," *The Massachusetts Baptist Year Book, Containing the Annual Reports of the Massachusetts Baptist State Societies with Minutes of Proceedings at the Anniversaries* (Boston, 1909), 29.

74. [Congregational] City Missionary Society, "Work among the Chinese," *Annual Report of the City Missionary Society, Boston, for the Year 1899* (Boston, 1900), 11.

75. Massachusetts Council of Churches, *Protestantism in East Boston*, 20.

76. Panunzio, *Soul of an Immigrant*, 204.

77. [Congregational] City Missionary Society, *Annual Report, 1913*, 40.

78. Gulinello, "Biography," 8, Gulinello family papers.

79. Virgil A. Olson, "Neither Jew nor Greek: A Study of an Ethnic Baptist Group, the Swedish Baptists, 1850-1950," *Baptist History and Heritage* 25(1990):36-37.

80. Massachusetts Baptist Convention, *The 95th Annual Report of the Massachusetts Baptist Convention* (Boston, 1897), 20, 27-28.

81. Gulinello, "Biography," 8, Gulinello family papers.

82. "Protestants Marrying Roman Catholics," *The Converted Catholic* 27.7(1910):264.

83. Thomas Sowell, *Ethnic America: A History* (New York, 1987), 111-112. He cites Herbert Gans, *The Urban Villagers: Group and Class in the Life of Italian-Americans* ([New York], [1962]), 35; Humbert S. Nelli, *Italians in Chicago, 1880-1930: A Study in Ethnic Mobility* (New York, 1970), 195-196, 198; and Joseph Lopreato, *Italian Americans* (New York, [1970]), 85.

84. Thernstrom, *Other Bostonians*, 167. Thernstrom cites Raymond Breton, "Institutional Completeness of Ethnic Communities and the Personal Relations of Immigrants," *American Journal of Sociology* 70(1964):193-205.

85. Maria Erling, "Swedish Popular Movements and Immigrant Culture: Links to the Protestant Establishment among Swedish Immigrants in New England, 1880-1920" (Ph.D. diss., Harvard Univ., 1992).

86. Francis Mazzeo, interview by author, Mar. 15, 1996, Concord, Mass.

87. Ladislaus Wlaslo to William Cardinal O'Connell, Aug. 5, 1920, TLS, RG 5.3 Parish Correspondence Files, Boston, Our Lady of Ostrobrama, 1916-39, Archives, Archdiocese of Boston, Boston.

88. John Daniels, *America via the Neighborhood* (New York, 1920), 247.

89. DeBilio, "Protestant Mission Work among Italians," 167-168.

90. DeBilio, "Protestant Mission Work among Italians," 131.

91. Massachusetts Council of Churches, *Protestant Ministry to Italian People*, 34-35. See also DeBilio, "Protestant Mission Work among Italians," 165, 167-168.

92. The Rev. Michael Shirley, interview by author, July 28, 1998, Amesbury, Mass.

Beyond the Machine

Martin Lomasney and Ethnic Politics

JAMES J. CONNOLLY

> *I think that there's got to be in every ward somebody that any bloke*
> *can come to—no matter what he's done—and get help. Help you un-*
> *derstand, none of your law and justice but help.*[1]
>
> —MARTIN LOMASNEY

OSTON WARD BOSS Martin Lomasney's credo has served not only to explain his own extraordinary political career but also as the most succinct statement of how urban and ethnic politics worked. Bosses helped immigrants integrate into American social and political life without forcing them to abandon their old-world values and customs. Lomasney's career provides a prime example of how this process worked. The legendary boss dominated the electoral life of Boston's immigrant-filled West End and North End from the 1880s through the early 1930s. Scholars have accepted his claim that he persisted despite constant charges of corruption because he had an intimate relationship with the working-class immigrants of his district. This allowed him to provide the kind of assistance that culturally alien charity workers and social reformers could not and earned him the steady loyalty of his ethnic neighbors.

Until recently, most historians took him at his word. Not only did they accept Lomasney's self-serving claim, reported through the less than reliable medium of Lincoln Steffens's *Autobiography*, they made it a cornerstone of the scholarly understanding of machine politics.[2] When sociologist Robert Merton first proposed that political machines endured despite their obvious corruption because they performed latent functions, he cited only one specific piece of evidence, Lomasney's explanation of his own success. Unlike condescending settlement residents and charity workers, Merton claimed, political bosses such as Lomasney thrived by providing needed assistance to their struggling immigrant constituents in a friendly, unthreatening fashion. Their beneficiaries provided votes in return. This functional explanation of machine politics, elaborated on by historians such as Oscar Handlin and John Allswang, shaped a generation of scholarly writing about urban politics. In most instances, these discussions of the ward boss featured Lomasney and his famous quotation.[3]

This machine model of urban politics has also shaped our understanding of the place of immigrants in American public life during the early twentieth century. The "help" Lomasney and his peers supposedly provided, which ranged from meeting newcomers at the dock and finding them a home and a job to interceding when trouble with the law arose, wedded grateful immigrants to the boss and his party. Political assimilation of most immigrants thus took place within the context of the machine, blocking other forms of mobilization, including a more radical, class-oriented politics and the independent reformism of middle-class Progressives. The hierarchical character of urban party politics also seemed to fit neatly with the old-world feudal traditions peasant immigrants brought with them, with obedience to the boss replacing fealty to the landlord. The result was a conservative, clannish political culture that changed little over time.[4]

Proponents of this understanding envisioned the political dimension of assimilation in a simplistic way. Immigrants arrived with preformed group identities, which bosses recognized and reinforced as they enclosed them within the machine's coalition. These collective self-understandings persisted, unchanged, as newcomers remained immersed in the parochial world of machine politics, safe from the predatory Americanization efforts of reformers. Assimilation took place largely outside the political realm, in private and economic life. When it was complete the Americanized children or grandchildren of immigrants entered the middle class and outgrew the need for help from the local boss. The political assimilation of these newcomers was merely a generational process, as their children and grandchildren Americanized, entered the middle class, and shed the dependency that necessitated boss politics.

Over the last two decades the urban political history that buttressed this account of the relationship between ethnicity and public life has encountered a powerful critique. Terrence McDonald has directly challenged this explanation of city politics, arguing that the prevailing climate of fiscal conservatism prevented bosses and machines from adopting the generous practices necessary to make a patronage-based approach work. Steven Erie's "life-cycle theory" of machine politics claims that patronage-driven machines could not operate effectively unless a sufficient supply of jobs and other resources were available from state governments and unless the pool of client-voters were limited. He contends that newer immigrants from southern and eastern Europe and other minority groups often received far less consideration from the local boss than did the more established Irish ethnics who dominated urban party operations. In fact, machines frequently thrived because the majority of new immigrants remained electorally inert. McDonald, Erie, and others have constructed an effective challenge to the traditional interpretation of big-city politics from the Gilded Age to World War II.[5]

The implications of this revisionist work for the scholarly understanding of ethnic political life remain undeveloped. If boss politics failed to incorporate substantial numbers of non-Irish immigrants, we cannot simply trot out the machine model to describe ethnic political culture. Nor can we simply focus on election results, seeking to quantify levels of voting support among various ethnic groups for particular candidates or parties, to measure changes in ethnic political culture. If we accept the premise that ethnicity is a malleable identity rather than a fixed, primordial characteristic, then straightforward attempts to trace group behavior become more difficult to sustain. Instead, we need to reconstruct ethnic politics from the bottom up, placing questions about group formation and mobilization at the center of the inquiry.

An examination of the relationship between Martin Lomasney and his ethnic neighbors is a good place to start. The literal prototype for Robert Merton's functional ward boss, Lomasney dominated politics in one of the most diverse sections of Boston for more than forty years. Most observers have attributed this feat to his ability to win the loyalty of struggling immigrants. But close inspection suggests the Lomasney method better fits the version of machine politics described by Steven Erie and his fellow revisionists. A majority of the poor Jews and Italians who filled his district did not vote and there is little evidence that he provided patronage or any other form of "help" to most of them unless he had to. Faced with a scarce supply of resources, Lomasney in fact had every incentive to discourage them from becoming citizens and voting.

We must look beyond the machine to understand ethnic politics, even in Lomasney's bailiwick. He only grudgingly incorporated Jews and Italians into his governing coalition when their voting strength began to threaten his control of the district. And these newcomers only began posing a danger to him when they started to think and act politically as groups, a process that developed slowly, unevenly, and largely in opposition to Lomasney and his machine. To some extent this was a social process, as the organizational infrastructure of a united community developed. But it was also a political development, driven by ambitious young activists who sought to establish themselves as representatives of specific ethnic communities even before these communities had fully taken shape. In doing so they also accelerated the emergence of politicized group consciousness in a local context. These efforts took root from the independent reform style of politics that permeated American public life during the Progressive era and the 1920s, rather than from the partisan tradition of the machine.

Reconstructing this process helps us understand the character of ethnic politics among specific groups in a particular time and place and also in modern America more generally. It resulted in part from the broader effort to construct group identities which were both overtly ethnic and legitimately American that was underway in many immigrant communities in response to the resurgent nativism of this period. It also flowed from institutional changes. Ethnic insurgencies developed more rapidly in Boston because of circumstances there, particularly the dominance of the Democratic Party, the Irish stranglehold on its operations, and local institutional changes stemming from Progressive reform. But the same patterns arose in most urban settings over the course of the twentieth century, as the ability of party machines to maintain stable ethnic coalitions—which was never as great as functional theory suggested—diminished further. These changes fueled a process in which ethnic politics became interest-group activism.[6]

On the surface, there seemed little room for a self-consciously ethnic politics in opposition to Martin Lomasney's machine. His organization, the Hendricks Club, dominated elections in Ward Eight, which encompassed Boston's immigrant-packed West End. The expansion of his district to include the Italian North End and a slice of the culturally diverse South End in 1916 had little affect on his power. No Lomasney-backed candidate ever failed to carry the district in a purely ward-based election from 1887, when he seized command of the local Democratic organization, until his death in 1933. Each Sunday before an election, Lomasney gave a rousing speech to his followers urging them to vote for a particular slate. The following Tuesday the ward invariably went to those candidates by a substantial margin. Lomasney's control over his Democratic district was so precise that he could deliver it to a Republican candidate, as he did in the 1905 Boston mayoral election, or divide up its precincts among two or more candidates.

Lomasney's record is all the more impressive when compared with those of his peers. A substantial revision of the city charter in 1909 sharply undercut the power of neighborhood party organizations. While a few ward politicians ascended to high office, most notably John F. Fitzgerald and James Michael Curley, most lost whatever grip they had on their district. Charlestown's Joseph Corbett, South Boston's Jeremiah McNamara, and the South End's Jim Donovan, all reputed to have been ward bosses on par with Lomasney during the 1890s, faded from view during the early twentieth century. Lomasney alone remained capable of controlling his ward into the 1920s, testimony to the unique social and political circumstances he faced and to his skill in exploiting them.

In many respects Lomasney became a remnant of an older style of politics. He remained rooted in a locally based organizational culture during an era in which many of his contemporaries began engaging in mass politics. While his loquacious rivals Fitzgerald and Curley both adopted a more publicity-friendly style that propelled them to wider acclaim and to seats in Congress and the mayor's office, the famously taciturn Lomasney served only on the city council and in the state legislature, and he often chose not to seek any office during the later stages of his career. This localistic orientation made Lomasney the quintessential ward boss and helps explain why he remained in full control of his district's political life long after his rivals in other districts lost power.

But power was not the same thing as popularity. The argument that Lomasney dominated the district because he had earned the full loyalty of his ethnic neighbors loses steam upon close inspection. A careful review of voting totals demonstrates that the level of support he received represented only a small fraction of the total population of his district. Even when considering the smaller universe of adult males, the size of the vote he delivered remains small, and its proportion of the whole shrank as the size of the nonvoting new immigrant population grew.

Charges that Lomasney cheated by bringing in outsiders to vote in his district appear to have some merit as well, indicating that the actual degree of support he earned within his district was even smaller than a superficial scan of election results suggests.

By the turn of the century, the social and political character of Lomasney's Ward Eight (the West End) was changing rapidly. Second-generation Irish began abandoning central Boston for an inner ring of semi-suburban neighborhoods, their places taken by Jewish newcomers from Russia and eastern Europe. This shift caused a steady decline in voter participation in the district. More than 70 percent of the 32,430 inhabitants of the district were Jewish by 1905, and according to one observer, these newcomers were just half as likely to register to vote as their Irish counterparts.[7] Although Ward Eight turnout in the city elections held from 1896 to 1915 averaged 75 percent of those registered and 75 percent of those eligible registered to vote, the portion of the entire district's male population participating in electoral politics dropped steadily as immigrants poured into the district. While 38.6 percent of the adult male population of the ward voted in 1896 and 41.9 percent in the mayor-city council contest of 1897, the proportion fell below 30 percent in non-mayoral elections after 1900 and down to 16.1 percent by 1914. On average, less than 28 percent of the district's adult male population voted in the twenty city elections during this period compared to 40 percent for the city as a whole.[8]

Raw numbers make the case even more starkly. Of the 10,565 men listed as residents of Ward Eight in 1900, just 2,810 cast votes in that year's city elections. At least 7,755 men in Lomasney's district did not—and in most cases could not—exchange their votes for his services. After 1909, when a revision of their city charter cut overall electoral participation in Boston sharply, the number of active voters in the ward shrank even further. Only 1,684 of the 10,454 men in the ward voted in the December 1914 city council elections.[9]

Lomasney's private records support the conclusion that Jewish nonparticipation fueled this decline. In a precinct-by-precinct accounting of turnout for the 1904 municipal election preserved in his scrapbook, he monitored not only the overall vote but also the "number of Hebrews" registered and voting. According to these figures, 1,094 Jews registered and 770 voted in the 1904 city contest, a 70 percent turnout rate. But this total pales in comparison to a West End Jewish population approaching 22,000. Lomasney may have earned the loyalty of most electorally active

Jews (his table does not report how they voted), but they represented only a small fraction of the total Jewish population.[10]

The extent of Lomasney's political control becomes less impressive in this context. When he delivered his ward to Republican mayoral candidate Louis Frothingham in 1905, a feat often cited as proof of the iron grip he held over the votes of the district, Frothingham won only 2,101 votes, or just 18 percent of Ward Eight's adult males. At least several hundred of those votes would have gone to the Republican candidate regardless of Lomasney's stance. The 1907 Republican mayoral candidate received 841 votes from Ward Eight despite Lomasney's opposition. Most Lomasney-backed local candidates rarely earned more than 2,500 votes and usually polled less than 2,000 in a district with more than 32,000 inhabitants in 1910.[11]

Measuring the proportion of adult men who voted rather than the proportion of eligible voters is appropriate when considering Merton's hypothesis. Although he did not specify whether his functionalist theory applied solely to voters or to the whole community, the prevailing interpretation has been the latter, that the boss served the interests of "immigrants" in general. If we are to test the proposition that the ward boss ruled because of the social functions he performed, then his efforts must be measured against the entire community in which he operated, not simply its electorally active element. Voters did not constitute the entire social universe in the West End or in any other urban context. Moreover, as political changes, mass immigration, and restrictions on the franchise caused voting rates to decline in the early twentieth century, the gap between the size and scope of the electorate and that of the population as a whole widened significantly. While this logic can be extended to support the argument that adult women should also figure in any measurements of the social functions of the machine, it can also be argued that some women exerted power in different fashion, through the medium of the household. Thus for purposes of comparison between voters and non-voters, I will restrict myself to the admittedly artificial measuring stick of the adult male population.[12]

Lomasney's vote totals remain unimposing even when we use the more traditional measurement of eligible voters—those adult men who had become American citizens after the required five-year waiting period. Only about two-thirds of those able to vote actually cast ballots in city elections between 1900 and 1910.[13] This meant that just 37 percent of those eligible voted for Louis Frothingham in 1905. Thus in all probability the Ward Eight boss delivered less than a third of the available votes in his most renowned demonstration of power.[14]

Ironically, efforts to reduce corruption and weaken boss politics ultimately increased Lomasney's local dominance. Boston's 1909 charter revision—the principal manifestation of Progressive-style political reform in the city—dramatically reshaped its public landscape. While the new arrangements, which included the elimination of ward-based, partisan, city council elections, damaged Lomasney's municipal clout and he resisted them furiously, his grip on the elections in his ward grew even stronger. These structural changes sharply reduced electoral participation throughout the city, including the West End, where turnout in city elections fell to 63 percent of those eligible and just 22 percent of all adult males in the district between 1910 and 1914. A smaller electorate made the ward even easier to control, as did the structural alterations in city politics that channeled political action by his opponents into extra-electoral forms.[15]

Measures designed specifically to eliminate Lomasney's base of power backfired as well. Hostile state legislators redrew the boundaries of his district to encompass not only the West End but also the North End and a portion of the South End in 1916, assuming that the sheer size and ethnic heterogeneity of the new Ward Five would stymie Lomasney's efforts to maintain the kind of client-patron politics on which bosses supposedly throve. But Lomasney adjusted to the new circumstances, parceling out nominations to representatives of each of the three largest ethnic groups in the district—Italians, Jews, and Irish—and remaining the dominant political figure in the district into the 1930s.[16]

Gerrymandering failed because its architects misunderstood the roots of Lomasney's power. Adding the immigrant-filled North and South Ends further reduced the proportion of active voters in his ward. In particular the annexation of the North End with its large community of Italians made it easier for Lomasney to capture the ward's elections. "Italians without a doubt take the least interest in politics of any nationality," noted a contemporary observer. In 1896 just 13 percent of Italian males with five years of residence in Boston had registered to vote. At the turn of the century, only 36 percent of the city's Italian population had even become citizens. Barriers of language and custom blocked their participation in American public life, a difficulty many never tried to overcome because they planned to return to Italy. As a result Italians had the lowest partici-pation rate of any of Boston's major ethnic groups, with registration totals remaining under 20 percent of the eligible electorate in the North End well into the 1920s.[17]

An examination of participation rates in the new ward illustrates the impact of redistricting. From 1916, when the new ward lines went into effect, until 1923, when they changed again, the proportion of active voters fell steadily. The extension of the franchise to women in 1920 only accel-erated this decline. By 1923, fewer than 10 percent of the district's entire adult population voted; the remaining 90 percent—30,492 of the 33,742 adult men and women in Ward Five—did not and were thus superfluous to Lomasney's political survival. Although municipal voting rates were declining throughout the city during the same period, the 13.4 percent average in Lomasney's Ward Five fell significantly below the citywide average for adult participation of 25.9 percent.[18]

In all likelihood, even these meager numbers were inflated. Numerous observers charged the Hendricks Club with augmenting its own vote totals and reducing opposition results through a wide range of illegal and semi-legal methods. While some of these claims were undoubtedly exaggerated, even accounts sympathetic to Lomasney describe illicit ac-tivities by the West End leader and his organization. The one practice that did appear widespread and received a certain degree of confirmation was "mattress voting," in which Lomasney allies residing outside his dis-trict checked into a West End hotel on the eve of the annual police listing of eligible voters. Their presence in the ward the following day allowed them to claim residence there for voting purposes. They then returned home, only to reappear on election day to cast their vote as Lomasney dictated.[19]

Two investigations confirmed that Lomasney's organization used this practice. A 1902 dispute over a congressional seat prompted hearings that featured several witnesses acknowledging that they had voted in Ward Eight despite residing elsewhere. The accompanying uproar sparked sev-eral press investigations, including one that found a West End hotel that housed eighty-five men in fifteen rooms on the eve of the disputed elec-tion. A similar controversy in 1919 prompted the U.S. House of Represen-tatives to reverse the outcome of another election after hearing testimony describing widespread mattress voting. Even Lomasney himself all but admitted that the practice went on, declaring that "when a single man wanted to change his residence and take up a new one it did not matter, when he was honest about it, whether he changed his mind again in a few days and moved back." A House Elections Committee concluded—and the full House agreed—that at least 316 of the 1,004 ballots cast in three West End precincts were fraudulent, a number sufficient to reverse the result. Other estimates ranged from 400 to 1,000 illegal votes, totals that suggest the actual number of Lomasney supporters truly living in his district was even smaller than election returns indicated.[20]

A large part of Lomasney's success stemmed from the absence of most of his neighbors from local voting booths. Unlike his political rivals in other wards Lomasney faced relatively few challenges to his power and he was able to absorb the few men who earned substantial followings into his organization by offering them patronage. Boston's Irish wards in particular featured rampant factionalism, usually erupting when the number of ambitious young politicians and would-be politicians exceeded the number of places on the ballot or the number of choice patronage slots. Since electoral politics was a far more central part of the public culture of second- and third-generation Irish Bostonians than it was first-generation Jews and Italians, competition for offices and patronage slots was fierce and organizational leaders in these districts regularly faced challenges to their power from those left out. Many of Boston's Irish politicians with reputations as ward bosses, including Joseph Corbett of Charlestown, Patrick Kennedy of East Boston, and William McNary and Jeremiah McCarthy in South Boston, saw their slates defeated almost as often as not in local elections. The few exceptions to this rule, most notably Jim Donovan in the South End and John Fitzgerald in the North End, presided over districts with large numbers of nonvoting recent immigrants, much like Lomasney.[21]

If Lomasney thrived because so few of his immigrant neighbors voted, it is unreasonable to assume that Lomasney supplied much "help" to the majority of his ethnic neighbors who did not vote. He undoubtedly distributed a substantial amount of patronage. No record exists of how many people received public or private sector jobs with Lomasney's assistance, nor can we ever determine precisely what other favors he provided. Public estimates of the time reported that Lomasney placed as many as 1,000 men on the city payroll and that his supporters drew between $75,000 and $300,000 in public salaries. But given the advantages Lomasney derived from an inactive ethnic electorate, he was unlikely to deploy a significant share of his resources to mobilize them, even as he promoted the notion that he dispensed jobs and favors generously.[22]

Local circumstances made the supply of patronage scarce as well. As Stephen Erie has noted, the period from the late nineteenth century through the early 1930s was one of constricted resources for urban machines, particularly if they lacked the support of the state government. Irish Democrats in Boston faced just such a difficulty because the Republican Party consistently controlled the Massachusetts state legislature and usually carried the governor's office as well. That left the city's burgeoning Irish political class competing for whatever morsels city hall could dispense. And even that supply dwindled as Progressive-era reforms tightened civil service laws and hiring practices, making it all the more difficult to maintain a cohesive political organization through available patronage.[23]

The absence of a citywide machine in Boston further exacerbated these problems. While Lomasney ran his own district with an iron hand, he needed support from politicians in other sections of the city to capture most state and city offices, particularly after the institution of at-large city council elections in 1909. Thus at least some of the patronage he managed to distribute had to go to politicians and supporters outside his ward. And as the ethnic makeup of his district shifted and many of Lomasney's West End allies moved to other sections of the city, some of his patronage went with them. (One reason he may have continued to assist them is because he relied on them to return to the West End each year to register and cast their votes.)

The limited evidence available supports this assessment. When Mayor James Michael Curley threatened to remove Lomasney men from the city payroll in 1922, the *Boston Telegram* published a partial list of supporters the West End boss had placed in municipal positions. The *Boston City Directory* for that year listed fewer than two-thirds of the eighty-seven people named as residents of Lomasney's district. The remainder lived in other sections of the city or had no listing at all within the city limits. While neither the *Telegram*'s list nor the *City Directory* are perfectly reliable sources, together they suggest that a substantial portion of Lomasney-controlled patronage flowed beyond the borders of his district, a claim Lomasney's local opponents repeated constantly over the course of his career.[24]

All of this suggests that however lavishly Lomasney spread his patronage, few of the thousands of Jews and Italians in his district benefited. There simply was not enough to go around. As one of his contemporaries explained, "every time I give a job I make one friend and ten enemies." Another, interviewed several years after Lomasney's death, recalled that if someone asked for a job or favor, Lomasney would check to see if he voted in the last election. If not, he would not help, a policy that excluded most non-Irish ethnics in the ward. Lomasney could maintain a cohesive organization with city work and other favors, but he could not provide directly for the vast majority of immigrant poor who packed his neighborhood during the early twentieth century. Indeed, there was no reason for him to want to help them, since his longevity stemmed to a substantial degree from their inactivity on election day and the absence of the factional challenges so pervasive in Irish wards.[25]

The study of ethnic politics in early-twentieth-century America must move beyond the machine, as the relationship between Lomasney and his immigrant neighbors shows. Not only did Lomasney fail to mobilize or assist most newcomers, he faced the active opposition of many ethnic leaders. Only when that hostility threatened his power did he accommodate some Jews and Italians with offices, a share of patronage, and, most often, symbolism and support for policies that cost him little of his scarce supply of jobs and other divisible benefits. The process of mobilizing "the Jewish vote" and "the Italian vote" took place outside and usually in opposition to the machine, as spokesmen for these groups urged their fellow ethnics to naturalize, register, and vote. The development and politicization of distinctive identities that made ethnic loyalty a demonstration of good citizenship preceded the machine's attempt to absorb the challengers, an effort that met with mixed success at best.

Lomasney provided a valuable foil for this project. By the early twentieth century he had earned a widespread reputation as a corrupt boss and had become a symbol of civic decline in the city. In *Americans in Process*, their 1902 study of immigrant life in the North and West Ends of Boston, settlement worker Robert Woods and his colleagues declared "the West End . . . so boss-ridden that there is rarely any public campaign at all. . . . This seems to represent the extreme step in setting aside our American precedents." These revelations set off a round of press investigations into West End public life that claimed to expose a range of corrupt political practices. Lomasney also became a target of Boston's Good Government

Association, launched in 1903 by local businessmen, which devoted a substantial amount of time and energy to investigating and criticizing the increasingly infamous Lomasney over the next decade. This context made attacking the "Czar of the West End" an effective strategy for ethnic insurgents who sought to demonstrate their loyalty to the precepts of American democracy.[26]

A small set of Jewish activists led the first self-consciously ethnic attack on Lomasney. Although the West End boss came to power while his district was still predominantly Irish, after 1900 it rapidly became a Jewish district. He faced increased difficulty as this change occurred, fueled in part by his reputation as "a secret anti-semite." A prospective "Hebrew uprising" earned repeated mention in press accounts of West End political life and Lomasney kept a close watch on Jewish registration and voting rates. The predicted insurgency developed, though circumstances allowed Lomasney to survive the challenge.[27]

A sharp shift in the makeup of Jewish Boston fueled this wave of political action. From the middle of the nineteenth century Boston had featured a small, mostly German Jewish population that sought invisibility. "We have no special Jewish interests to defend," the local *Jewish Chronicle* declared in 1892, "and we would not antagonize our Christian neighbors by continually forcing our religion to the surface." But 70,000 eastern European Jews entered Boston between 1880 and 1914, bringing with them distinctive languages and customs that undercut aspirations of Jewish assimilation. Suddenly the West End became a district teeming with newcomers from Russia and other parts of eastern Europe and thus a highly visible symbol of Jewish Boston. Tensions along class and national lines developed and the cohesiveness that marked nineteenth-century Boston Jewry faded. Jewish leaders faced instead the long-term challenge of unifying their community. The immediate task was to construct a public identity for themselves and their coreligionists that struck a balance between being Jewish and being respected American citizens, an effort that would itself fuel a sense of group identity and community.[28]

Attempts to develop an independent Jewish politics began almost as soon as a substantial number had settled in the West End. In 1891 Samuel Borofsky urged early Jewish settlers in the North and West Ends to form Hebrew political clubs that could exercise power outside the purview of the Irish-run Democratic machine. The development of Zionism during the 1890s and early 1900s, which fostered a strong sense of Jewish identity,

increasingly merged with the call for a distinctly Jewish political movement. Jacob de Haas, a staunch Zionist and editor of the *Boston Advocate*
(which became the *Jewish Advocate* under his direction), emerged as a
particularly emphatic supporter of concerted Jewish political action both
at home and abroad.[29]

Lomasney was one of the impediments to that process. The majority of
Jewish newcomers crowded into the tenements of the West End, where
the tradition of boss rule had poisoned popular perceptions of local politics. From the outside, Boston's Jews began to appear to be either the
ignorant dupes of the boss or his willing co-conspirators. Neither view
fostered the respect and acceptance of Jews as solid citizens that the Jewish press and Boston's emerging Jewish leadership sought to cultivate.
Opposition to the "Czar of the West End"—a nickname that Lomasney
hated and which had obvious connotations for Russian Jews—thus became the basis upon which Jewish spokespersons attempted to construct
Jewish political independence.[30]

The anti-Lomasney offensive began in earnest in 1905, when a controversy arose between Robert Silverman, a Jewish settlement worker in the
West End, and Walter Harrington, headmaster of a local grammar school
and a political ally of Lomasney. Silverman accused Harrington of "mis-
appropriation of funds." When the school board narrowly dismissed the
charges, angry Jewish leaders claimed that it did so because of political
pressure by Lomasney. Harrington's subsequent libel lawsuit against Silverman intensified the controversy further.[31]

Jewish leaders rallied behind Silverman. David Ellis, a Jewish Democrat
on the school committee, quit the party and made the case a central
theme of his independent reelection bid. Louis Brandeis arranged for a
lawyer from his firm to represent Silverman for free. Most importantly,
de Haas and the *Jewish Advocate* used the issue to underscore Jewish opposition to Lomasney and support for the principles of good government
and Progressive reform. The controversy pitted "the people"—in this
case Boston's Jews—against a political boss and his machine, the paper
claimed. The *Advocate* also insisted that it was "the paramount duty on
the part of Jewish voters" to support David Ellis and his fellow reformers
in the ensuing school committee election against "the tools of some corporation or political machine."[32]

De Haas and others continued to cultivate a Jewish politics rooted in
opposition to bossism and support for reform in the wake of the Silver-

man case. "These bosses are enemies of the immigrant," the *Advocate* proclaimed. "Remember what our people suffered through the influence of ward bosses," the paper warned; "the bosses want you today but forget your interests tomorrow." There was little doubt which boss was the chief villain in these declarations: the paper regularly celebrated even the slightest Lomasney defeat. The school controversy also marked the emergence of Louis Brandeis as a forceful voice for Jewish political unity and activism. Previously quiet on these issues as he built his legal career, the future Supreme Court justice gave a preelection address in 1905 to a Jewish audience entitled "What Loyalty Demands." In it he argued that Jewish traditions and the ideals of American citizenship were consistent and urged Jews to forsake the corrupt machine and support reform.[33]

Action followed rhetoric in 1906, when Jewish leaders backed Henry Levenson for the state legislature in Ward Eight. A successful businessman and president of the West End Educational Union, Levenson presented himself as "the people's independent candidate" running against the Lomasney machine and sought to mobilize Jewish voters on that basis. "This is a campaign of the people against the boss," he declared, and he left no doubt who the people were in this case. As one of his supporters claimed, the goal of his candidacy was to win "representation for the Jews." Levenson received support from the *Advocate* and from numerous prominent West End Jews, including Silverman, settlement workers Horace Kallen and Meyer Bloomfield, and several synagogue leaders, all of whom angrily attacked Lomasney not only for the corrupt public life in the district but also its deteriorating sanitary conditions.[34]

Although Levenson lost, the attempt threw a scare into Lomasney. The Jewish candidate ran strongly in the three predominantly Jewish precincts of the ward, earning 535 votes in those sections. He trailed Lomasney himself, who captured 1,079 votes, but outpolled the boss's running mate in one of the three precincts. Levenson's total dropped slightly because Lomasney arranged for two other Levensons, Abraham and Jacob, to appear on the ballot. Although not close to defeating a Hendricks Club man, Levenson's showing far outdistanced the usual anti-machine candidate in the West End. His performance was evidently impressive enough to prompt Lomasney to nominate David Mancovitz for the state legislature in 1908, the first Jew to receive machine support for an office above the Common Council level.[35]

Levenson's substantial showing and Lomasney's response suggested the power that even the threat of Jewish political unity contained. The *Advocate* began to insist that it was the voice of "the solid Jewish vote in Boston" and to emphasize the "natural political morality of the Jews" that led them to support reform measures and candidates. Several prominent Jews persuaded the Citizens Municipal League, a nonpartisan nominating body created by reformers after the 1909 charter revision, to support Mark Stone (a Jew) or risk forfeiting Jewish support for the entire reform ticket. Jewish leaders and organizations started working outside the electoral process, pressuring the city council and state legislature on issues ranging from regulation of kosher food to concerns over rising antisemitism. The pressure they brought to bear stemmed from their assertion that they represented a large and cohesive Jewish vote. Although an exaggeration, since most Jews did not vote and those who did divided themselves between parties, the claim was becoming plausible enough to carry weight. In the short run it made them a more effective interest group. In the long run it formed the basis for continued efforts to mobilize Jewish voters into a single bloc, efforts that gradually bore fruit.[36]

Lomasney was astute enough to recognize this development and accommodate Jewish interests to a certain degree. He included Jews on slates for local offices and took supportive positions on issues directly affecting the group. He criticized American foreign policy for tolerating czarist Russia's mistreatment of Jews, supported kosher food legislation, and opposed immigration restriction. The Jewish representatives he placed at city hall and in the state house regularly offered measures designed to benefit Jews. For instance Ward Eight Common Council member Jacob Rosenberg sponsored orders providing for Jewish chaplains at city institutions, leaves of absence for Jewish holidays, and the issuance of permits for the slaughter of live fowl on Jewish feast days during his 1907 term. But Lomasney could afford to make these gestures because they did not dilute the precious supply of patronage jobs reserved for his closest allies.[37]

More concrete accommodation of Jewish demands would have proven difficult for Lomasney had two developments not intervened. The first was the redistricting of 1916, which placed Lomasney in the newly designated Ward Five, which encompassed all of the Italian North End and a part of the South End. This new, vastly larger district included a wider range of ethnic groups, making Jews a smaller portion of Lomasney's total constituency. The second change was demographic. Just as Jews began to increase their voting power, they also started leaving the West End for the more suburban neighborhoods of Roxbury and Dorchester, where they soon established a substantial political presence. By the middle of the 1910s, the Jewish population of the West End stopped growing; the number of Jews in the district, above 30,000 in 1910, had slipped to 20,000 in 1920 and only 8,000 in 1930, by which time Jewish voting rates were beginning to jump sharply. (Only a little over 3,000 would remain by 1938). Middle-class Jews moved earlier, siphoning off the population most likely to naturalize, register, and vote and most likely to challenge Lomasney's power through participation in Jewish insurgent politics. This combination of developments allowed Lomasney to fend off the first ethnic challenge to his power.[38]

The redistricting that helped Lomasney escape the consequences of Jewish political mobilization created new ethnic complications. While the new ward boundaries diluted the Jewish presence in the district, they encompassed the 27,000 Italians of the North End. The threat was not immediate since the prospects for the mobilization of "an Italian vote" to challenge Lomasney seemed even dimmer than the chances of creating a substantial Jewish vote in the West End had been. Few Italians voted and those who did were sharply divided along provincial lines. But by the late 1920s, voting rates among local Italians jumped sharply. While Lomasney never faced a fully unified and mobilized Italian insurgency, the political life of the North End grew more competitive and far less manageable as a result of these changes.[39]

The North End was a far from cohesive community during the early twentieth century. The district's social and political life was dominated by a plethora of mutual benefit societies, many tied to local loyalties from the old country. These provincial ties made coordinated political action all but impossible, particularly among first-generation immigrants. Many had no intention of remaining long in the United States and so had little incentive to participate in political social life or attempt to overcome the traditional boundaries that separated Italian immigrants. Not until the 1920s, as the children of these immigrants came of age, did Italian North Enders begin to demonstrate a politically significant sense of community, and even then internal divisions remained powerful.[40]

The absence of cohesion among Italians during the first decades of the twentieth century did not prevent politically ambitious politicians from claiming to represent "Italians." Led by a small tier of *prominenti*, including labor leader Dominic D'Alessandro, newspaper editor James Donnaruma, state representative George Scigliano, and lawyers Jerome Petitti and Frank Leveroni, the campaign sought to challenge the dominance of the neighborhood's entrenched Irish Democratic machine. The focus of their attacks was the organization's leader, ambitious and controversial John "Honey Fitz" Fitzgerald, who became mayor of Boston in 1905. Using Fitzgerald as a foil in much the same way that West End Jews attacked Lomasney, North End Italian spokesmen decried him as a "dictator" responsible for the "oppression" of the Italian people and urged local Italians to "cooperate for the benefit of their district." When Fitzgerald's administration faced corruption charges, Donnaruma's paper, the *Gazzetta del Massachusetts*, seized on the controversy to strengthen the attack on the mayor and demonstrate the political independence of North End Italians. Hoping to capitalize on the antagonism against Fitzgerald, local leaders formed the "Partito Italiano Independente" and began sponsoring anti-machine candidates.[41]

The ward boundary changes of 1916 diluted Italian strength before these efforts could bear much electoral fruit. Italians constituted only a third of the new, larger ward's population. Thus even if Italians unanimously supported their own, their candidates were unlikely to carry the district without significant additional support. Since Italian voting rates remained even lower than those of the Jews, the prospect of a substantial and cohesive Italian vote was slight, giving them little leverage against the Hendricks Club. Lomasney was able either to ignore Italian upstarts who gained a following or to absorb them into his organization. In the short run at least, he encountered few difficulties with ethnically based challenges emanating from the North End.[42]

Although these early insurgencies met with little success on election day, they set a course for subsequent attempts to mobilize Italians. North Enders formed a variety of groups designed to seize control of the Americanization process away from native-born reformers and place it in the hands of Italians themselves. By 1921 several organizations were working to Americanize Boston Italians, notably the United Independent Italian American Citizens Club, the Young Men's Italian Association, and the Woman's Italian Club. A part of this work entailed naturalization and voter registration, a process that took place outside the purview of the machine. As the "United Independent Italian American Citizens Club" name suggests, it encouraged these new citizens to think of themselves in ethnic terms but also as independent, patriotic American citizens rather than the pawns of an organization or party.[43]

External sources of Italian mobilization also emerged, many through the work of Boston mayor James Michael Curley. Lomasney and Curley were rivals, but while Lomasney's base of power remained rooted in his home ward, Curley's ambitions carried him well beyond the boundaries of his neighborhood, landing him in the mayor's office and then the governorship. As part of his effort to cultivate a citywide following, Curley circumvented Democratic ward leaders, spending lavish sums on improvement projects in ethnic districts for which he took the lion's share of the credit. After Lomasney backed his opponents in the mayoral elections of 1917 and 1921, Curley made a concerted attempt to create an independent Italian vote in opposition to Lomasney.

Upon his return to the mayor's office in 1921, Curley became a prominent presence in the North End. With great fanfare he issued loan orders for increased street cleaning and repaving in the district, the construction of a playground and a bathhouse, and improved sewer and water services. He also worked to improve parks and to replace lost trolley service with new bus routes. For each of these steps, Curley made a point of publicly consulting community leaders who were not linked to Lomasney's organization. All of these gestures earned Curley warm praise in local Italian circles. The Mazzini-Garibaldi Republican Club happily noted that "he had appropriated for the good of the Italian people of this city over $500,000." He supplemented spending with Americanization efforts, directed from city hall and designed to naturalize and register new voters, who presumably would owe little allegiance to the Lomasney machine.[44]

Within the Italian community, the calls for an independent, anti-machine politics initiated during the Progressive era continued as well. Both the *Italian Voice* and the *Italian News* joined the anti-Lomasney chorus and urged Italian unity on election day. "We know from experience that whatever representation the Italians have had in politics, that representation has been given in the form of a bribe and with the understanding that the representative should strictly obey the orders of the boss," the *Voice* complained. The *News*, formed in 1921 as the self-conscious articulation of second-generation Italian American interests, routinely attacked Lomasney and celebrated even the slightest sign of his weakness in the Italian quarter. Both papers were motivated by their sympathy for the Republican Party (although the *News* was ostensibly

nonpartisan), but the common stress on the need for Italians to unite
and reject the boss as a way of demonstrating their good citizenship
added to a growing chorus demanding independent Italian political
action.[45]

Early efforts to challenge Lomasney in the name of the Italian people
met with only limited success, serving mostly to keep alive the drumbeat
for Italian independence. After a failed anti-machine primary bid in 1922
by North Enders George Costanza and Michael Carchia showed promise,
with Costanza finishing just 300 votes shy of a nomination, Republican
Saverio Romano and the *Italian News* lobbied fiercely for all Italians to
unite behind him and against the machine in the general election. Urging
North Enders to vote on the basis of their ethnic loyalty rather than party
affiliation, the *News* endorsed Romano as the "real type of man who
should represent Italo-American voters." Romano himself made little
mention of his party affiliation, instead seeking the support of "the individual unbossed citizens" of the district to support his candidacy. Though
he lost, his effort added volume to the calls for Italian independence from
Lomasney.[46]

East Boston Italian (and former North Ender) Vincent Brogna's 1926
state senate run had better results. He ran for the seat in the Second
Suffolk District, which included Lomasney's ward, on an Italian-oriented
"Beat the 'Boss'" platform. During the campaign the *Italian News* vilified
Lomasney, blaming him for the poor physical condition of the North End,
and celebrated Brogna's effort as "the beginning of a re-awakening which
will lead to both political and moral salvation." Brogna also lost, unable to
carry non-Italian sections. But that failure did not prevent the *News* from
declaring the attempt itself a "triumph" because Brogna carried several
Italian precincts. "An overwhelming majority of Italo-American voters
[went] on record as expressing their disapproval of Lomasney," the paper
exulted, adding that Brogna's performance "can be interpreted as a great
victory for the political redemption of Boston Italians." It also predicted
that "the day is not far when the Italians of Boston will finally assert themselves against the merciless bosses who grind them down."[47]

While there was some reason for hope, the *News*'s optimism was premature. Brogna was not the first candidate to carry the Italian vote against
a Hendricks Club candidate. Joseph Langone did so on the Republican
ticket for state representative in 1920, finishing ahead of Lomasney himself in the North End. Anthony Squilaciotti carried the Italian precincts of

the ward over the two machine candidates in the 1926 Democratic state representative primary as well. But Lomasney brought Langone into his organization the following year and endorsed his next bid for a seat at the state house while Squilaciotti faded after his one brief whiff of success. The Italian electorate remained too small and often too divided to pose a serious threat to Lomasney through the mid 1920s. Whenever a challenger gained a significant following Lomasney absorbed him readily.[48]

It is easy to dismiss the Italian independence movement as a calculating factional ploy, as some observers at the time did. Some challengers may also have been stalking horses planted in the race by Lomasney to divide Italian support. But even they stressed opposition to Lomasney and "Italian independence," underscoring and reinforcing the power of such appeals in a context where the bulk of Italians had no connection to the machine. Although some voices argued for unified support of the Republican Party against the West End Democratic machine, most emphasized independent, nonpartisan action.[49] The fact that editors viewed these appeals as effective tools for cultivating an Italian audience and that political insurgents saw them as an effective way of mobilizing Italian supporters reflects the public culture forming among Boston Italians during the 1920s. They were coming of age politically, as self-consciously independent "Italian" voters rather than as cogs in a partisan machine.

The election of 1928 constituted a watershed in the emergence of a significant ethnic politics in the North End. The campaign of Democratic nominee Al Smith and the New Deal era that followed triggered a surge of naturalization and registration among "new immigrant" voters throughout the nation over the subsequent decade. As Gerald Gamm has noted, no group better fit that description than Boston Italians, whose voting rates jumped dramatically beginning in 1928. Two years earlier, just 20 percent of the 6,493 adult men and less than 7 percent of 4,623 adult women in the North End had registered to vote. With Smith's campaign the figure for males jumped to 26 percent while the proportion of women rose slightly to 7.4 percent. Those percentages grew steadily in succeeding elections, with the strongest surge coming between 1930 and 1934. By 1936, 51 percent of the men and 28 percent of the women had registered; by 1940 those figures reached 57 percent and 38 percent.[50]

Smith's presidential bid evoked themes that matched those used by the anti-machine Italian insurgents in the North End. On the campaign trail Smith stressed his Progressive record as governor of New York, partly to overcome his origins as a Tammany machine stalwart. Although he spoke infrequently of his ethnic and religious background on the campaign trail, he made no effort to hide it; that heritage made him an extraordinarily attractive candidate in urban immigrant America. His campaign also targeted specific ethnic groups to an unprecedented extent. In the North End, this effort took the form of the Smith Italian League of Massachusetts, which operated separately from both the Democratic Party and the Hendricks Club. As its name and its organizational independence suggest, it placed greater stress on ethnic identity than on partisan loyalty. Lomasney enemy George Costanza headed the group, which sought to capitalize on the New Yorker's combination of ethnic and reform credentials to mobilize local Italians. Smith's candidacy resonated so powerfully in the North End because it echoed the central claims of Italian independence— that ethnic loyalty and good citizenship were not only compatible, they were mutually reinforcing.[51]

Several North End political entrepreneurs rode the Smith wave after 1928, the most successful of whom was Edward Bacigalupo. An ambitious young Italian "social worker," he gained a following in the North Bennett Street section of the North End, which he parlayed into an effective political movement in the wake of the upheaval of 1928. "Unite, Italo-American voters of Ward 3, against Lomasney and his candidate, who have insulted our noble race," Bacigalupo's campaign literature announced during his bid for the City Council in 1929. (Ward Five had become Ward Three in 1926). Although he lost, he carried the two most Italian precincts of the ward by a 1,370 to 291 margin over the Hendricks Club candidate, a feat he repeated the following year in the Democratic primary race for state representative even though Lomasney put an Italian candidate up against him. These successes within the North End, while not enough to overcome the machine's power in the rest of the ward, reflected the sharp rise in Italian political participation and cohesiveness after 1928. Bacigalupo, who constantly stressed the theme of Italian independence and who reportedly represented "the younger element" in the ward, capitalized on this growing ethnic vote to become Lomasney's first serious Italian challenger.[52]

The West End boss responded as he so often had before, by offering Bacigalupo a share of the spoils of his machine. At first Bacigalupo accepted, agreeing not to run for any office in 1931 in exchange for Hendricks Club backing in 1932 for the state legislature. Machine support carried him to office and it appeared that Lomasney had survived another threat to his preeminence in the North End. But Bacigalupo bolted in 1933 after the Hendricks Club chose to back another candidate. In part the split may have been precipitated by Lomasney's death that year, which deprived the West End machine of its driving force. Yet it also reflected the changing political character of the district. Bacigalupo had developed enough of a following among Italian Americans to challenge the machine, and insurgency now appeared to offer an effective route to political success.[53]

A new political organization backed Bacigalupo's challenge to the Hendricks Club. Created in the fall of 1933, the Italian Political Association was hailed in the North End press as a body "destined to become a colossal force for the influence and affirmation of the race." The new group was nonpartisan and devoted to supporting candidates who served "the best interest of Italo-Americans." It was launched with the blessing of James Michael Curley, who was just finishing a term as mayor and preparing a gubernatorial bid for 1934. Mobilizing Italians independently, outside the purview of the Hendricks Club, gave him a better chance of carrying the district in future elections. After making a show of considering other candidates it endorsed Bacigalupo for City Council and urged united Italian support of his candidacy.[54]

Bacigalupo found himself challenged by three other Italians, each of whom represented a separate new political organization claiming to serve the group's interests. Emboldened by Lomasney's death and no doubt encouraged by the increasing voting strength of Italians, several ambitious politicians had formed North End political groups in the hopes of capturing Ward Three's city council seat in 1933. Bacigalupo represented the newly formed Italian Political Association in the race. He faced challenges from Dominic Meo, carrying the endorsement of the Young Men's Democratic Club of Ward Three, and the Hend-Jun Club, a North End offshoot of the Hendricks Club (the name was a contraction of "Hendricks Junior") led by Lomasney lieutenant Frank Leonardi. The Hend-Jun Club organized immediately after the Italian Political Association and appears to have been a response to its emergence. The new wing of the old machine endorsed West Ender John I. Fitzgerald, Lomasney's longtime ally. A third Italian candidate, Ralph Del Gaudio of the North End, entered the competition as well.[55]

Despite factional intrigue that threatened to splinter the Italian vote, Bacigalupo clearly emerged as the "Italian" candidate. He totaled 1,769

votes in the two precincts encompassing most of the North End, far out-
distancing his closest rival (Meo, with 532 votes). Hendricks Club candidate John Fitzgerald carried the ward as a whole, benefiting again from
the organization's strength in the West and South Ends, but trailed badly
in the North End precincts with only 460 votes despite the efforts of Frank
Leonardi and the Hend-Jun Club. By 1933 the Lomasney machine had
clearly lost whatever loyalty it might have once engendered among North
End Italians.[56]

This scramble to represent "the interests of the Italian people" not only
reflected their growing voting strength but added to it. The Hend-Jun
Club listed "stimulating registration of voters" as one of its chief goals and
worked assiduously to achieve it, while the Italian Political Association
reported adding 644 new names to Ward Three voting rolls, including 414
in the North End, by early October. These local efforts continued over the
next several years, contributing as much or more to surging Italian voting
rates during the 1930s as did national developments such as the Smith
candidacy and the New Deal.[57]

Italian mobilization did not immediately translate into political offices
for Italian candidates. In many ways the notion of an "Italian vote" was a
useful fiction, one that allowed aspiring politicians to claim more influence than they had. Provincial divisions among Italians remained sharp
through the 1930s and beyond, and these differences often took on political significance. This factionalism made North End politics resemble the
splintered public life of Boston's contentious Irish districts. The size of
Ward Three also hurt Italians—even a perfectly unified ethnic vote would
leave them short of a majority in the district. But as the Irish and Jews left
and Italians spread into the West and South Ends, Italians became more
successful. The Hendricks Club gradually lost its influence and in 1939
North End Italian independent Joseph Russo earned a seat on the City
Council, sealing its demise. In the period after World War II, Italians
would begin to dominate North End politics and become a distinctive
force in city affairs.[58]

Although the earlier Italian independent campaigns failed to carry the
ward, they threw into sharp relief patterns that were now shaping ethnic
politics in new, immigrant Boston. By the 1920s, an interest-group based
political style had arisen in opposition to partisanship nationally, and
North End Italians drew on this new form. Campaigns "in the interest of

the Italian people"—however implausible at the time—replaced calls to partisan arms as a typical mode of winning political support in the district and establishing the legitimacy of a group or candidate. James Michael Curley had by this time mastered the art of speaking for and winning the support of the Boston Irish without the support of a party machine as well. Italian leaders and their counterparts in other groups followed suit, fueling the contentious group politics that would define Boston through the much of the twentieth century.[59]

The intensification of avowedly ethnic politics in early-twentieth-century Boston must be understood as the product of modern, interest-group activism. Progressive reforms remade public life in ways that encouraged political mobilization outside of the partisan framework that dominated nineteenth-century American politics. The growth of "ethnic politics" among Boston's Jews and Italians arose in this fashion, largely in opposition to partisan-based machine politics. Before they could assume a significant place in the city's public life during the New Deal era, their ethnic identities had to become politically salient, a process that was grudgingly accepted rather than encouraged by Lomasney's machine. Only when a coherent, self-consciously "ethnic" Jewish or Italian politics developed could they begin to demand real accommodation from Democratic leaders, a process that sharpened group conflict.

The particular circumstances of Boston's public life shaped this process of ethnic mobilization. Lomasney and his Irish counterparts in the city never aggressively sought to incorporate ethnic newcomers into the Democratic coalition because Boston was a one-party city through the early twentieth century. Democrats faced little competition from the Republican Party, which abandoned any serious effort to win immigrant support early in the Progressive era. Lomasney and his colleagues had no reason to mobilize newcomers and further divide their already scarce supply of offices and patronage. As a result, recent immigrants became voters slowly and largely in opposition to the Democratic machine. In this respect, the experience of Boston's newer immigrants differed from those in other cities where party competition was more balanced. Both parties aggressively competed for the support of Chicago's ethnics, for instance, in a battle the Democrats finally won by the early 1930s by building a cross-ethnic "house for all peoples." Boston's Irish Democratic leaders had no need for Italians and Jews, leaving them to be mobilized instead as ethnic insurgents who earned a place at the table only when they grew strong enough to seize one. Consequently, an effective multi-ethnic coalition never developed in Boston and divisions among European ethnic groups in local public life remained particularly pronounced.[60]

The politicization of Italian and Jewish identities also took place within a distinctive moment in American ethnic political culture. These group definitions took shape in an era when new, nonpartisan avenues of public action had developed to challenge traditional party politics. Irish immigrants to Boston during the nineteenth century had been mobilized into a far different political world, one more open to their participation in party affairs—and ultimately to their domination of them. But even their politics became less party driven and more focused on group grievances with the political transformations of the early twentieth century. Migrants and immigrants coming to the city since World War II have entered a public environment with much weaker parties and no political machines, one that has fostered an even more pronounced sense of group differences. Recent public life has also been informed by a different idea of the relationship between distinctive cultural groups and mainstream American life. Becoming "ethnic" before World War II did not entail a rejection of the dominant culture as it does in today's multicultural America.

The ability of new immigrant leaders in Lomasney's district to turn the independent, nonpartisan style fueled by Progressivism to ethnic ends is one episode in the larger process of immigrant adaptation to American life during this era. Faced with criticism from reformers and Americanizers, who generally demanded complete assimilation, they used this new political form to construct categories of public identity and action that claimed full American citizenship while preserving an ethnic allegiance. Presenting themselves as political independents working in opposition to Lomasney and boss rule not only immunized them from charges that they were mindless dupes of the machine, it also helped them demonstrate the compatibility of civic patriotism and ethnic loyalty. They thus became ethnic Americans, loyal to their old-world heritage and a part of mainstream American public culture simultaneously. The uncritical equation of ethnic politics with machine politics has obscured this essential part of immigrant adaptation to American life.

NOTES

1. Quoted in Lincoln Steffens, *The Autobiography of Lincoln Steffens* (New York, 1931), 2:618.
2. On the reliability of Steffens's *Autobiography*, see Justin Kaplan, *Lincoln Steffens: A Biography* (New York, 1974), 305. On Steffens's interest in celebrating political bosses, see Christopher Lasch, *The New Radicalism in America, 1889-1963: The Intellectual as a Social Type* (New York, 1965), 251-285.
3. Robert K. Merton, *Social Theory and Social Structure*, rev. ed. (New York, 1968), 128; Oscar Handlin, *The Uprooted: The Epic Story of the Great Migrations that Made the American People*, 2d ed. (Boston, 1973), 190-195; John Allswang, *Bosses, Machines, and Urban Voters: An American Symbiosis* (Port Washington, N.Y., 1977). On the importance of functionalism for urban political historiography, see Terrence McDonald, "The Problem of the Political in Recent American Urban History: Liberal Pluralism and the Rise of Functionalism" *Social History* 10(1985):330-342.
4. Handlin, *The Uprooted*, 187-198; John Bodnar, *The Transplanted: A History of Immigrants in Urban America* (Bloomington, 1985), 197-204; Ira Katznelson, *City Trenches: Urban Politics and the Patterning of Class in the United States* (Chicago, 1981).
5. Terrence McDonald, *The Parameters of Urban Fiscal Policy: Socioeconomic Change and Political Culture in San Francisco, 1860-1906* (Berkeley, 1986); Stephen Erie, *Rainbow's End: Irish-Americans and the Dilemmas of Urban Machine Politics, 1840-1985* (Berkeley, 1988); Alan DiGaetano, "The Rise and Development of Urban Political Machines: An Alternative to Merton's Functional Analysis," *Urban Affairs Quarterly* 24(1988):242-267. See also Bruce Stave et al., "A Reassessment of the Urban Political Boss: An Exchange of Views," *History Teacher* 21(1988):293-312, for a statement of both sides in this debate.
6. On the transformation of American political life and the rise of nonpartisan interest group politics, see Elizabeth Sanders, *The People's Lobby: Organizational Innovation and the Rise of Interest Group Politics, 1890-1925* (Chicago, 1997). On the effort of immigrants to construct "ethnic-American" identities, see Kathleen Neils Conzen et al., "The Invention of Ethnicity: A Perspective from the U.S.A.," *Journal of American Ethnic History* 12(1992):3-41; and Russell A. Kazal, "Revisiting Assimilation: The Rise, Fall, and Reappraisal of a Concept in American Ethnic History," *American Historical Review* 100(1995):437-471. On ethnic groups as interest groups, see Nathan Glazer and Daniel Patrick Moynihan, *Beyond the Melting Pot: The Negroes, Puerto Ricans, Jews, Italians, and Irish of New York City*, 2d ed. (Cambridge, Mass., 1970).
7. Robert A. Woods, ed., *Americans in Process: A Settlement Study by Residents and Associates of the South End House* (Boston, 1902), 63-64; Massachusetts Bureau of Statistics and Labor, *Census of Massachusetts: 1905, Population and Social Statistics* (Boston, 1909), 1:xciii; *Jewish Advocate*, Aug. 26, 1910. The census figures are for Russians, a proxy that may underestimate the total number of Jews in the district. Gerald H. Gamm, "In Search of Suburbs: Boston's Jewish Districts, 1843-1994," in *The Jews of Boston*, ed. Jonathan D. Sarna and Ellen Smith (Boston, 1995), 139, puts the total Jewish population in the West End at 24,000.

8. The average for the entire city was compiled and computed from the annual reports of the Boston Board of Election Commissioners for this period. The 1896 to 1915 range best suits this study because the boundaries of Lomasney's district remained unchanged during that time.

Every one of the board's annual reports appeared in print as individual publications usually within a year or two of the year covered. For reference purposes, these items will be cited individually or in a group, thus: BBEC, AR 1896-1916. Page numbers will also be cited when appropriate. All of the reports were printed in Boston.

9. BBEC, AR 1900-1914.

10. "City Election, December 13th," typescript, Martin Lomasney Scrapbook [microfilm], vol. 10, n.p., Massachusetts Historical Society.

11. BBEC, AR 1905, 171; BBEC, AR 1907, 211.

12. See Philip J. Ethington, "Recasting Urban Political History: Gender, the Public, the Household, and Political Participation in Boston and San Francisco during the Progressive Era," *Social Science History* 16(1992):301-333, for a discussion of the importance of the household in urban politics.

13. U.S. Bureau of the Census, *Twelfth Annual Census of the United States: Population Schedule* (Washington, D.C., 1900), 11; U.S. Bureau of the Census, *Thirteenth Annual Census of the United States: Population Schedule* (Washington, D.C., 1910), 890; BBEC, AR 1900, 1905, 1910. Only the 1905 report included eligible voter figures; calculations for the remaining years relied on the 1900 and 1910 federal censuses, adding naturalized adult males to native-born totals.

14. BBEC, AR 1905.

15. On the 1909 charter and its impact, see James J. Connolly, *The Triumph of Ethnic Progressivism: Urban Political Culture in Boston, 1900-1925* (Cambridge, Mass., 1998), 105-132. Eligible voters for 1910-1914 calculated from U.S. Bureau of the Census, *Thirteenth Annual Census: Population Schedule*, 890.

16. Gustave R. Serino, "Italians in the Political Life of Boston: A Study of the Role of an Immigrant and Ethnic Group in the Political Life of an Urban Community" (Ph.D. diss., Harvard Univ., 1950), appendix II-B.

17. There were 27,000 Italians in the North End, 90 percent of the total population. Gerald H. Gamm, *The Making of New Deal Democrats: Voting Behavior and Realignment in Boston, 1920-1940* (Chicago, 1989), 79, 82, 185; Frederick A. Bushee, *Ethnic Factors in the Population of Boston* (Boston, 1903), 132; Serino, "Italians in the Political Life of Boston," 34. See also Woods, *Americans in Process*, 64-65. On repatriation among Italian immigrants, see Bodnar, *The Transplanted*, 53.

18. BBEC, AR 1916-1923.

19. Leslie G. Ainley, *Boston Mahatma: The Public Career of Martin Lomasney* (Boston, 1949), 57-58; Benjamin Loring Young, "Martin Lomasney as I Knew Him," *Proceedings of the Massachusetts Historical Society* 75(1963):63; William Foote Whyte, *Street Corner Society: The Social Structure of an Italian Slum* (Chicago, 1955), 237-238.

20. *Boston Post*, Feb. 21, 1903; *Boston Globe*, Mar. 11, 1919; U.S. Congress, *Congressional Record*, 66th Cong., 1st sess., 1919, 7396-7398, 7401. Though it is difficult to calculate its precise impact, another source of inflated turnout was repeat voting. See Whyte, *Street*

Corner Society, 313-316, for evidence of this practice by both the machine and Italian challengers.

21. James J. Connolly, "Boston's Other Irish Wards: Democratic Wards without Bosses" (master's thesis, Univ. of Massachusetts—Boston, 1989); Maurice Baskin, "Ward Boss Politics in Boston, 1896-1921" (senior honors thesis, Harvard Univ., 1975), 31-52.

22. *Boston Traveler*, Oct. 23, 1908; *Boston Post*, Mar. 22, 1903, Jan. 10, 1904; Edward Dixon Flyer, Sept. 24, 1906, Lomasney Scrapbook, vol. 14, p. 126.

23. Erie, *Rainbow's End*, 76.

24. *Boston Telegram*, May 13, 1922. One of the city contractors Curley did manage to cut from the city payroll was Lomasney ally Bernard Grant, who resided in suburban Brookline. *Boston Globe*, May 23, 1922.

25. Woods, *Americans in Process*, 169; Whyte, *Street Corner Society*, 194.

26. Woods, *Americans in Process*, 163.

27. Woods, *Americans in Process*, 189.

28. Quoted in Jacob Neusner, "The Rise of the Jewish Community of Boston, 1880-1914" (honors thesis, Harvard Univ., 1953), 117. See also Jacob Neusner, "The Impact of Immigration and Philanthropy upon the Boston Jewish Community (1880-1914)," *Publication of the American Jewish Historical Society* 146(1956):71-85; and William Alan Braverman, "The Ascent of Boston's Jews, 1630-1918" (Ph.D. diss., Harvard Univ., 1990), chap. 6.

29. Braverman, "Ascent of Boston's Jews," 211-219.

30. Woods, *Americans in Process*, 163.

31. *Jewish Advocate*, Sept. 29, 1905; *Proceedings of the Boston School Committee for 1905* (Boston, 1906), 374-379, 401; *Jewish Advocate*, Oct. 13, 1905; William A. Braverman, "The Emergence of a Unified Community, 1880-1917," in *The Jews of Boston*, 86; Allon Gal, *Brandeis of Boston* (Cambridge, Mass., 1980), 87-90.

32. *Jewish Advocate*, Oct. 6, Dec. 8, 1905.

33. *Jewish Advocate*, Feb. 22, 1906, Oct. 20, 1905; Gal, *Brandeis of Boston*, 93.

34. *Boston Post*, Oct. 14, 1906; Levenson Campaign Flyer, Lomasney Scrapbook, vol. 14, n.p.; *Boston Herald*, Oct. 1906.

35. Braverman, "Ascent of Boston's Jews," 223, 353.

36. *Jewish Advocate*, Dec. 13, 1905; Braverman, "Ascent of Boston's Jews," 235; *Boston Herald*, Jan. 2, 1910; Marlene Rockman, "The Kosher Meat Riots: A Study in the Process of Adaption of Jewish Immigrant Housewives to Urban America, 1902-1917" (master's thesis, Univ. of Massachusetts—Boston, 1980), 35-37.

37. *Boston Herald*, June 1, 1911; *Proceedings of the Boston Common Council for 1907* (Boston, 1908), 238-239, 544, 557.

38. Gamm, *Making of New Deal Democrats*, 50, 60-61, 66.

39. Gamm, *Making of New Deal Democrats*, 79.

40. On North End social life and the persistence of provincial divisions, see William M. DeMarco, *Ethnics and Enclaves: Boston's Italian North End* (Ann Arbor, 1981).

41. Ward 6 Regular Democratic Club Flyer, Lomasney Scrapbook, vol. 11, n.p. See also Connolly, *Triumph of Ethnic Progressivism*, 56-61.

42. Jewish voting rates were split by class, with working-class rates lower than those of the

middle class. But even Jewish working-class rates were substantially higher than those of any Italian cohort. Gamm, *Making of New Deal Democrats*, 60, 82.

43. *Italian News*, May 21, 1921, Oct. 14, 1922, May 1, 1921.

44. Connolly, *Triumph of Ethnic Progressivism*, 166-167.

45. *Italian Voice*, Jan. 24, 1920; *Italian News*, Jan. 19, 1921.

46. *Italian News*, Sept. 16, Nov. 4, 1922; Saverio R. Romano Flyer, Lomasney Scrapbook, vol. 30, p. 153.

47. *Italian News*, Aug. 21, Sept. 18, 1926.

48. Serino, "Italians in the Political Life of Boston," 57; Gamm, *Making of New Deal Democrats*, 215.

49. Serino, "Italians in the Political Life of Boston," 88, 50-51. Erie notes that the absence of two-party competition meant the dominant party had no incentive to mobilize new immigrants. *Rainbow's End*, 96.

50. Gamm, *Making of New Deal Democrats*, 82, 219

51. *Gazzetta del Massachusetts*, Oct. 6, 1928. For Smith's career, see Oscar Handlin, *Al Smith and His America* (Boston, 1958); Donn C. Neal, *The World beyond the Hudson: Alfred E. Smith and National Politics, 1918-1928* (New York, 1983); Elizabeth Israels Perry, *Belle Moskowitz: Feminine Politics and the Exercise of Power in the Age of Alfred E. Smith* (New York, 1987), 184-213; and John F. McClymer, "Of 'Mornin' Glories' and 'Fine Old Oaks': John Purroy Mitchel, Al Smith, and Reform as an Expression of Irish-American Aspiration," in *The New York Irish*, ed. Ronald H. Bayor and Timothy J. Meagher (Baltimore, 1996), 274-294.

52. Bacigalupo Flyer, Lomasney Scrapbook, vol. 34, p. 37; BBEC, AR 1929, 39; BBEC, AR 1930, 56.

53. *Gazzetta del Massachusetts*, Sept. 10, 17, 24, 1933.

54. *Gazzetta del Massachusetts*, Sept. 2, Oct. 28, 1933.

55. *Gazzetta del Massachusetts*, Sept. 10, 1932; *Italian News*, Sept. 8, Nov. 3, 1933.

56. BBEC, AR 1933, 43.

57. *Italian News*, Sept. 8, 1933; *Gazzetta del Massachusetts*, Oct. 7, 1933; Gamm, *Making of New Deal Democrats*, 82-83.

58. John F. Stack, Jr., *International Conflict in an American City: Boston's Irish, Italians, and Jews, 1935-1944* (Westport, Conn., 1979), 75; Whyte, *Street Corner Society*, 194-205.

59. On Curley, see Connolly, *Triumph of Ethnic Progressivism*, 133-189. See Whyte, *Street Corner Society*, 230-232, on the use of ethnic appeals among Italians.

60. Serino, "Italians in the Political Life of Boston," 50-51; J. Joseph Huthmacher, *Massachusetts People and Politics, 1919-1933* (New York, 1969), 15-18; John M. Allswang, *A House for All Peoples: Ethnic Politics in Chicago, 1890-1936* (Lexington, 1971).

Lines in the Sand

*Ethnicity, Race, and Culture
at Revere Beach*

MARK HERLIHY

S GREATER BOSTON'S, and perhaps New England's, most popular summer pleasure ground from the late nineteenth century until the 1960s, Revere Beach provided diverse people with an experience that in theory all could have shared. Public beaches, after all, are among the most open of open spaces, and the strip of dance halls, mechanical rides, cheap eateries, and souvenir shops that once lined Revere Beach Boulevard served as a regional mecca of modern, mass, commercial culture. A closer look, however, reveals that despite Revere Beach's general popularity—the resort attracted 200,000 visitors on a typical weekend during its heyday—subgroups from throughout the region experienced and perceived it differently. Previous studies of leisure in American cities have stressed the degree to which modern amusements blunted differences among audiences and visitors and homogenized culture. John Kasson, for example, argued that seaside resorts such as Coney Island "help[ed] knit a heterogeneous audience into a cohesive whole." Immigrants, Kasson asserted, considered a trip to Coney a "means to participate in mainstream American culture." "Though traces of class and ethnic backgrounds still clung to Coney Island's amusement seekers," he contended, "in arriving at the resort they crossed a critical threshold, entering a world apart from ordinary life, prevailing social structures and positions."[1]

At Revere Beach visitors could certainly transcend their differences, but seaside resorts, Coney Island included, provided spaces where distinctions among visitors were reinforced, celebrated, exploited, or otherwise made manifest. Ethnicity, for example, could influence the kinds of food people consumed at the beach. Despite rules prohibiting religious and political expression, members of various ethnic groups also used the site to affirm their particular faiths. In these and other ways, immigrants resisted the homogenizing influence that the new mass culture allegedly exerted.

When people ventured to Revere Beach, they often brought with them their customs, their heritages, their demands to utilize space as they saw fit, and even their prejudices. They did so because a trip to the beach could be a reminder of, and not an escape from, "prevailing social structures and positions." If many saw an outing at the resort as an opportunity to reinvent themselves amid the anonymity of the crowd, just as many recognized a chance to associate with people who shared their ethnic heritage. By examining the immigrant dimension of Revere Beach's history, particularly the experiences of Jews and Italians who frequented the beach in large numbers, we can learn more about how Massachusetts's immigrants appropriated and contested public space. We can also see that they used leisure and recreation as a means both to embrace and to resist assimilation into "mainstream American culture."

Immigrants did not only use space at Revere Beach. Insofar as they developed, worked at, and were the principal patrons of amusement venues along the boardwalk, they helped to create the phenomenon that Revere Beach became. They fashioned a culture—a decidedly commercial one, privileging fun and entertainment—at odds with the "higher" purposes that planners and officials believed an urban beach should serve. Indeed, the history of Revere Beach reveals both the differential uses of urban space by immigrants and a long-standing struggle between recent immigrants and more established groups to control and define the seaside leisure experience of Greater Bostonians.

Beginning in the 1950s, as African Americans and Asian Americans began to come to Revere Beach, the already ethnically contested area became racially contested as well. These new arrivals laid claim to a space that had traditionally been a white working-class leisure preserve, redefining and broadening the "public" for which Revere Beach had been created. Race, however, was also (and remains) an important, if not openly acknowledged, dimension of the discourse surrounding the decline of Revere Beach as a popular summer pleasure ground after World War II. Indeed, by focusing on the later history of the beach, when interracial friction convinced some people that the beach was unsafe, we gain insights into the relationship of demographic shifts to changing perceptions of urban public space.

Revere Beach's Renaissance

Immigrants have played an important role in the history of Revere Beach for the last century. Steady immigration to Boston beginning in the mid nineteenth century led to severe crowding in the city's inner wards, spurring the development and privatization of scenic areas and open spaces throughout eastern Massachusetts. Boston's celebrated Emerald Necklace, virtually complete by 1895, provided a creative response to these conditions.[2] This ring of interconnected parks, green spaces, and ocean-side pleasure grounds preserved many open spaces for the region's inhabitants. As a municipal park system, however, it could not meet the needs of a growing metropolis. Frederick Law Olmsted, the system's architect, perhaps understood this better than anyone; he believed that provisions for open space throughout metropolitan Boston would become necessary at some point. "It is practically certain," he wrote in 1870, "that the Boston of today is the mere nucleus of the Boston that is to be. It is practically certain that it is to extend over many miles of country now thoroughly rural in character."[3]

Throughout the latter portion of the nineteenth century, the need to preserve open spaces intensified. The privatization of oceanfront property presented a particularly acute problem. The Trustees of Public Reservations, formed in 1891 to protect scenic areas, noted in its first annual report that "most of the shore towns have no park, common, or open space of any kind to which the people have a right to resort."[4] The most striking development, according to the Trustees, was the purchase and development of coastal land by the wealthy. As the organization reported:

There is a general movement of moneyed people from the cities and towns of the whole country east of the Mississippi River to the shore towns of Massachusetts. Individuals, companies, and associations are buying lands everywhere along the shore. Besides what is being done openly by buyers who are known and recognized, in most of the towns some citizen acts as agent for principals who prefer not to be known. Several of these agents say they are buying for New York men; but capitalists from various interior cities are investing here. . . . It is largely a movement of people with means to enable them to build and maintain comfortable mansions for either summer occupancy or permanent residence by the sea.[5]

In the late 1890s, the wealthy adopted the "vacation habit," fueling the purchase of oceanfront property on which to build "comfortable mansions."[6] For people of modest means, however, this trend did not bode well. As the Trustees warned, there is "a great population inland hedged away from the beach, and all conditions [point] to a time, not remote, when nobody can walk by the ocean in Massachusetts without payment of a fee."[7]

Boston planners, reformers, and civic leaders in the 1890s noted the privatization of the region's coast, as well as other encroachments upon open spaces, with alarm. In March 1892 landscape architect Charles Eliot, son of Harvard president Charles W. Eliot, argued that as the region's open spaces became developed "the mass of the townspeople in the State . . . are more and more shut out from the beauty and the healing influence of nature's scenery and more and more shut up in their tenements and shops. Is this for the advantage of the State? Is it not rather a foreboding condition of things?"[8]

Eliot and other old-line Yankees, including Sylvester Baxter, Philip A. Chase, and Charles Francis Adams, Jr., led a movement that resulted in the creation of the Metropolitan Park Commission (MPC) in 1893. Granted broad powers to acquire, improve, and maintain open spaces within a ten-mile radius of Boston, the commission focused much of its early attention and resources on Revere Beach. Just five miles up the coast from Boston and accessible by public transportation, it had the potential to become metropolitan Boston's most popular summer pleasure ground. By the turn of the century, after the MPC spent $1 million clearing the beach of private dwellings and commercial establishments and building a mammoth bathhouse, it became just that.

Revere Beach constituted a priority for the MPC because, as Baxter noted, it was the "nearest ocean-side pleasure ground for a population numbering at least half a million."[9] After surveying open spaces throughout Greater Boston, a temporary MPC board, made up of Adams, Chase, and William B. de las Casas, with Baxter serving as secretary and Eliot as landscape architect, deemed Revere Beach one of "the most important features" of the regional park system within their purview. In Chase's estimation, the beach took precedence because of "the benefit to the largest number of people in providing them with facilities for summer recreation."[10]

More than anyone else, immigrants, Jews and Italians particularly, stood to gain from the improvement of Revere Beach. In the late nineteenth century, the beach was surrounded by communities with high concentrations of recent arrivals from abroad, people who would consider it their personal playground. Just north of Revere stood Lynn, whose laborers, many newcomers among them, gave the town the moniker "City of Shoes." Chelsea, south of the reservation, was "the poorest of the Boston harborside immigrant and industrial cities," according to Sam Bass Warner, Jr., and beginning in the 1890s home to Jews from eastern Europe. Groups that constituted ethnic majorities in various sections of Boston—Italians from the North End and East Boston and Irish from Charlestown—frequently visited Revere Beach. [11]

In the City of Revere, Jews and Italians have been a strong presence since the late nineteenth century. Italians, of whom there were only 21 in Revere in 1895 but who made up about half of the city's population in 1940, settled in a section close to the northern end of the beach and in other areas. The dedication of the lavish Saint Anthony's parish in 1926 symbolized their rise to power in the city. There were 137 Polish and Russian immigrants in Revere in 1885, most of them Jews, and 1,646 by 1915. In 1940, Jews constituted approximately 25 percent of the city's population. [12] Traditionally, they occupied an area of the city close to the beach around Shirley Avenue.

One of the Jewish families that settled in Revere in the 1890s was that of writer Mary Antin, who achieved fame with the 1912 publication of her autobiography, *The Promised Land*. Antin, along with her mother, sister, and brother, emigrated from Polotzk, Russia, in 1894, and joined her father in Boston; he had come three years earlier seeking work and a better future for his family. Shortly after the Antins reunited, they moved to Crescent Beach (an early name for Revere Beach), where her father operated a refreshment stand. They "came to live on the edge of the sea," in what she alternately described as "a little cottage" and a "shanty" in *The Promised Land*. She recalled the beach as "historic ground in the annals of my family," expressing a sentiment that other immigrants who visited or worked at the beach would have shared. [13]

Temporary MPC board members did not refer specifically to immigrants as the principal beneficiaries of an improved Revere Beach. In advocating for a metropolitan system of parks, it was perhaps unwise to single out any particular constituency. They used the example of Revere Beach, however, to make the case that a regional approach to land management and the preservation of open spaces was imperative. In a land-

mark 1893 report, in which they argued for the establishment of a permanent MPC (to create what would become the country's first regional park
system), the board members asserted that

> A proper park system . . . cannot be developed within local lines. . . .
> All enjoy the results; all consequently should participate according to
> their means and needs in bringing those results about.
>
> This proposition the commissioners do not deem it necessary to
> elaborate further than by a single illustration. The summer . . . is the
> season of the year when all feel the need of open-air reservations. . . .
> The natural trend of movement at that season in eastern Massachu-
> setts speaks unmistakably for itself, and shows what the popular de-
> mand is; rich and poor instinctively find their way towards the ocean;
> the excursion steamers are thronged, the beaches are black with visi-
> tors. Nor is this movement confined to those who dwell in the
> crowded districts of Boston. It takes in all of the suburbs of Boston.
> [I]n answer to this natural demand . . . the beaches should be set aside
> and sacredly preserved through combined action. To expect the local
> municipalities—sometimes towns neither rich nor populous—to
> carry the burden of such a public work as the proper improvement of
> Revere or Nantasket Beach, is neither right nor practical. It must be
> borne by the district . . . or the burden most assuredly will not be as-
> sumed at all.[14]

After the Massachusetts legislature established a permanent MPC, Revere Beach underwent a remarkable transformation. Before the commission took the area by eminent domain in 1895, it was almost completely
overrun by eighty-one privately owned shops, bathhouses, hotels, and
shanties that extended down to the waterline. So close were they to the
water that, "At high tide, people were compelled to use a narrow passage-
way at the rear of the buildings" in order to move up and down the
beach.[15] These structures marred the view of the ocean and assaulted
the environment and senses in other ways. Garbage receptacles and cesspools underneath the buildings polluted the air and water and produced
"a notorious smell, which 1,000,000 or more people have experienced . . .
in summer whenever the wind was southeast."[16] The *Boston Herald* reported in July 1897 that

Revere Beach, circa 1893. Before the Metropolitan Park Comission (MPC) redesigned the area in 1896, clam shacks, hotels, and saloons, many built on piles, crowded in on the beach, and extended down to the waterline.
Photograph from *Report of the Board of Metropolitan Park Commissioners* (Boston, January 1893). Collection of the Massachusetts Historical Society.

Under many of these buildings there were cesspools or barrels for sewage. Some of these had never been covered, many of them were improperly covered. Half the cottagers and other housekeepers were in the habit of throwing slops and swill at random from the back door. Some persons dug little holes in the sand beside their houses, and buried swill and fresh clam shells in them. Under the piazza of one of the hotels, which has accommodated as many as 3000 sightseers on a Sunday afternoon, there was an immense cesspool, which reeked with filth. There was no sewer main along the beach crest. The sand, being very porous, absorbed all this sewage and decaying vegetable and animal matter readily.[17]

Railroad tracks and a highway upon the crest of the beach hemmed in these structures on the landside. Eliot, in charge of the Revere Beach improvement, maintained that the tracks and the highway had gone up "without regard either to the safety and convenience of the public. . . . The railroads cared only for a location which would enable them to use the beach as an attraction to draw passengers. No account was taken of the fact that swarms of people must induce a demand for buildings, and so the buildings have had to find sites where best they could, generally between the highway and the sea." Private development and poor planning, Eliot believed, had blighted Revere Beach. He claimed that the "present condition of this fine beach is a disgrace" and called for a "thorough reformation" of the area. Baxter argued that "Something should be done . . . to make Revere Beach what it is capable of becoming for the great public."[18]

When planners target an area for renewal, they often invoke moral and cultural as well as practical reasons for the changes they propose. In its discussions of Revere Beach, the MPC rang this note with particular gusto. Baxter argued that the beach, "so far as environment is concerned, is today in a most deplorable condition"; he cited the poor placement of the railroad and the "cheapest kind of shanties" built on the beach; and he asserted that development along the shore "attracted rough and disorderly elements . . . so that, except in a few favored spots, women and children" stayed away. Baxter's concern over morals at the beach stemmed most likely from the gulf between his own cultural predilections and those of the immigrants who claimed the beach as their space. Baxter, however, was not alone in his low regard for the beach prior to the MPC's takeover. The cultural and class biases of reformers like Baxter distorted views of the moral climate at Revere Beach—as they would of any place. The *Boston Traveler*, for example, reported in 1897 that "Everybody knows what [Revere Beach] used to be [like]. Husbands forbade their wives, parents their children, to visit the place."[19]

Mary Antin's recollections of life at Revere Beach paint a picture that differs radically from these views of the area. She never suggests that the beach threatened the morals of those who ventured to it. Antin, age thirteen when she arrived in Revere, describes the beach not only as a space in which children could cavort freely and safely but also as one that could reactivate latent play impulses. "Let no one suppose that I spent my time entirely, or even chiefly, in inspired solitude. By far the best part of my day was spent in play—frank, hearty, boisterous play, such as comes natural to American children," she wrote. "In Polotzk I had already begun to be considered too old for play, excepting set games or organized frolics. Here I found myself included with children who still played, and I willingly returned to childhood. There were plenty of playfellows."[20]

Photographic evidence also suggests that Revere Beach, before the MPC intervention, may have been more genteel and safer than Baxter and others claimed. Pictures of large expanses of the beach before the MPC improvement show well-dressed people strolling along the beach or sitting on benches enjoying the sights. In these photos women and children appear to have free rein throughout the area.

While one could contest the MPC's critique of Revere Beach's moral climate, the site's need for public health and accessibility improvements was incontrovertible. In planning the redesign of Revere Beach, Eliot mostly addressed the physical aspects of the area, but he nonetheless betrayed an upper-class bias on occasion. In an 1891 paean to old, country estates, he wrote that "New England, in the old days before the growing up of the great cities, possessed many towns in and near which dwelt people of polite cultivation and polished manners, whose sober, but often stately, mansions yet remain." He had a similarly genteel view of what constituted a proper seaside experience and aesthetic. Writing about development along Maine's coast, Eliot claimed that "nowhere is lack of taste quite so conspicuous as on the seashore." As for Revere Beach, he hoped both that private land opposite the water would be "occupied by hotels, restaurants, shops, apartment houses, and private dwellings" and that it would be "possible to impose some restrictions" on such development.[21]

Like his mentor, Frederick Law Olmsted, Eliot believed that picturesque landscapes exerted a salutary and civilizing effect on people, even when they did not realize it, and that immigrant and working-class residents of crowded urban centers were most in need of nature's balm. Eliot envisioned Revere Beach as a powerful antidote to city life, presenting visitors with a vast open expanse that was "rarer and grander than the landscape of a field." As he later put it: "Nothing . . . presents a more striking contrast to the jumbled, noisy scenery of a great town" than "the grand and refreshing sight of [Revere Beach] with its long, simple, curve, and its open view of the ocean."[22] So that the resort could serve this high purpose, Eliot called for the wholesale removal of all structures on the waterside of the railroad tracks and the repositioning of the tracks to a spot several hundred yards away, behind buildings that remained standing opposite the beach. The MPC built a roadway over the area occupied by the tracks and a promenade between that and the shore. The only structures permitted between these new features and the water were a few sun shelters and a pavilion that the MPC built for band concerts. Eliot even insisted that the bathhouse be placed along the outer edge of the boulevard so that nothing would mar the ocean views.

With the funds and resources at his disposal, Eliot designed a space intended to bring the glories of nature to the masses of metropolitan Boston. He set forth this view in the MPC's *Annual Report* of 1896:

> It is sometimes said to be useless to spend time, pain and money in making sure that public domains are made as beautiful as they can be made, because "ordinary people will never appreciate the difference." But what if fine results are not accurately valued and their causes discerned by the multitude? . . . When he comes into the presence of unaccustomed beauty or grandeur, the average man does . . . consciously or unconsciously experience a reaction, which is of benefit to him. It is on this account, and not in order to satisfy competent students of aesthetics, that our democracy has ordered the setting apart of Revere Beach and the other reservations. It is precisely for the sake of "the common people" that these reservations ought to be made to exhibit their grand or beautiful scenery just as effectively as possible. The principle that the most effective management is none too good for "the common people" already governs the trustees of our schools, libraries, and art museums.[23]

The elitism, paternalism, and sense of noblesse oblige that Eliot betrays here echo many of Olmsted's pronouncements on landscape architecture; they are also typical of the views held by many reformers of the era.[24] As David Schuyler has urged, however, we must not let this dimension of planners' thought or rhetoric lead us to overlook the positive impulses that animated their best work. Schuyler maintains that landscape architects and urban planners in Eliot's day considered themselves to be reformers who believed "that the physical spaces humans occupy influence their patterns of behavior." According to Schuyler, historians are quick to criticize Eliot and others for trying to use the built environment to "induce immigrants and lower-class residents of cities to emulate the behavioral patterns, the refinement and culture, of an educated class," but they often fail to recognize that their "words and work . . . convey a positive vision of what American society could become and reveal a deep commitment to the nation's republican destiny."[25]

No matter our hindsight today, at the turn of the century the transformation of Revere Beach won accolades throughout metropolitan Boston and beyond. As news of the improvements spread, the numbers of visitors

*Revere Beach, 1896. To improve the beach, the MPC cleared it of 81 struc-
tures, moved train tracks along its crest several hundred yards inland, and,
where the tracks once stood, laid down a boulevard and a promenade. The
result was an area divided into distinct zones—for bathers, pedestrians,
and vehicles—and one which was safer and more accessible for the public.*
Photograph from *Report of the Board of the Metropolitan Park Commissioners*
(Boston, January 1898). Collection of the Massachusetts Historical Society.

to the beach swelled to the point that, on a Sunday at the turn of the century, a crowd of 150,000 was typical.[26] The MPC could claim a victory:
as its most popular reservation—one that had undergone extensive alterations—Revere Beach demonstrated the virtues of public control of
important natural resources and the benefits that can derive from judi-
cious planning. In an exhibition at the 1900 Paris Exposition, the MPC
touted the beach and the Middlesex Fells Reservation to illustrate its
work.[27] To civic leaders and urban planners in other American cities, such
as Chicago's Daniel Burnham, Revere Beach's renaissance served as a
model of enlightened civic action.

Challenging the MPC's Vision

Despite the MPC's celebrated success at constructing an ocean-side park
where overwrought city folk could enjoy nature's balm and a view of the
open sea, entrepreneurs, correctly gauging public desire, turned Revere

Beach into a regional mecca of commercial entertainment and amusement. Almost as soon as the MPC's improvements were completed, a bustling strip of dance halls, mechanical rides, amusement parks, and cheap eateries arose along the boulevard opposite the water. These attractions, as much as the improved beach area, made Revere Beach the "public park of greatest resort" within the MPC system and gave the area its lasting fame.[28] The commercial attractions also posed a serious challenge to the MPC's plans to maintain Revere Beach Reservation (as it was officially designated) as an antidote to the city.

Observers soon noted the prominence and appeal of commercial amusements near the reservation. "Side-show business is so dominant as to vie with the shore in attractiveness," wrote Arthur Shurtleff, of the Olmsted firm, after visiting the site on July 4, 1901.[29] At that time, the Olmsted firm was planning to redesign other waterfront areas throughout metropolitan Boston; Shurtleff believed that a trip to Revere Beach a few years after its reclamation and improvement would provide insights about popular uses of seaside park space. His comment spoke volumes about the MPC's inability to shape culture at the reservation and about the powerful appeal of the commercial amusements.

The redefinition of urban public space to include uses that planners never intended, a common theme in the literature on parks and leisure, has a long history in Boston and elsewhere.[30] Historically, efforts to control the uses of park space have met with resistance. As the Olmsted firm noted in an 1888 report, "In every city of our Northern States which has a public park ... great dissatisfaction is constantly expressed by numbers of people with the restrictions which those in charge think it necessary to impose upon the use of its turf."[31] This "dissatisfaction" represented a popular rejection of the pastoral ideal of parks used solely for the quiet contemplation of nature and passive recreation.

At seaside reservations and parks where commercial amusement venues sprang up opposite the ocean and occasionally spilled onto the beach itself, the process of redefinition proved especially dramatic as a space intended to serve as an escape from the city became thoroughly urbanized. The amusement venues strung along the boardwalk offered an experience and an aesthetic diametrically opposed to that of the abutting reservation. Given the extent of the MPC's improvements, the beach at Revere constituted a built environment to some degree, but it still gave visitors the opportunity to experience nature—sun, water, sand—in pristine

Commercial amusements along the boardwalk at Revere Beach challenged the MPC's vision of the resort as a refuge from crowded urban areas and as a space in which visitors could commune with nature.
Postcard, "Crescent Gardens Ball Room and Theatre." Courtesy of the author.

form and within a wide open space. Despite the noise and the spectacle created by thousands of visitors, the sound of the surf and the panorama of the ocean provided a striking aural and visual backdrop. Along the boardwalk at the turn of the century, however, visitors could marvel at exhibitions showing new scientific breakthroughs such as infant incubators, take turns on mechanical rides that harnessed electricity for the pursuit of pleasure, pose for a group photo "in a live automobile" (as one advertisement put it), or, in the evening, be dazzled by lights that illuminated the buildings along the boardwalk and a series of arches spanning the boulevard.[32] Architecturally, these amusement venues presented in extreme form the "jumbled, noisy scenery" of the cities from which Eliot had imagined the beachgoer escaping.

The boardwalk at Revere Beach represented and showcased the emergence of modern, mass, commercial culture in Greater Boston. The natural sublime of the reservation contrasted with a kind of technological sublime on the boulevard, creating a unique leisure landscape full of contradictions. In this respect, it was a representative space. At Atlantic City, at Coney Island, and at many other seaside and lakefront resorts throughout the country and abroad, commercial amusement venues arose opposite the water. The popularity of these shore resorts suggests the degree to which reformers, nature enthusiasts, and proponents of park development overestimated the lure and purported healing powers of nature; it also hints that nature, by itself, proved an insufficient draw.[33] Indeed, seaside parks such as Revere Beach have exemplified powerful juxtapositions of culture and landscape. Coexisting in tension, beaches and boardwalk amusements have satisfied popular longings for nature and artifice; for the open sea and the claustrophobia of the funhouse; for the ebb and flow of the tide and the latest technological marvel.

Amusement venues at Revere Beach transformed the look and feel— the very experience—of going to the beach. Indeed, as Shurtleff's comment about the "Side-show business" suggests, park officials and planners came to realize that visitors to the reservations not only desired to commune with nature but also wanted to partake of the pleasures of commercialized leisure. Developments at Revere Beach proved the point dramatically. They also evinced a profound change in manners and mores in American culture. As John Kasson has argued, commercial amusements at seaside resorts offered the "purest expression" of an emerging cultural order, one predicated on frivolity, consumption, and mixed-sex socializing, and one that challenged an older, more puritanical order that had valued production, work, restraint, and modesty. At the turn of the century, according to Kasson, leisure entrepreneurs such as those at Coney Island and Revere Beach "pioneered a new cultural institution that challenged prevailing notions of public conduct and social order, of wholesome amusements, of democratic art—of all the institutions and values of the genteel culture."[34]

Immigrants were largely responsible for developing and patronizing the boardwalk amusements at Revere Beach. Just as foreign newcomers were the chief supporters and patrons of early motion pictures in American cities, they also provided early and strong support for commercialized public amusements at seaside resorts. At Revere Beach, Jewish businessmen, including Mary Antin's father, operated small concession stands, while other newcomers from western and eastern Europe worked at establishments such as Wonderland, an enormous amusement park that attracted over 100,000 visitors when it opened in 1906. Old-line Yankee businessmen, keen to capitalize on the thousands of visitors to Revere Beach, owned some of the large amusement venues, but the success

Spectacles like Gorman's Diving Horses periodically spilled onto the beach itself, further compromising the MPC's goal of showcasing the area's natural beauty. Postcard, "Souvenir Revere Beach Carnival, 1906." Courtesy of the author.

of such ventures depended on the labor and patronage of recent immigrants.

MPC records make almost no mention of the national origins of visitors to Revere Beach, although a notable exception can be found in MPC police personnel records. In 1912, we find Herbert West, superintendent of the Revere Beach Division, praising officer Geromino F. A. Biggi for his work as a crossing guard at Revere. Biggi "is a valuable addition to the department as he can speak the Italian language" with visitors, wrote West.[35]

Employing the same rhetoric of democracy that helped create the metropolitan park system in the first place, newspaper and magazine accounts almost always failed to distinguish among groups of visitors to the beach. Instead, journalists dubbed Revere Beach "the people's beach" or the "people's paradise." One writer, for example, described it as a place "where all races, kindreds and conditions are welcome," where "Care-free humanity . . . rubs elbows with a multitude of others of its kind," and where one can find "a cross-section of American democracy." Ubiquitous in the published accounts of the use of public leisure spaces in the early part of the century, such rhetoric could soar to even greater heights. "When you bathe in Coney [Island]," noted one observer, "you bath in the American Jordan. It is holy water. Nowhere else in the United States will you see so many races mingle in a common purpose for a common good. [Here] Democracy ... has its first interview skin to skin. Here you find the real meaning of the Declaration of Independence, the most good for the greatest number."[36] By portraying public spaces as sites of social leveling—where all visitors, irrespective of their socioeconomic status and ethnic backgrounds, coexisted peacefully—journalists celebrated the manner in which urban leisure venues provided diverse people with a shared experience.

On rare occasions the press acknowledged the rich ethnic dimension of life at Revere Beach and revealed the fragmented nature of the resort's public. In a poem in the *Boston Traveler* about the Narrow Gauge, for example, an author noted that "There's a long way" to travel on the train "for the Hebrew / who gets off at the Beach," a clear reference to Jews living near the southern end of the beach. Writing for the *Boston Herald* in 1925, Edward Ross went into much greater detail in a piece about a colony of impoverished immigrants living directly behind the amusement venues. He described the hundreds of families that made up this "strange and densely-populated foreign colony" as "a new Italy, a new France, a new Poland"; he recorded the homes they made in shacks and shanties and even in an abandoned streetcar, on "swampy lots . . . bought on the '$10 down and $10 a month' plan."[37] This colony "forms as polyglot a community as can be found in all Massachusetts," he wrote, adding,

> Various are the tongues one may hear on the summer air; diverse the racial characteristics of the men and women who . . . exchange gossip in this colony. . . . Blue-eyed Poles chat animatedly with black-eyed French. Brown-eyed Italian children, clad in the most abbreviated of bathing dresses, play in the crusted mud of the lanes with hazel-eyed Spanish youngsters. American slang and even stronger expletives combine in a sort of "lingua franca" which passes current all up and down the colony.[38]

While Ross stressed the degree to which the "many races" in the colony "mingle fraternally," he noted that pronounced differences existed among the various groups: "There are strange contrasts and intermixtures and, eager and ambitious as they all are 'to be Americans,' the customs and habits of the birthland persist in multitudinous details." Italians, for example, built grape arbors on their property, allowing the visitor who "really does know his Rome or his Florence" to "find a most enchanting bit of color that will carry him straight back to the land of his memories."[39] Ross also noted that the homes of some Jewish families displayed a six-pointed star.

The differences among ethnic groups that Ross emphasized were of course not unique to Revere Beach. As historian Arthur Mann has documented, members of particular immigrant groups that congregated in poor sections of Boston and surrounding communities in the late nineteenth century "were distinguished by speech, mannerisms, dress [and] religion" and were "held together by the desire to be among people of like kind and the fear of a prejudiced and hostile world." Immigrants who visited and lived at Revere Beach (who, according to Ross, were "inveterate bathers") manifested their differences on the beach and along the boardwalk. People's memories clearly reveal this ethnic dimension. Phyllis Okoomian, for example, recalled family trips to Revere from their home in Everett and picnics at the beach featuring traditional Armenian food. "[My mother] used to make stuffed grape leaves and she'd bring along a lemon and some sardines in a can. . . . She'd bring other Armenian food. We always had hard-boiled eggs on the beach," Okoomian recollected, adding, "Sometimes in the evening my mother would prepare dinner . . . roast lamb and Armenian pilaf, and she would take salad ingredients and make it there at the beach . . . and we would have dinner at the beach." Jack Cook, who lived in Revere for sixty-one years, remembered that "If you walked along the beach, you would hear Yiddish near the Shirley Avenue section of the beach. Further along would be the Italian section."[40]

Oral testimony reveals also that people of different ethnic groups used the beach to affirm their religious heritage. From 1896 on, MPC rules explicitly forbade preaching and praying aloud at Revere Beach and other reservations. These rules were tested and enforced early in the history of the beach. On at least two occasions, for example, the MPC board denied requests by Reverend J. O. Bixby to "maintain [a] gospel wagon" at the beach.[41] The board's position in this regard presumably stemmed from a desire to maintain the reservation as a public space, with no particular group given preference. The regulations regarding religion were typical of those that had been in effect at parks maintained by the Boston Park Department and authorities throughout the country.

People nevertheless used the beach to express their religious faith. Catholics in Revere and surrounding communities recall Easter Sunday as the unofficial opening of the beach season; even if the weather was still too cool for swimming, they traditionally promenaded along the beach in their finery. Members of Revere's large Jewish population and Jews from other towns remember meeting at the beach on certain holy days to read from prayer books and to perform the traditional symbolic act of atonement by emptying their pockets into the ocean.

Religion became central to heated and ongoing debates in the early twentieth century about whether to permit boardwalk amusements to operate on Sundays. These battles were waged primarily between members of the city's Law and Order League, made up largely of Protestants, and businessmen who controlled the arcades, the dance halls, and other attractions along the boulevard. The community at large also had strong and mixed feelings, which many had the opportunity to air in the spring of 1906. William Duffney, a Revere businessman, put up $50 in gold to be divided among the individuals who furnished the three best responses to the question "Should we have a liberal interpretation of the Sunday law in Revere?" Printed in full in the *Revere Journal,* the responses exposed the tensions and conflicts among groups within the community—tensions that the boardwalk attractions created or, at the very least, exacerbated. The debate over Sunday amusements became, for example, an occasion for nativists to register their displeasure with the manner in which the influx of Catholic immigrants was changing the demographics of the region. According to one sarcastic, pro-Sabbath writer, "How our Latinian newcomers must enjoy their old-fashioned continental Sunday—'To church in the forenoon and to the circus or bull fight in the afternoon.'"[42]

Some strict Sabbatarians also believed that prohibiting the operation of amusements on Sundays would allow visitors to enjoy the true and intended benefits of Revere Beach Reservation. They maintained, as had Eliot, Baxter, and other MPC officials, that the primary value of the beach was the salutary effect of its beauty on those who beheld it. Instead, however, the boardwalk amusements drew visitors away from the beach and the precepts of the Sabbath. To portray contemporary attitudes toward the Sabbath, the author of a 1907 *Boston Transcript* article painted the following picture of a Sunday at Revere Beach:

Three o'clock in the afternoon. Temperature 82 in the shade. Humidity slightly above normal. Wind about southwest. Water "fine—come on in." But only three thousand persons have patronized the State Bathhouse; the other ninety-seven thousand are anywhere between Beachmont and Point of Pines. Along the Boulevard myriads mass in a moving picture six persons wide and three miles long. When they tire of peanuts and frankfurts and "chewing candy" and ice cream and soda, they will buy a souvenir cane and go over to Wonderland, where are some thousands already. For Wonderland is wide open, open as is the beach to the bay.[43]

Another commentator writing in the same year asserted that the "sign of a strong citizenship is the 'Christian Cross,' and not 'Wonderland.'" He elaborated his theme in some detail:

I am for any law which would bring under reasonable regulations the teeming thousands of the tenement districts of the cities out into the parks such as the state provides at Waverley, the Fells or along the banks of the Charles. It would pay the state, in the quality of its citizenship, to provide these people with free transportation to the spots where they would come into contact with uplifting nature. . . . The modern Sunday vaudeville, with its acrobats, cheap jokes and the like, are creatures of an anti-Lord's Day mammon, contrary to the spirit of the "Sign of the Cross" and irreconcilable with the fundamental law of this state. There are better influences for men, women and children, and families can find needed relief from cares in the hallowed precincts of nature's God, where sturdy citizenship will be built and health promoted.[44]

Similarly, one of the *Revere Journal* responses pleaded for enforcement of the Sunday laws so that "the coarse rant of the 'barker' may yield to the musical prattle of the children; that the din of the show places may be hushed by the gentle rhythm of the sea-tide; and that in the peace of our contemplation we may more fully appreciate the natural beauties of our seashore, and the purpose for which it was created."[45]

Commentators on both sides of the debate had to acknowledge that amusements changed the atmosphere of the beach on Sundays. In 1902, one *Boston Post* cartoon rendered the topic in graphic terms. Under the caption "Lifting the Lid at Revere," the image shows the selectmen using a rope to pull up a giant covering, beneath which music blares, barkers hawk hot dogs, and crowds of people mill about along the boardwalk. It accompanied a news item reporting that the Revere Law and Order League had failed to convince the city's selectmen to rescind their action sanctioning the operation of amusements on Sunday. At least one proponent of a more liberal interpretation of the Sunday laws conceded that these kinds of changes were problematic. This essayist believed that the amusements should be allowed to operate on Sundays, but that "Everything should be conducted . . . in a seemly and respectful manner" and that "barkers should be eliminated on that day."[46]

Support for the Sunday amusements came largely from Jews, Italians, and other immigrants who typically had only that one day free from work. Oral evidence also suggests that members of these same ethnic groups valued the beach and the boardwalk as a space in which they could express overtly political sentiments. Boston native Francis Foley, for example, recalled being at the beach on the evening of June 19, 1953, and hearing over a public address system that the Rosenbergs had been executed; the lights then dimmed along a portion of the boardwalk as a gesture of protest or solidarity.[47] Although it would be difficult to find evidence to corroborate this account, it seems highly plausible. Given the degree to which ethnicity structured life at the beach and along its boardwalk, proprietors of certain amusement venues—and in particular Jews who owned some of the concession stands—might have adopted this unusual mode of dissent.

While certain issues—such as the Sunday debates—may have enjoyed support across ethnic lines in Revere's immigrant community, conflict between groups existed and could become violent. Journalist Alan Lupo remembered that his father, Max, a 1927 graduate of Revere High School, and other Jews endured harassment that at times led to altercations. Lupo recalled that his father spoke of one "Jewish-Italian fistfight that went on for about an hour" outside Revere High in 1926. According to his father, as Lupo explained, Italian guys "used to poke fun at or harass the Jewish kids after school. And my father and his twin brother got tired of running home," so they decided to stand up for themselves one day. The irony of the story, Lupo said, is that his father later became friends with one of his chief tormentors. For Lupo, the story illustrates an important dimension of urban life. As he put it:

One of the wonderful things about Revere, as with some other communities that have so many ethnic groups and so many immigrant
groups . . . , is that yes, there's tension, and people have to kind of
dance around a little bit and spar and box, and hopefully not worse
than that, but hopefully they end up getting together and they have
wonderful tales about one another.[48]

A self-described "Winthrop guy," Lupo recalled hitchhiking to Revere
Beach with friends when he was eleven or twelve (circa 1950) and hanging
out at the amusement venues. His childhood, like his father's, was punc-
tuated with episodes of inter-ethnic conflict, but he also remembered
youths of various backgrounds overcoming differences. "We had a lot of
fights based on turf, on religion, on ethnicity," he recalled. "We also made
a lot of friends across those borders, friends that lasted a lifetime, and Revere was a wonderful lab dish for that sort of behavior on both sides."[49]

Racially Redefining Revere Beach

Throughout much of its history Revere Beach served primarily as a white
working- and middle-class leisure space where racial minorities held a
subordinate status. Throughout the first half of the twentieth century,
non-white racial groups routinely filled the role of the exotic "other"
against whom white ethnics could define themselves and affirm their
identity as members of a superior race. Wonderland, like expositions and
fairs throughout the country, featured a number of attractions depicting
the "Storied East" and showcasing "A Congress of Strange Oriental People," in contrast to which western cultures could be understood as rational
and normal.[50] Combining apparent education and entertainment with
racism, these amusements exploited and reinforced popular notions of
Asians as exotic "others" perpetuated in literature, theater, folklore, and
film. Even newspapers of the time ran articles describing the purported
strangeness of Asians as a sign of their subhuman status.[51] In the July 13,
1907, issue of the *Revere Journal*, for instance, a story entitled "The Land of
the Noises" appeared next to a report on a new attraction at Wonderland.
"In China night is as alive as the day and is filled with whoops, noisy con-
versations, the singsong accompanying work, boisterous repartee and
every other unmusical sound," the piece reported. "In addition, the dark-
ness is one long howl of dogs, cackle of geese, braying of donkeys, croak-

ing of frogs, the squealing of pigs, the drumbeats of the policeman. . . . Individually the people are full of varieties of unsuppressed violent demonstrativeness, and collectively they are only a terrific tribal turbulence."[52] Such portrayals of Asians, passing as news and conveyed in a matter-of-fact tone, reinforced messages presented at Wonderland's Asian-themed attractions.

African Americans, especially from the South, also appeared in crude caricature at Revere Beach. One exhibition at Wonderland amounted to little more than an outdoor minstrel show. The promoters described it:

> One of the big new spectacular shows for the season of 1908 at Wonderland is Manning's Darktown with its picturesque scenes on the Mississippi Levees, in which fifty black, chocolate, brown and yellow symphonies will appear. This aggregation is certain to stir the eye and heart. There will be banjo choruses, songs of Dixieland, dancing in the moonlight, alligator hunts, chicken stealing forays, and all sorts of "cut-ups" and revelries. Ole grand daddy will be there with his white hair and white whiskers and cane and mule, and so will be a bunch of little black berries and a pickanniny band. There will be a sensational steamboat race between the Natchez and the General Lee, with fire and explosion on board the City of New Orleans. How the Darktown Fire Brigade will work to put out the fire will be a revelation to the departments hereabouts. The whole show is a scream from beginning to ending, a source of never ending delight and unalloyed merriment.[53]

Manning's Darktown presented audiences with the same contradictory images routinely used to depict blacks in American popular culture—fun loving and violent, thievish but also obsequious and proficient at particular tasks. The blacks here—either old and frail or very young—are asexual, and their close association with nature (the children are "little black berries") and ease with animals underscore their subhuman status.

The African dodger game, in which patrons paid for chances to throw balls at human targets, ritualized the degradation of racial minorities. A visitor to Revere Beach in 1916 offered this account of the game:

> Well, anyway . . . the next thing we saw was [an] African dodger, and outside his place was a colored man ashoutin' at the top of his lungs,

"Hit him one," "He's a Mexican," "The only original," and all that, and men throwin' baseballs right at the top of his head which was stuck through a hole in a sheet. Sometimes he got hit but most times he didn't, and I'll bet his head was sore, though I s'pose he got good money for it.[54]

To this observer, the game was as natural a part of the Revere Beach attractions as the flying horses, the derby racers, and the fortune-teller. Others described the African dodger game at Revere in a similarly matter-of-fact manner. Explaining how competition for patron's dollars had changed the nature of the boardwalk amusements in recent years, a journalist in 1921 portrayed the dodgers—present at Revere Beach and other resorts as late as 1940—as mere features of a changing leisure landscape.[55] While noting that roller coasters and other rides had become faster and more exciting, the writer also observed that "Not long ago the African dodger was a rather morose person with the vantage of at least a 25-foot space between him and his pelters; today he holds provocative parley with the crowd at the intimate distance of but twelve or fifteen feet; or three dodgers, grimacing and ducking, are targeted side by side."[56]

Blacks must have felt some discomfort at Revere Beach with amusements such as the African dodger featured along the boardwalk, and at least until the end of World War II few came to the beach except to perform or work. Throughout the first half of the twentieth century, the beach thus remained a predominantly white working- and middle-class leisure space, part of a larger racially defined social geography within Greater Boston.[57] Because no one apparently questioned or challenged this white dominance before World War II, Revere Beach, unlike resorts elsewhere, did not become racially contested and charged. In Chicago, by contrast, the determination of a group of blacks to swim at a public beach that "unwritten law" had "designated . . . as exclusively white" touched off a five-day race riot that left 23 blacks and 15 whites dead, and 500 residents injured.[58] After World War II, however, conflicts arose.

The extension of the subway line out to Revere Beach in 1954 made a trip from Boston easier than ever. African Americans, perhaps emboldened by gains in the Civil Rights movement, began coming in increasing numbers throughout the following decades. When they arrived, they claimed the beach as a space in which they would enjoy pleasure rather than serve as its source. But the process of racially redefining the beach was slow, incomplete, and fraught with instances of tension and violence. African American writer Jewelle Gomez, a Roxbury native, wrote in 1993 about trips to Revere Beach in the 1950s:

> At nine years old I didn't realize that my grandmother, Lydia, and I were doing an extraordinary thing by packing a picnic and riding the elevated train from Roxbury to Revere Beach. It seemed part of the natural rhythm of summer to me. I didn't notice until much later how the subway cars slowly emptied most of their Black passengers as the train left Boston's urban center and made its way into the Italian and Irish suburban neighborhoods to the north. It didn't seem odd that all of the Black families sorted themselves out in one section of the beach and never ventured onto the boardwalk to the concession stands or the rides, except in groups.[59]

For Gomez, making forays into a recreational space that had been primarily, if not exclusively, the preserve of whites was a liberating experience, an exercise in racial empowerment. Referring to these outings with her grandmother as "Black females in a white part of town," Gomez recalled the older woman's confident and unselfconscious appropriation of space at Revere Beach, claiming that she "looked as if she had been born to the shore, a kind of aquatic heiress." These images and memories resonate all the more powerfully, Gomez contended, because "nothing in the popular media had made the great outdoors seem a hospitable place for Blacks or women. It was a place in which, at best, we were meant to feel uncomfortable, and at worst—hunted."[60]

In her generally upbeat accounts of experiences at Revere Beach, Gomez also included evening trips with relatives and friends when she was eleven or twelve and, in her teens, visits on Easter Sundays with male companions and other black couples.[61] Nonetheless, she also spoke of how the threat of violence hung over trips she took to the beach in the 1960s. Gomez remembered a

> sense that kids, teenagers, would be really in danger going there . . . that sometimes it would be perfectly fine, but that other times . . . rowdies would, you know, pick fights with the guys . . . or that you could walk down the beach, and this never happened to me person-

ally, but I had heard stories of friends who walked down the beach and had people yell "nigger" at them. So it never felt exactly like it was safe, yet we continued to lay claim to it.[62]

A rumor that a black youth was beaten up at Revere Beach added to the worry. Gomez remembered it as "one of those stories . . . that lived through the winter to become part of the discussion of the summer to determine if we should go or not."[63]

Although cautionary tales about racially motivated violence influenced how blacks perceived the beach, many remained undeterred in their quest to claim the resort as a space that belonged to them as well as to whites. As the 1960s progressed, "there was much more of a sense of a political movement, a black movement," Gomez explained. She added: "I think a lot of [black] teenagers were unconsciously kind of feeling . . . much more . . . [like] well, 'I'm not going to take any shit.' So we would just go out there." Some whites resented the new stance, and throughout the 1960s and into the 1970s a number of incidents involving black and white youths occurred at the beach. "Back in the '60s," Revere native Robert Upton recalled, "you had the race riots in Selma, Alabama. . . . [T]hrough the news all the time you could see the discussion, the controversy, the racial tension that was very prevalent in my time in the '60s and early '70s. Revere Beach was a place where a lot of that was played out."[64]

Much of the conflict occurred at amusement venues along the boardwalk, where black and white youths encountered one another in a confined space that seemed to heighten racial tensions. Gomez remembered the boardwalk as "kind of anxiety-provoking"—people were packed tightly together and disputes arose over places in the lines that formed around rides. She recalled that boys in particular competed aggressively for position. "There was all this testosterone flying around. . . . [G]uys were always pushing each other and trying to get to the front of the line," she explained, adding that black males felt the need to "protect their dignity and not look like the white guys were pushing them around." No matter what happened, Gomez recollected, "the black kids always felt like it really didn't matter if the line was set up and it was orderly—we [still] didn't get picked to go, we were like the last to get picked to go."[65]

Interracial dating or socializing of any kind was extremely rare among her peers, and "there was no social place where [you] would meet non-black kids" Gomez recalled. Most whites who visited Revere Beach

were also used to associating only with members of their own race. Stephen Hagen, a native of Revere, for example, could not recall having any
black classmates when he attended the city's public schools in the 1940s.
"You just never saw black people at Revere Beach in the '40s," he said. "You
didn't see any black people around Revere period . . . at the beach or
otherwise."66

Despite the difficulties Gomez and her friends experienced or perceived, Revere Beach, after World War II, was one of the few places in metropolitan Boston where members of different races socialized together.
Revere Beach did encompass several spots where whites and blacks tried
to share space amicably in the 1960s. Bob Upton recalled one area in front
of the Himalaya, "the ride on Revere Beach where Motown music would
blare." Upton said, "We would enjoy Motown Music, Diana Ross and the
Supremes, Smokey Robinson—all the rest of the Motown music was fan-
tastic. And you could see there was a quite a mix of African Americans,
blacks and whites mixed. . . . [R]ight in front of the Himalaya there was always a lot of dancing and there was always a lot of fun." Such interracial
socializing was experimental, according to Upton, and it created a "lot of
tension." He explained that "There was a lot of talk of racial mixing. There
was lot of black and white, male and female. . . . That represented change
and that represented controversy, and that controversy was certainly part
of Revere Beach's history, there's no question about that."67

Although racially motivated incidents occurred at Revere Beach in the
1950s and 1960s, the beach nevertheless served as a space to which both
blacks and whites could lay claim. Given the novelty of sharing public
leisure space with whites that her trips to Revere Beach constituted, and
the tension that surrounded those trips, Gomez expressed surprise "that
there weren't more confrontations and bloodshed . . . and that black kids
kept going back every Easter." She maintained that "the beach was a common ground" acknowledged by blacks and whites as having universal appeal. "The beach," she explained, "allowed us to have a space that we, the
two separate groups, could openly acknowledge as a place [we] desired, a
place [we] desired to be . . . and it created a kind of triangular connection
and I think that was good."68

Sociologists would support Gomez's assertion that beaches function as
a "common ground" where tensions between groups do not always lead to
confrontations. In the 1970s, Robert B. Edgerton conducted a comprehen-
sive study of a southern California beach that he maintained "attracted a

greater diversity of people from all walks of urban life than any other beach" in the region. In his research, he sought to determine "how it is possible for these many thousands of strangers of all ages and ethnic groups to come to a strip of sand, remove almost all their clothing, spend a day in close proximity to one another, often drink alcohol and smoke marijuana, and yet manage to avoid conflict with one another." He concluded that "remarkably little serious trouble occurs" at the beach in part because visitors share a tacit understanding that beach space is available for all to appropriate: "Beachgoers . . . regularly behave in ways that serve to ignore, avoid, or minimize trouble. . . . [T]hey establish private territories on the sand and with a few exceptions they keep to themselves within these territories. Except for the most innocuous kinds of greetings or requests, beachgoers rarely interact with strangers."[69]

Under certain circumstances, of course, beaches can serve not as common grounds but as battlegrounds, and they can be literally and sometimes brutally contested. Carson Beach in South Boston, for example, became a focal point of the city's racial violence in the summer of 1975. Court-ordered busing, begun in the fall of 1974 as a means to desegregate Boston's public schools, enflamed racial tensions in this period, and the ensuing strife spilled onto the beaches.[70] Unable to control the racial makeup of the student body in their children's schools, working-class whites attempted to control certain public leisure spaces. Blacks in the city, intent on claiming public space for themselves, naturally resisted such efforts, and racially charged battles ensued. In South Boston, home to some of the city's most attractive beaches and most vociferous anti-busing protests, these battles erupted periodically. The summer of 1975 was a particularly tense and dangerous time at the beach, with racial animosity most clearly evident on August 10, a Sunday, when forty people were hurt and ten arrested at Carson Beach after blacks and whites, separated by a wall of police officers, hurled stones and bottles at each other.[71]

Revere Beach never saw this level of racially motivated violence and tension. Court-ordered busing did not apply to Revere. African Americans and other racial minorities also never ventured to Revere Beach in numbers, or in a manner, that might make white beachgoers perceive that "outsiders" were appropriating their leisure space. Gomez notes that on a "big day" at the beach there would only be twenty to thirty African Americans present—a mere fraction of the enormous crowds that came to the beach on a typical summer day. Of course, since most blacks in Greater

Boston lived outside the general vicinity of Revere Beach, the majority
would have found it more convenient to venture to beaches in the city.
Nonetheless, the presence of Gomez, her family members and friends,
and other blacks at the beach—despite the incivilities and the threat of
violence they endured—marks an important chapter in the redefinition
and expansion of Revere Beach's "public."[72]

Race and the Decline of Revere Beach

Even though Revere Beach may have seemed idyllic compared to Carson
Beach, problems that arose after the arrival of blacks in the 1950s and '60s
negatively affected the beach's reputation. Skirmishes between blacks, intent on asserting their right to enjoy public leisure spaces throughout the
Boston region, and whites, who resented incursions on a space that historically had been theirs, gave the beach a bad reputation. Citing safety
reasons, some blacks stayed away from all the area's beaches. "People have
to feel safe to go," Barbara Bullette, a Roxbury mother, told the *Boston
Globe* in 1995. For blacks of modest means who did not own automobiles,
the decision to avoid local beaches could have serious consequences. Bullette believed that because many blacks of her generation no longer went
to the beaches with their children, the younger generation would lose out
on a valuable experience. "Since we grew up going to Revere Beach, Carson Beach, Wollaston Beach, we can't understand how the kids can't go to
the beach, and they can't understand the need to go to a beach," she said.
"How can I put it? You don't miss what you don't know." White attitudes
toward Revere Beach also changed. Going to the beach in the late 1950s,
according to Stephen Hagen, "was really frowned upon. . . . [Y]ou had to
sort of sneak to go down to the beach. . . . I mean we did it, but it was not
the place your parents really wanted you to be going to much."[73]
    A host of factors led to the decline of Revere Beach after the World War
II-era, including mass-automobility, which expanded people's leisure
options; water pollution and poor maintenance by the Metropolitan District Commission (the MPC became the MDC in 1919); rising insurance
costs for mechanical rides; and even the popularity of backyard swimming pools. Perceptions among whites that the increasing presence of
African Americans made the space unsafe also had an impact. "When the
T started to [bring blacks from Boston] quite frankly, there was racial
prejudice," recalled Hagen. "I think one of the unsaid things was 'Oh,

don't go to the beach. I don't want you going to the beach,' partly because
. . . people who were different were coming down there. I think that really
was part of it."[74] Alan Lupo agreed:

> There had been incidences of racial tension and there had been some
> fights as I recall some years ago between, I would guess, blacks and
> whites, maybe between Latinos and blacks, or Latinos and whites,
> frankly I don't remember. I just remember vaguely there were some
> problems. It never stopped me from going to Revere Beach, I'm sure
> that there were white people, as there are white people in all kinds of
> communities in the United States, who, when they see some people
> of color, showing up at a place that had been strictly white, decide
> that they should no longer go there.[75]

Race clearly figured in the demise of other amusement centers, such as
Chicago's Riverview amusement park in 1967 and Olympic Park outside
Newark in 1965. In June 1964 the *New York Times* reported that concessionaires at Coney Island believed the "Growing influx of Negro visitors"
was the primary reason for the resort's fading popularity. "Once a small
minority," the *Times* asserted, blacks now "comprise half the weekend
tourists, and the concessionaires believe that the presence of Negroes has
discouraged some white persons from visiting the area."[76]

Despite this widespread belief among whites that the influx of young
racial "outsiders" contributed significantly to Revere Beach's decline in
popularity, popular histories of the resort overlook this dimension of its
history. In *Revere Beach: The Changing Tide,* a video documentary, commentators who review reasons for the eclipse of the beach as a major
recreation center in the 1960s and '70s do not broach race as an issue.[77]
Even in oral histories, when interviewers do touch on the idea that race
contributed to the area's demise, they may sometimes skirt the issue, using
words and phrases such as "riffraff," "bad elements," "kids from other parts
of Boston," and "different kinds of people" as code words for non-whites.

Fiction writers, who can ascribe sentiments and beliefs to characters,
have more freedom to express ideas. In the novel *Revere Beach Boulevard,*
by Revere native Roland Merullo, characters take turns narrating the story
and several express their feelings about Asian immigrants, who began
coming to the city in the 1980s. The first narrator, Father Dominic Bucci,
of Saint Anthony's Parish in Revere, introduces the notion of ethnic and

racial succession in the book's prologue, asserting that the novel is partly "about the changing face of the blue-collar neighborhood I was born into and never left" in "our tattered beach city." [78]

Other characters in the novel make no attempt to conceal their disdain of immigrants. Vittorio Imbesalacqua, the family patriarch and a life-long Revere resident, reveals his contempt for Vietnamese and Cambodians in this conversation with his nephew:

> "The city changed on us," I said, because paper cups and scratched-off lottery tickets were laying in the gutter, and you could hear the sound of police cars in the air half the time, and I wasn't getting used to having things like that in the city of Revere.
> "Uncle, you have no idea."
> "All the new people moving in," I said, but he didn't make no answer.[79]

Eddie Crevine, another character in the novel, laments the passing of a romanticized golden era of Italian American community life in Revere. He recalls "the way the city used to be years ago, all the [Italian] families like one family, eating at each other's houses, watchin out for each other's brothers and sisters and cousins, the good old ways of doing things." Crevine's comments are ironic—he's a mobster with a well-earned reputation for brutality—but the sentiment he expresses, the feeling that a sense of community life has disappeared in Revere, pervades the book.

The character's feelings about the city match their feelings about the beach, which are also inextricably linked to the changing demographics of the area. The central character, Peter Imbesalacqua, harbors no animosity toward recent immigrants. He even claims at one point that a Cambodian gas station attendant reminds him of himself when he was younger. Nevertheless, the Revere Beach he remembers fondly is inseparable from his feeling of belonging to a close-knit community that he understands implicitly:

> I held a memory of the old Revere Beach in my mind's eye, the Dodgems, the Wild Mouse, the Cyclone, the smell of fried dough and pepper steak, the families who used to come down here by the tens of thousands on a warm Saturday morning like this and spread out their blankets and chairs. It was my little kingdom, this three-

mile stretch of sand, one of the jewels I held inside me—the beach, my family, the city of Revere.[80]

Peter's half-brother Alphonse later presents a very different image of the beach—one capturing its condition in the present. Shortly after observing "two skinny Cambodian kids chasing a crippled seagull along the shore while their mother or grandmother or aunt squatted on her heels near the edge of the water," Alphonse offers the most searing indictment of a beach and city bereft of community spirit:

> We rode back along Revere Beach Boulevard in a bitter silence. It seemed to me somehow that the ghosts of all the old amusements were standing up to watch us pass. . . . Young men and women in shorts and T-shirts were jogging the sidewalk with Walkmans over their ears, kids sprinting up the sand, waves breaking, seagulls calling, but it simply was not the place it had once been. There was no life here now, just poses, snapshots, suntan oil and show-off bodies and greasy paper plates in the gutter. A shallower, greedier America. There was no Revere here anymore.[81]

While *Revere Beach Boulevard* suggests that shifting demographics are related to changing perceptions of urban public space and culture generally, and of Revere Beach in particular, more evidence is needed to test that hypothesis. It would be unfair to make generalizations about the reactions of white ethnics to the arrival of Asian immigrants in Revere based on what characters in a novel say and think.

The testimony of many past residents and visitors demonstrates another perspective worth documenting. Some of these individuals offer a decidedly more positive assessment of the recent history of Revere and the beach. Alan Lupo believes the beach has "come back" and that because it attracts visitors of many different races, it functions as "the ultimate melting pot":

> What you see now is inevitable, you see the newest group of people, be they Revere citizens or be they people from somewhere else who now have access by public transportation or car, taking advantage of a public beach. . . . There had been some problems some years ago, but the beach seems peaceful. I go there a lot. My wife and I walk the

beach occasionally. We certainly drive up and down the boulevard. Once in a while we go to the beach as swimmers. I do not sense the kind of tension that may have existed there twenty years ago. I see black people, Latino people, Asian people, white people, all sharing the beach, all sharing the boulevard, all sharing the few foodstands that are left. . . . I think that's terrific. I think it's a wonderful thing to happen.[82]

In recent years, the beach *has* improved. In 1992, the MDC completed its "Revere Beach Renaissance," a $13 million rehabilitation. Owing to this project and the improved water quality, the beach has been attracting more visitors. If concerns about safety are still an issue, they did not affect the estimated 300,000 people who came to Revere Beach's centennial celebration (July 19-21, 1996) to enjoy the festivities and to pay homage to a leisure space that had played an integral part in their lives. Shortly after the celebration, the *Revere Journal*'s David Procopio waxed poetic while describing the event's significance. "For three days," he wrote, "people put aside what divided them and embraced a common thread, a love of the beach."[83] Revere Beach may remain a contested area—public space is by definition subject to the claims of individuals occupying varied social positions—but in a real way, as Gomez, Lupo, and others suggest, it may serve as a true common ground for those who visit it.

NOTES

1. John F. Kasson, *Amusing the Million: Coney Island at the Turn of the Century* (New York, 1978), 4, 39, 41. Gunther Barth makes the same claim for department stores, baseball parks, and vaudeville theatres in his *City People: The Rise of Modern City Culture in Nineteenth-Century America* (New York, 1980).
2. See Cynthia Zaitzevsky, *Frederick Law Olmsted and the Boston Park System* (Cambridge, Mass., 1982), for a detailed analysis of Boston's municipal parks.
3. Frederick Law Olmsted, "Public Parks and the Enlargement of Towns" (1870), reprinted in *Civilizing American Cities: A Selection of Frederick Law Olmsted's Writings on City Landscapes,* ed. S. B. Sutton (Cambridge, Mass., 1971), 68.
4. *First Annual Report of the Trustees of Public Reservations, 1891* (Boston, 1892), 54. The creation of the Trustees for Public Preservation and its role in promoting preservation and a regional approach to park planning is discussed in David Schuyler, *The New Urban Landscape: The Redefinition of City Form in Nineteenth-Century America* (Baltimore, 1986), 143-146; and Norman T. Newton, *Design on the Land: The Development of Landscape Architecture* (Cambridge, Mass., 1971), 320-326.

5. *First Annual Report of the Trustees of Public Reservations*, 56.

6. On seaside vacations, see Cindy S. Aron, *Working at Play: A History of Vacations in the United States* (New York, 1999); Janet E. Schulte, "Summer Homes: A History of Family Summer Vacation Communities in Northern New England" (Ph.D. diss, Brandeis Univ., 1993); and Richmond Barrett, *Good Old Summer Days: Newport, Narragansett Pier, Saratoga, Long Branch, Bar Harbor* (Boston, 1952). Joseph E. Garland, *The North Shore: A Social History of Summers among the Noteworthy, Fashionable, Rich, Eccentric and Ordinary on Boston's Gold Coast, 1823-1929*, rev. ed. (Beverly, Mass., 1998), describes the transformation of coastal communities outside of Boston into havens for wealthy vacationers and permanent residents. On conspicuous consumption in the late 19th century, see Thorstein Veblen, *The Theory of the Leisure Class* (1899; New York, 1979).

7. *First Annual Report of the Trustees of Public Reservations*, 55.

8. Charles Eliot, handwritten notes for speech delivered Mar. 8, 1892, Special Collections, Frances Loeb Library, Harvard University.

9. *Report of the Board of the Metropolitan Park Commissioners* (Boston, 1893), 37.

10. *Record of Land Inspection Reports by the Preliminary Board of the Metropolitan Park Commission*, Oct. 12, 1892, 89, Metropolitan District Commision Archives, Boston, Mass. (Hereafter, MDC Archives.)

11. Sam Bass Warner, Jr., *Province of Reason* (Cambridge, Mass., 1984), 21-22. The industrial history of Lynn has been well chronicled. See Mary Blewett, *Men, Women, and Work: Class, Gender, and Protest in the New England Shoe Industry, 1780-1910* (Urbana and Chicago, 1988); John T. Cumbler, *Working-Class Community in Industrial America: Work, Leisure, and Struggle in Two Industrial Cities, 1880-1930* (Westport, 1979); Paul Faler, *Mechanics and Manufacturers in the Early Industrial Revolution: Lynn, Massachusetts, 1780-1860* (Albany, 1981); and Alan Dawley, *Class and Community: The Industrial Revolution in Lynn* (Cambridge, Mass., 1976). For demographic analyses of some of these communities in the beginning of the 20th century, see Robert A. Woods and Albert J. Kennedy, *The Zone of Emergence: Observations of the Lower- and Middle- and Upper-Working-Class Communities of Boston, 1905-1914*, 2d ed. (1962; Cambridge, Mass., 1969).

12. David Procopio, "The End of Something," *Traditions: Commemorating Revere's Past, A Special Supplement to The Revere Journal*, Aug. 2, 1995. The Italian American presence in Revere is very much the subject of *Revere Beach Boulevard* (New York, 1998), Revere native Roland Merullo's novel about the fictional Imbesalacqua family. The book is the first in Merullo's "Revere Beach Trilogy."

13. Mary Antin, *The Promised Land* (1912; Boston, 1969), 189.

14. *Report of the Metropolitan Park Commissioners*, xii-xii.

15. H. J. Kellaway, "Revere Beach Reservation of the Metropolitan Park System, Boston," *Engineering Record* 48(Oct. 24, 1903):17, 487.

16. "No Foul Odors," *Boston Herald*, July 14, 1897.

17. "No Foul Odors."

18. *Report of the Metropolitan Park Commissioners*, 108-109, 37.

19. *Report of the Metropolitan Park Commissioners*, 37; *Boston Traveler*, Aug. 21, 1897.

20. Antin, *The Promised Land*, 191.

21. Charles Eliot, "Some Old American Country Seats—IV," *Garden and Forest*, Mar. 12, 1890, 122; Charles W. Eliot, *Charles Eliot: Landscape Architect* (Boston, 1902), 313, 670.

22. Metropolitan Park Commission, *Annual Report, 1896* (Boston, 1896); Eliot, *Landscape Architect*, 677.

23. Metropolitan Park Commission, *Annual Report, 1896*.

24. On the way Olmsted linked reform with park building, see Geoffrey Blodgett, "Frederick Law Olmsted: Landscape Architecture as Conservative Reform," *Journal of American History* 62(1976):869-889; and Roy Rosenzweig and Elizabeth Blackmar, *The Park and the People: A History of Central Park* (Ithaca, 1992).

25. Schuyler, *The New Urban Landscape*, 6-7.

26. "In Farthest Nantasket," *Boston Evening Transcript*, May 11, 1912.

27. A 36-page pamphlet on the work of the MPC was published for the Paris Exposition and made available to "students of municipal affairs" who wanted to know more about the commission's work. This pamphlet—Arthur A. Shurtleff, *A History and Description of the Boston Metropolitan Parks* (Boston, 1900)—remains one of the best sources for general information on parks in and around Boston.

28. *Annual Report of the Board of Metropolitan Park Commissioners* (Boston, 1915), 119. For Eliot's ideas on boardwalk development, see Commonwealth of Massachusetts, *House No. 50: Report of the Board of the Metropolitan Park Commissioners* (Boston, 1893), 109, and his letter to William B. de las Casas, Aug. 19, 1896, in Eliot, *Landscape Architect*, 670.

29. Arthur A. Shurtleff, Report following visits to Revere Beach and Nantasket Beach Reservations, July 4, 1901, Records of the Olmsted Associates, Series B, Job #1527, Nantasket Beach Reservation, Manuscript Division, Library of Congress, Washington, D.C.

30. See, for example, George Chauncey, *Gay New York: Gender, Urban Culture and the Making of the Gay Male World, 1890-1940* (New York, 1994); Lizabeth Cohen, *Making a New Deal: Industrial Workers in Chicago, 1919-1939* (New York, 1993), especially chap. three; David Nasaw, *Children of the City at Work and Play* (New York, 1985); Robert Richardi Weyeneth, "Moral Spaces: Reforming the Landscape of Leisure in Urban America, 1850-1920" (Ph.D diss., Univ. of California, Berkeley, 1984); and Rosenzweig and Blackmar, *The Park and the People*. For some examples of the redefinition of urban space in Boston, see Stephen Hardy, *How Boston Played: Sport, Recreation, and Community, 1865-1915* (Boston, 1982).

31. *Report of the Landscape Architects on Provisions for the Playing of Games*, City of Boston. Department of Parks, *Fourteenth Annual Report of the Board of Commissioners for the Year 1888*, 23.

32. John Kasson brilliantly describes the manner in which machinery was converted from an instrument of production to one of consumption at a seaside resort. *Amusing the Million*, 72-82.

33. The commercial, "honky-tonk" development in close proximity to Niagara Falls perhaps best demonstrates the manner in which culture has been used to supplement and complement visitors' encounters with nature.

34. Kasson, *Amusing the Million*, 3-4, 8.

35. Herbert West to George L. Rogers, Oct. 5, 1912, "Correspondence and Reports from the Superintendents of the Revere Beach Division to the Secretary of the MPC and to other MPC and MDC personnel," MDC Archives.

36. Edward Ross, "Revere Beach 'People's' Own Pleasure Paradise," *Boston Sunday Herald,* Sept. 5, 1926; "When you bathe . . ." quoted in Ric Burns, *Coney Island,* video documentary (Alexandria, Va., 1991).

37. Reuben Green, *Boston Traveler,* cited in Peter McCauley, *Revere Beach Chips* (Revere, 1996); Edward Ross, "Unique Colony Flourishes on Muddy Marshes," *Boston Herald,* Aug. 16, 1925.

38. Ross, "Unique Colony Flourishes."

39. Ross, "Unique Colony Flourishes."

40. Arthur Mann, *Yankee Reformers in the Urban Age* (Cambridge, Mass., 1954); Ross, "Unique Colony Flourishes"; Phyllis Okoomian, interview with author, Sept. 1, 2001; Jack Cook, interview with author, June 19, 1997.

41. See Minutes of Meetings, MPC Board of Commissioners, June 23, 1896, MDC Archives.

42. *Revere Journal,* May 26, 1906.

43. Walter Leon Sawyer, "A Puritan at Revere," *Revere Journal,* Aug. 17, 1907. The article originally appeared in the *Boston Transcript.*

44. Byron B. Johnson, "Analyzes the Sunday Law," *Revere Journal,* Jan. 5, 1907. This article first appeared in the *Waltham Free Press-Tribune.*

45. *Revere Journal,* June 9, 1906.

46. *Revere Journal,* May 26, 1906.

47. Francis Foley, interview with author, June 18, 1997.

48. Alan Lupo, interview with author, Aug. 9, 2001 .

49. Alan Lupo, interview with author, Aug. 9, 2001.

50. Edward and Frederick Nazzaro, *Revere Beach's Wonderland,* 18, 37; Robert W. Rydell, *All the World's a Fair: Visions of Empire at American International Expositions, 1876-1916* (Chicago, 1984).

51. For a history and analysis of depictions of Asia and Asians, see Robert G. Lee, *Orientals: Asian Americans in Popular Culture* (Philadelphia, 1999); Gina Marchetti, *Romance and the "Yellow Peril": Race, Sex, and Discursive Strategies in Hollywood Fiction* (Los Angeles, 1993); and James Moy, *Marginal Sights: Staging the Chinese in America* (Iowa, 1993).

52. *Revere Journal,* July 13, 1907. The *Journal* noted that the article appeared originally in the *Montreal Standard.*

53. *Souvenir Program, Wonderland, Revere Beach, Mass., Season of 1908* (n.p., n.d.).

54. "Flipping the Flaps at 10 Cents a Flop," *Boston Sunday Herald,* July 30, 1916.

55. See Henry W. Harris, "Artful Dodger at Revere Snatches a Last Snooze," *Boston Sunday Globe,* May 26, 1940. David Nasaw describes Coney Island's version of this "game" in *Going Out: The Rise and Fall of Public Amusement* (New York, 1993).

56. "Edging the Thrills," Clipping from unidentified newspaper, Aug. 21, 1921, George H. Beebe Communication Reference Library, Boston University, Boston, Massachusetts.

57. Other leisure venues in and around the city, for example, shared the beach's distinction of drawing an overwhelmingly white crowd. Fenway Park, home of the Boston Red Sox, "has never been a place where minorities feel welcome or comfortable, even today," author Dan Shaughnessy wrote in 1996. "In 1991, *Globe* interns counted the number of blacks in the house during a Red Sox home stand and found no more than

80 black fans at any game. On a Friday night against the Blue Jays, *Globe* reporters counted 71 black faces out of a crowd of 34,032. That's .2 percent of the crowd." See Shaugnessy, *At Fenway: Dispatches from Red Sox Nation* (New York, 1996), 66.

58. William M. Tuttle, Jr., *Race Riot: Chicago in the Red Summer of 1919* (New York, 1972), 5.

59. Jewelle Gomez, "A Swimming Lesson," in her *Forty-Three Septembers* (Ithaca, 1993), 25.

60. Gomez, "A Swimming Lesson," 26-27.

61. Jewelle Gomez, interview with author, Feb. 20, 1998.

62. Gomez, interview with author, Feb. 20, 1998.

63. Gomez, interview with author, Feb. 20, 1998.

64. Gomez, interview with author, Feb. 20, 1998; Robert Upton, interview with author, Apr. 1, 2000.

65. Gomez, interview with author, Feb. 20, 1998.

66. Gomez, interview with author, Feb. 20, 1998; Stephen Hagen, interview with author, June 25, 1997.

67. Upton, interview with author, Apr. 1, 2000.

68. Gomez, interview with author, Feb. 20, 1998.

69. Robert B. Edgerton, *Alone Together: Social Order on an Urban Beach* (Berkeley, 1979), 2, 188, 198.

70. Boston's busing crisis has been well chronicled. For a particularly illuminating account, see J. Anthony Lukas, *Common Ground: A Turbulent Decade in the Lives of Three American Families* (New York, 1985).

71. Curtis Wilkie, "40 hurt, 10 arrested at beach protest," *Boston Globe*, Aug. 11, 1975.

72. An even more dramatic example of racial redefinition of leisure space occurred at Atlantic City in the 1960s, an era when African Americans began coming to the resort in significant numbers. The *New York Times* reported in 1971 "scenes that would have surprised visitors a generation ago: blacks riding in motorized rolling chairs driven by whites, and sitting in cafes where they were once unwelcome." Quoted in Charles Funnell, *By the Beautiful Sea: The Rise and High Times of that Great American Resort, Atlantic City* (New Brunswick, 1983), 157.

73. Dolores Kong, "Putting troubles of the past to rest," *Boston Globe*, June 26, 1995; Hagen, interview with author, June 25, 1997.

74. Hagen, interview with author, June 25, 1997.

75. Lupo, interview with author, Aug. 9, 2001.

76. Martin Tolchin, "Coney Island Slump Grows Worse," *New York Times*, July 2, 1964. On Riverview and Olympic Park, see Nasaw, *Going Out.*

77. Kevin Carey and Tim Young, *Revere Beach: The Changing Tide* (1995).

78. Merullo, *Revere Beach Boulevard*, 3-4.

79. Merullo, *Revere Beach Boulevard*, 18.

80. Merullo, *Revere Beach Boulevard*, 204-205.

81. Merullo, *Revere Beach Boulevard*, 224, 228.

82. Lupo, interview with author, Aug. 9, 2001.

83. David Procopio, "A Celebration for All," *Revere Journal*, July 24, 1996.

CONTRIBUTORS

Jonathan Chu's grandmothers avoided, in the full legal sense of the term, the consequences of the Chinese Exclusion Act by being born in Hawai'i; his grandfathers, by immigrating there before it became a territory of the United States. An Associate Professor of History at the University of Massachusetts—Boston, he has written on seventeenth- and eighteenth-century Massachusetts. He is currently at work on a book on the legal and economic consequences of the Revolution.

James J. Connolly is Associate Professor of History at Ball State University in Muncie, Indiana. He is the author of *The Triumph of Ethnic Progressivism: Urban Political Culture in Boston, 1900-1925* (1998) as well as articles and essays on urban and ethnic politics. He is currently working on a book to be entitled *The Idea of the Machine: A Cultural History of Party Politics in Industrial America.*

Kristen A. Petersen is the Executive Director of the Bay State Historical League. She received the Ph.D. in the history of American civilization from Brown University and is the author of *Waltham Rediscovered: An Ethnic History of Waltham, Massachusetts* (1988).

Janette Thomas Greenwood is Associate Professor and Chair of the History Department at Clark University. She is author of *Bittersweet Legacy: The Black and White "Better Classes" in Charlotte, 1850-1910* (1994) and is currently working on a book-length treatment of Southern black migration to New England in the era of the Civil War.

Mark Herlihy is Assistant Professor of History at Endicott College. He earned a Ph.D. in American Civilization at Brown University in 2000 and is completing a book on Revere Beach to be published by University of Massachusetts Press.

Paula M. Kane is Associate Professor and Marous Chair of Religious Studies at the University of Pittsburgh, where she holds a joint appointment in History and Religious Studies. Her books include *Separatism and Subculture: Boston Catholicism, 1900-1920* (1994) and *Gender Identities in*

American Catholicism (2001). Her current project is a study of stigmata and related mystical phenomena in the modern era.

JOHN F. MCCLYMER is Professor of History at Assumption College in Worcester, Massachusetts. He is the author of several books, most recently *The Triangle Strike and Fire* (1998) and *The High and Holy Moment: The First National Woman's Rights Convention, Worcester, Massachusetts, 1850* (1999), as well as numerous articles.

REED UEDA is Professor of History at Tufts University. He is also a member of the Steering Group of the Inter-University Committee on International Migration of the Center for International Studies at the Massachusetts Institute of Technology.

CONRAD EDICK WRIGHT is Ford Editor of Publications at the Massachusetts Historical Society, Boston. An historian of the late colonial, Revolutionary, and early national periods, he has written *The Transformation of Charity in Postrevolutionary New England* (1992) and a forthcoming group biography of the members of four Harvard College classes, *Revolutionary Generation: College Men and the Consequences of Independence.*

INDEX